GREENS GUIDE
TO
SHERIFF COURT DISTRICTS

AND LOCAL AUTHORITY AREAS IN SCOTLAND

GREENS GUIDE
TO
SHERIFF COURT DISTRICTS

AND LOCAL AUTHORITY AREAS IN SCOTLAND

Second Edition

BY

CHARLES McCAFFRAY

W GREEN
EDINBURGH
1992

First published 1980 as
INDEX TO SHERIFF COURT DISTRICTS IN SCOTLAND
Second edition 1992

ISBN 0 414 00960 6

A catalogue record for this book is available
from the British Library

Computertypeset by MFK Typesetting Ltd., Hitchin, Herts.
Printed in Great Britain

INTRODUCTION

Publication in 1980 of the first edition of Charles McCaffray's "Index to Sheriff Court Districts in Scotland" provided a much needed and user friendly tool for all court practitioners. His book has become a familiar and essential part of the lawyer's library, equally valuable to Sheriff Officers and others concerned with jurisdiction in Scotland. The success of this checklist and its format has been well deserved and its many users will be grateful for this updated second edition.

Ian D Morrison
Past President
Scottish Law Agents Association

CONTENTS

THE SHERIFFDOMS AND SHERIFF COURTS
OF SCOTLAND

Grampian, Highland and Islands

Aberdeen	Lerwick
Banff	Lochmaddy
Dingwall	Peterhead
Dornoch	Portree
Elgin	Stonehaven
Fort William	Stornoway
Inverness	Tain
Kirkwall	Wick

South Strathclyde, Dumfries and Galloway

Airdrie	Kirkcudbright
Ayr	Lanark
Dumfries	Stranraer
Hamilton	

Tayside, Central and Fife

Alloa	Falkirk
Arbroath	Forfar
Cupar	Kirkcaldy
Dundee	Perth
Dunfermline	Stirling

North Strathclyde

Campbeltown	Kilmarnock
Dumbarton	Oban
Dunoon	Paisley
Greenock	Rothesay

Lothian and Borders

Duns	Linlithgow
Edinburgh	Peebles
Haddington	Selkirk
Jedburgh	

Glasgow and Strathkelvin

Glasgow

SHERIFF CLERKS' OFFICES

The Sheriff Clerk
Sheriff Court House
Castle Street
ABERDEEN   RE Box No 61   Fax: (0224) 575915
                                                         Tel: (0224) 572780

The Sheriff Clerk
Sheriff Court House
Graham Street
AIRDRIE   RE Box No 416   Fax: (0236) 47497
                                                         Tel: (0236) 51121

The Sheriff Clerk
Sheriff Court House
Mar Street
ALLOA   RE Box No 433   Fax: (0259) 21947
                                                         Tel: (0259) 722734

The Sheriff Clerk
Sheriff Court House
ARBROATH   RE Box No 442   Fax: (0241) 74413
                                                         Tel: (0241) 76600

The Sheriff Clerk
Sheriff Court House
AYR   RE Box No 16   Fax: (0292) 282442
                                                         Tel: (0292) 268474

The Sheriff Clerk
Sheriff Court House
BANFF   RE Box No 1325   Fax: (02612) 8394
                                                         Tel: (02612) 2140

The Sheriff Clerk
Sheriff Court House
CAMPBELTOWN   Fax: (0586) 54967
                                                         Tel: (0586) 52503

The Sheriff Clerk
Sheriff Court House
County Buildings
CUPAR   RE Box No 545   Fax: (0334) 56807
                                                         Tel: (0334) 52121

The Sheriff Clerk
Sheriff Court House
Ferry Road   Fax: (0349) 65230
DINGWALL   RE Box No 584   Tel: (0349) 63153

The Sheriff Clerk
Sheriff Court House   Fax: (0862) 810958
DORNOCH   RE Box No 652   Tel: (0862) 810224

The Sheriff Clerk
Sheriff Court House
Church Street   Fax: (0389) 64085
DUMBARTON   RE Box No 597   Tel: (0389) 63266

The Sheriff Clerk
Sheriff Court House
Buccleuch Street   Fax: (0387) 62357
DUMFRIES   RE Box No 617   Tel: (0387) 62334

The Sheriff Clerk
Sheriff Court House
6 West Bell Street   Fax: (0324) 202006
DUNDEE   RE Box No 33   Tel: (0382) 29961

The Sheriff Clerk
Sheriff Court House
1/6 Carnegie Drive   Fax: (0383) 621205
DUNFERMLINE   RE Box No 17   Tel: (0383) 724666

The Sheriff Clerk
Sheriff Court House
George Street   Fax: (0369) 2191
DUNOON   Tel: (0369) 4166

The Sheriff Clerk
Sheriff Court House   Use Jedburgh
DUNS   RE Box No 1222   Tel: (0835) 63231

The Sheriff Clerk Sheriff Court House Lawnmarket **EDINBURGH**	RE Box No 308	Fax: (031) 226 2029 Tel: (031) 226 7181
The Sheriff Clerk Sheriff Court House **ELGIN**	RE Box No 652	Fax: (0343) 541015 Tel: (0343) 2505
The Sheriff Clerk Sheriff Court House Hope Street **FALKIRK**	RE Box No 17	Fax: (0324) 613736 Tel: (0324) 20822
The Sheriff Clerk Sheriff Court House Market Street **FORFAR**	RE Box No 674	Fax: (0307) 62268 Tel: (0307) 62186
The Sheriff Clerk Sheriff Court House High Street **FORT WILLIAM**	RE Box No 1405	Fax: (0397) 706214 Tel: (0397) 702087
The Sheriff Clerk Sheriff Court House 1 Carlton Place **GLASGOW**	RE Box No 213	Fax: (041) 429 2217 Tel: (041) 429 8888
The Sheriff Clerk Sheriff Court House Nelson Street **GREENOCK**	RE Box No 16	Fax: (0475) 24511 Tel: (0475) 87978
The Sheriff Clerk Sheriff Court House Court Street **HADDINGTON**	RE Box No 732	Fax: (062 082) 6350 Tel: (062 082) 2936

The Sheriff Clerk
Sheriff Court House
Almada Street   Fax: (0698) 284403
HAMILTON   RE Box No 16   Tel: (0698) 282957

The Sheriff Clerk
Sheriff Court House
The Castle   Fax: (0463) 710602
INVERNESS   RE Box No 25   Tel: (0463) 230782

The Sheriff Clerk
Sheriff Court House   Fax: (0835) 64110
JEDBURGH   RE Box No 1222   Tel: (0835) 63231

The Sheriff Clerk
Sheriff Court House
St Marnock Street   Fax: (0563) 43568
KILMARNOCK   RE Box No 20   Tel: (0563) 20211

The Sheriff Clerk
Sheriff Court House   Fax: (0592) 642361
KIRKCALDY   RE Box No 17   Tel: (0592) 260171

The Sheriff Clerk
Sheriff Court House
High Street   Fax: (0557) 31764
KIRKCUDBRIGHT   RE Box No 812   Tel: (0387) 62334

The Sheriff Clerk
Sheriff Court House
Watergate   Fax: (0856) 4835
KIRKWALL   Tel: (0856) 2110

The Sheriff Clerk
Sheriff Court House
County Buildings   Fax: (0555) 4319
LANARK   RE Box No 832   Tel: (0555) 61531

The Sheriff Clerk
Sheriff Court House
LERWICK

Fax: (0595) 3340
Tel: (0595) 3914

The Sheriff Clerk
Sheriff Court House
Court Square
LINLITHGOW   RE Box No 881

Fax: (0506) 848457
Tel: (0506) 842922

The Sheriff Clerk
Sheriff Court House
LOCHMADDY

Tel: (087 63) 340

The Sheriff Clerk
Sheriff Court House
Albany Street
OBAN   RE Box No OB8

Fax: (0631) 62037
Tel: (0631) 62414

The Sheriff Clerk
Sheriff Court House
St James Street
PAISLEY   RE Box No 48

Fax: (041) 887 6702
Tel: (041) 887 5291

The Sheriff Clerk
Sheriff Court House
High Street
PEEBLES   RE Box No 971

Fax: (0721) 29583
Tel: (0721) 20204

The Sheriff Clerk
Sheriff Court House
Tay Street
PERTH   RE Box No 20

Fax: (0738) 23601
Tel: (0738) 20546

The Sheriff Clerk
Sheriff Court House
Queen Street
PETERHEAD   RE Box No 1376

Fax: (0779) 72435
Tel: (0779) 76628

The Sheriff Clerk
Sheriff Court House
PORTREE

Fax: (0478) 3203
Tel: (0478) 2191

The Sheriff Clerk
Sheriff Court House
Castle Street
ROTHESAY

Fax: (0700) 4112
Tel: (0700) 2982

The Sheriff Clerk
Sheriff Court House
Ettrick Terrace
SELKIRK   RE Box No 1011

Fax: (0750) 22884
Tel: (0750) 21269

The Sheriff Clerk
Sheriff Court House
Veiwfield Place
STIRLING   RE Box No 15

Fax: (0786) 70456
Tel: (0786) 62191

The Sheriff Clerk
Sheriff Court House
Dunottar Street
STONEHAVEN   RE Box No 1023

Fax: (0569) 62273
Tel: (0569) 62758

The Sheriff Clerk
Sheriff Court House
Lewis Street
STORNOWAY

Fax: (0851) 4296
Tel: (0851) 2231

The Sheriff Clerk
Sheriff Court House
Lewis Street
STRANRAER   RE Box No 1261

Fax: (0776) 6792
Tel: (0776) 2138

The Sheriff Clerk
Sheriff Court House
County Buildings
TAIN

Fax: (0862) 3348
Tel: (0862) 2518

The Sheriff Clerk
Sheriff Court House
Bridge Street
WICK

Fax: (0955) 4063
Tel: (0955) 2846

LOCAL AUTHORITY OFFICES

REGIONAL COUNCILS

Borders Regional Council
Regional Headquarters
NEWTON ST BOSWELLS
Melrose
Roxburghshire
TD6 OSA   RE Box No 1310   Fax: (0853) 22145
                                        Tel: (0853) 23301

Central Regional Council
Veiwforth
STIRLING
FK8 2ET   RE Box No ST22   Fax: (0786) 51344
                                        Tel: (0786) 73111

Dumfries and Galloway Regional Council
Regional Council Offices
English Street
DUMFRIES   Fax: (0387) 60034
DG1 2DD   Tel: (0387) 61234

Fife Regional Council
Regional Headquarters
Fife House
North Street
GLENROTHES
Fife   Fax: (0592) 758582
KY7 5LT   Tel: (0592) 754411

Grampian Regional Council
Woodhill House
Westburn Road
ABERDEEN   Fax: (0224) 697445
AB9 2LU   RE Box No AB42   Tel: (0224) 682222

Highland Regional Council
Regional Buildings
Glenurquhart Road
INVERNESS   Fax: (0463) 223201
IV1 5NX   RE Box No IN5   Tel: (0463) 234121

Lothian Regional Council
  Regional Headquarters
  George IV Bridge
  EDINBURGH   Fax: (031) 229 0516
  EH1 1UG   RE Box No ED81   Tel: (031) 229 9292

Strathclyde Regional Council
  Strathclyde House
  20 India Street
  GLASGOW   Fax: (041) 227 2870
  G2 4PF   Tel: (041) 204 2900

Tayside Regional Council
  Tayside House
  28 Crichton Street
  DUNDEE   Fax: (0382) 28735
  DD1 3RA   Tel: (0382) 23281

ISLANDS AREAS

Orkney Islands Council
  Council Offices
  School Place
  KIRKWALL
  Orkney   Fax: (0856) 4615
  KW15 1NY   Tel: (0856) 3535

Shetland Islands Council
  Town Hall
  LERWICK
  Shetland   Fax: (0595) 4349
  ZE1 OHB   Tel: (0595) 3535

Western Isles Islands Council
  Council Offices
  Sandwick Road
  STORNOWAY
  Isle of Lewis   Fax: (0851) 5349
  PA87 2BW   Tel: (0851) 3773

DISTRICT COUNCILS

Angus District Council
County Buildings
Market Square
FORFAR
Angus   Fax: (0307) 64834
DD8 3LG   Tel: (0307) 65101

Annandale and Eskdale District Council
District Council Chambers
High Street
ANNAN
Dumfriesshire   Fax: (04612) 5876
DG12 6AQ   RE Box No 406   Tel: (04612) 3311

Argyll and Bute District Council
Kilmory
LOCHGILPHEAD
Argyll   Fax: (0546) 3956
PA31 8RT   Tel: (0546) 2127

Badenoch and Strathspey District Council
Council Offices
Ruthven Road
KINGUSSIE
Inverness-shire   Fax: (0540) 661004
PH21 1EJ   Tel: (05402) 555

Banff and Buchan District Council
St Leonard's
Sandyhill Road
BANFF   Fax: (02612) 5664
AB4 1BH   RE Box No 1328   Tel: (02612) 2521

Bearsden and Milngavie District Council
Municipal Buildings
Boclair
Milngavie Road
GLASGOW   Fax: (041) 942 6814
G61 2TQ   Tel: (041) 942 2262

13

Berwickshire District Council
Council Offices
8 Newtown Street
DUNS
Berwickshire   Fax: (03618) 3711
TD11 3DU   RE Box No 1208   Tel: (03618) 2600

Caithness District Council
Council Offices
Market Square
WICK
Caithness   Fax: (0955) 2481
KW1 4AB   Tel: (0955) 3761

City of Aberdeen District Council
Town House
ABERDEEN   Fax: (0224) 644346
AB9 1FY   RE Box No AB52   Tel: (0224) 642121

City of Dundee District Council
City Chambers
City Square
DUNDEE   Fax: (0382) 203302
DD1 3BY   RE Box No DD50   Tel: (0382) 23141

City of Edinburgh District Council
City Chambers
High Street
EDINBURGH   Fax: (031) 220 1849
EH1 1YJ   RE Box No 125   Tel: (031) 225 2424

City of Glasgow District Council
City Chambers
George Square
GLASGOW   Fax: (041) 227 5666
G2 1DU   RE Box No 269   Tel: (041) 221 9600

Clackmannan District Council
Greenfield
ALLOA
Clackmannanshire   Fax: (0259) 721315
FK1 2AD   RE Box No 436   Tel: (0259) 722160

Clydebank District Council
District Council Offices
CLYDEBANK
Dunbartonshire
G81 1TG

Fax: (041) 952 0573
Tel: (041) 941 1331

Clydesdale District Council
District Offices
South Vennel
LANARK
ML11 7JT

Fax: (0555) 2546
Tel: (0555) 61511

Cumbernauld and Kilsyth District Council
Council Offices
Bron Way
Cumbernauld
GLASGOW
G67 1DZ

Fax: (02367) 36258
Tel: (02367) 22131

Cumnock and Doon Valley District Council
Council Offices
Lugar
CUMNOCK
Ayrshire
KA18 3JQ

Fax: (0290) 22461
Tel: (0290) 22111

Cunninghame District Council
Cunninghame House
IRVINE
Ayrshire
KA12 8EE

Fax: (0294) 311058
Tel: (0294) 74166

Dumbarton District Council
Crosslet House
Argyll Avenue
DUMBARTON
G82 3NS

Fax: (0389) 42298
Tel: (0389) 65100

Dunfermline District Council
City Chambers
DUNFERMLINE
Fife
KY12 7ND

Fax: (0383) 620761
Tel: (0383) 722711

East Kilbride District Council
Civic Centre
East Kilbride
GLASGOW   Fax: (03552) 45548
G74 1AB   Tel: (03552) 28777

East Lothian District Council
County Buildings
HADDINGTON
East Lothian   Fax: (062082) 5735
EH41 3HA   RE Box No 743   Tel: (062082) 4161

Eastwood District Council
Council Offices
Eastwood Park
Rouken Glen Road
Giffnock
GLASGOW   Fax: (041) 620 0884
G46 6UG   Tel: (041) 638 6511

Ettrick and Lauderdale District Council
PO Box 4
Council Chambers
Paton Street
GALASHIELS
Selkirkshire   Fax: (0896) 57003
TD1 3AS   RE Box No 708   Tel: (0896) 4751

Falkirk District Council
Municipal Buildings
FALKIRK   Fax: (0324) 27356
FK1 5RS   RE Box No FA6   Tel: (0324) 24911

Gordon District Council
Gordon House
Blackhall Road
INVERURIE
Aberdeenshire   Fax: (0467) 24285
AB5 9WA   RE Box No 775   Tel: (0467) 20981

Hamilton District Council
Municipal Buildings
102 Cadzow Street
HAMILTON
Lanarkshire   Fax: (0698) 891491
ML3 6HH   Tel: (0698) 282323

Inverclyde District Council
Municipal Buildings
GREENOCK
Renfrewshire
PA15 1LY   RE Box No GR11

Fax: (0474) 20101
Tel: (0475) 24400

Inverness District Council
Town House
INVERNESS
IV1 1JJ   RE Box No IN7

Fax: (0463) 233813
Tel: (0463) 239111

Kilmarnock and Louden District Council
PO Box 13
Civic Centre
KILMARNOCK
Ayrshire
KA1 1BY   RE Box No KK23

Fax: (0563) 36829
Tel: (0563) 21140

Kincardine and Deeside District Council
Viewmount
Arduthie Road
STONEHAVEN
Kincardineshire
AB3 2DQ   RE Box No 1025

Fax: (0569) 66549
Tel: (0569) 62001

Kirkcaldy District Council
Town House
KIRKCALDY
Fife
KY1 1XW   RE Box No KY12

Fax: (0592) 268951
Tel: (0592) 261144

Kyle and Carrick District Council
Burns House
Burns Statue Square
AYR
KA7 1UT

Fax: (0292) 610650
Tel: (0292) 81511

Lochaber District Council
Lochaber House
High Street
FORT WILLIAM
Inverness-shire
PH33 6EL

Fax: (0397) 704016
Tel: (0397) 703881

Midlothian District Council
District Headquarters
1 Eskdaill Court
DALKEITH
Midlothian   Fax: (031) 654 2598
EH22 1DE   Tel: (031) 663 2881

Monklands District Council
Municipal Buildings
Dunbeath Road
COATBRIDGE
Lanarkshire   Fax: (0236) 23950
ML5 3LF   RE Box No 509   Tel: (0236) 24941

Moray District Council
District Headquarters
ELGIN
Morayshire   Fax: (0343) 540183
IV30 1BX   Tel: (0343) 3451

Motherwell District Council
PO Box 14
Civic Centre
MOTHERWELL
Lanarkshire   Fax: (0698) 75125
ML1 1TW   Tel: (0698) 66166

Nairn District Council
The Courthouse
High Street
NAIRN   Fax: (0667) 52056
IV12 4AU   Tel: (0667) 55523

Nithsdale District Council
Municipal Chambers
Buccleuch Street
DUMFRIES   Fax: (0387) 67225
DG1 2AD   Tel: (0387) 53166

North East Fife District Council
County Buildings
St Catherine's Street
CUPAR
Fife   Fax: (0334) 54016
KY15 4TA   RE Box No 548   Tel: (0334) 53722

Perth and Kinross District Council
Council Buildings
2 High Street
PERTH
PH1 5PH   RE Box No PE28   Fax: (0738) 35225
                                                  Tel: (0738) 39911

Renfrew District Council
Municipal Buildings
Cotton Street
PAISLEY
Renfrewshire   Fax: (041) 848 1450
PA1 1BU   Tel: (041) 889 5400

Ross and Cromarty District Council
Council Offices
High Street
DINGWALL
Ross-shire   Fax: (0349) 63465
IV15 9QN   RE Box No 586   Tel: (0349) 63381

Roxburgh District Council
District Council Offices
High Street
HAWICK
Roxburghshire   Fax: (0450) 78526
TD9 9EF   Tel: (0450) 75991

Skye and Lochalsh District Council
District Council Offices
Park Road
PORTREE
Isle of Skye   Fax: (0478) 2543
IV51 9EP   Tel: (0478) 2341

Stewartry District Council
Council Offices
KIRKCUDBRIGHT   Fax: (0557) 30005
DG6 4PJ   Tel: (0557) 30291

Stirling District Council
Municipal Buildings
STIRLING   Fax: (0786) 50863
FK8 2HU   Tel: (0786) 79000

Strathkelvin District Council
PO Box 4
Tom Johnston House
Civic Way
Kirkintilloch
GLASGOW
G66 4TJ

Fax: (041) 777 8576
Tel: (041) 776 7171

Sutherland District Council
District Offices
GOLSPIE
Sutherland
KW10 6RB

Fax: (04083) 3120
Tel: (04083) 3192

Tweeddale District Council
District Offices
Rosetta Road
PEEBLES
EH45 8HG

Fax: (0721) 20620
Tel: (0721) 20153

West Lothian District Council
District Headquarters
South Bridge Street
BATHGATE
West Lothian
EH48 1TS

Fax: (0506) 33587
Tel: (0506) 53631

Wigtown District Council
District Offices
Sun Street
STRANRAER
Wigtownshire
DG9 7JJ

RE Box No 1264

Fax: (0776) 4819
Tel: (0776) 2151

INDEX
To Place Names in Scotland

Abbey St Bathans, Duns,
Berwickshire; Lothian and Borders
at Duns.
Borders Region
Berwickshire District.

Aberarder, Inverness; Grampian,
Highland and Islands at Inverness.
Highland Region
Inverness District.

Aberargie, Perth; Tayside, Central
and Fife at Perth.
Tayside Region
Perth and Kinross District.

Aberchirder, Huntly,
Aberdeenshire; Grampian,
Highland and Islands at Banff.
Grampian Region
Banff and Buchan District.

Abercrombie, Anstruther, Fife;
Tayside, Central and Fife at
Cupar.
Fife Region
North East Fife District.

Aberdalgie, Perth; Tayside, Central
and Fife at Perth.
Tayside Region
Perth and Kinross District.

Aberdeen; Grampian, Highland
and Islands at Aberdeen.
Grampian Region
City of Aberdeen District.

Aberdour, Burntisland, Fife;
Tayside, Central and Fife at
Dunfermline.
Fife Region
Dunfermline District.

Aberfeldy, Perthshire; Tayside,
Central and Fife at Perth.
Tayside Region
Perth and Kinross District.

Aberfoyle, Stirling; Tayside,
Central and Fife at Stirling.
Central Region
Stirling District.

Aberlady, Longniddry, East
Lothian; Lothian and Borders at
Haddington.
Lothian Region
East Lothian District.

Aberlemno, Forfar, Angus;
Tayside, Central and Fife at
Forfar.
Tayside Region
Angus District.

Aberlour, Banffshire; Grampian,
Highland and Islands at Elgin.
Grampian Region
Moray District.

Abernethy, Nethybridge,
Inverness-shire; Grampian,
Highland and Islands at Inverness.
Highland Region
Badenoch and Strathspey District.

Abernethy, Perth; Tayside, Central
and Fife at Perth.
Tayside Region
Perth and Kinross District.

Abernyte, Perthshire; Tayside,
Central and Fife at Perth.
Tayside Region
Perth and Kinross District.

Aberuthven, Auchterarder,
Perthshire; Tayside, Central and
Fife at Perth.
Tayside Region
Perth and Kinross District.

Abington, Biggar, Lanarkshire;
South Strathclyde, Dumfries and
Galloway at Lanark.
Strathclyde Region
Clydesdale District.

Aboyne, Aberdeenshire; Grampian,
Highland and Islands at
Stonehaven.
Grampian Region
Kincardine and Deeside District.

Abriachan, Inverness; Grampian,
Highland and Islands at Inverness.
Highland Region
Inverness District.

Acairseid Mhor, Eriskay, Isle of
South Uist; Grampian, Highland
and Islands at Lochmaddy.
Western Isles Islands Council.

Achachork, Portree, Isle of Skye;
Grampian, Highland and Islands at
Portree.
Highland Region
Skye and Lochalsh District.

Achahoish, Lochgilphead, Argyll;
North Strathclyde at Dunoon.
Strathclyde Region
Argyll and Bute District.

Achanalt, Garve, Ross-shire;
Grampian, Highland and Islands at
Dingwall.
Highland Region
Ross and Cromarty District.

Acharacle, Strontian, Argyll;
Grampian, Highland and Islands at
Fort William.
Highland Region
Lochaber District.

Acharn, Aberfeldy, Perthshire;
Tayside, Central and Fife at Perth.
Tayside Region
Perth and Kinross District.

Achateny, Acharacle, Strontian,
Argyll; Grampian, Highland and
Islands at Fort William.
Highland Region
Lochaber District.

Achfary, Lairg, Sutherland;
Grampian, Highland and Islands at
Dornoch.
Highland Region
Sutherland District.

Achiltibuie, Ullapool, Ross-shire;
Grampian, Highland and Islands at
Dingwall.
Highland Region
Ross and Cromarty District.

Achilty, Strathpeffer, Ross-shire;
Grampian, Highland and Islands at
Dingwall.
Highland Region
Ross and Cromarty District.

Achmore, Isle of Lewis; Grampian,
Highland and Islands at
Stornoway.
Western Isles Islands Council.

Achmore, Killin, Perthshire; Tayside, Central and Fife at Stirling.
Central Region
Stirling District.

Achmore, Stromeferry, Ross-shire; Grampian, Highland and Islands at Dingwall.
Highland Region
Ross and Cromarty District.

Achnacarry, Spean Bridge, Inverness-shire; Grampian, Highland and Islands at Fort William.
Highland Region
Lochaber District.

Achnairn, Lairg, Sutherland; Grampian, Highland and Islands at Dornoch.
Highland Region
Sutherland District.

Achnaloich, Connel, Argyll; North Strathclyde at Oban.
Strathclyde Region
Argyll and Bute District.

Achnamara, Lochgilphead, Argyll; North Strathclyde at Dunoon.
Strathclyde Region
Argyll and Bute District.

Achnasheen, Garve, Ross-shire; Grampian, Highland and Islands at Dingwall.
Highland Region
Ross and Cromarty District.

Achnashellach, Strathcarron, Ross-shire; Grampian, Highland and Islands at Dingwall.
Highland Region
Ross and Cromarty District.

Achosnich, Kilchoan, Acharacle, Argyll; Grampian, Highland and Islands at Fort William.
Highland Region
Lochaber District.

Achrimsdale, Brora, Sutherland; Grampian, Highland and Islands at Dornoch.
Highland Region
Sutherland District.

Achtertyre, Balmacara, Kyle, Ross-shire; Grampian, Highland and Islands at Dingwall.
Highland Region
Skye and Lochalsh District.

Ackergill, Wick, Caithness; Grampian, Highland and Islands at Wick.
Highland Region
Caithness District.

Adabrock, Port of Ness, Isle of Lewis; Grampian, Highland and Islands at Stornoway.
Western Isles Islands Council.

Addiewell, West Calder, West Lothian; Lothian and Borders at Linlithgow.
Lothian Region
West Lothian District.

Advie, Grantown-on-Spey, Inverness-shire; Grampian, Highland and Islands at Inverness.
Highland Region
Badenoch and Strathspey District.

Ae, Dumfries; South Strathclyde, Dumfries and Galloway at Dumfries.
Dumfries and Galloway Region
Nithsdale District.

Ahmor, Lochmaddy, Isle of North Uist; Grampian, Highland and Islands at Lochmaddy.
Western Isles Islands Council.

Aigas, Beauly, Inverness-shire; Grampian, Highland and Islands at Inverness.
Highland Region
Inverness District.

Aignish, Isle of Lewis; Grampian, Highland and Islands at Stornoway.
Western Isles Islands Council.

Aird, Ardvassar, Isle of Skye; Grampian, Highland and Islands at Portree.
Highland Region
Skye and Lochalsh District.

Aird, Isle of Benbecula; Grampian, Highland and Islands at Lochmaddy.
Western Isles Islands Council.

Aird, Point, Isle of Lewis; Grampian, Highland and Islands at Stornoway.
Western Isles Islands Council.

Aird, South Dell, Isle of Lewis; Grampian, Highland and Islands at Stornoway.
Western Isles Islands Council.

Aird, Timsgarry, Isle of Lewis; Grampian Highland and Islands at Stornoway.
Western Isles Islands Council.

Aird, Tong, Isle of Lewis; Grampian, Highland and Islands at Stornoway.
Western Isles Islands Council.

Airdhantuim, Isle of Lewis; Grampian, Highland and Islands at Stornoway.
Western Isles Islands Council.

Airdrie, Lanarkshire; South Strathclyde, Dumfries and Galloway at Airdrie.
Strathclyde Region
Monklands District.

Airds Bay, Taynuilt, Argyll; North Strathclyde at Oban.
Strathclyde Region
Argyll and Bute District.

Airlie, Kirriemuir, Angus; Tayside, Central and Fife at Forfar.
Fife Region
Angus District.

Airth, Falkirk, Stirlingshire; Tayside, Central and Fife at Falkirk.
Central Region
Falkirk District.

Aith, Bixter, Shetland; Grampian, Highland and Islands at Lerwick.
Orkney Islands Council.

Alcaig, Conon Bridge, Ross-shire; Grampian, Highland and Islands at Dingwall.
Highland Region
Ross and Cromarty District.

Aldourie, Inverness; Grampian, Highland and Islands at Inverness.
Highland Region
Inverness District.

Alexandria, Dunbartonshire; North Strathclyde at Dumbarton.
Strathclyde Region
Dumbarton District.

Alford, Aberdeenshire; Grampian,
Highland and Islands at Aberdeen.
Grampian Region
Gordon District.

Allandale, Bonnybridge,
Stirlingshire; Tayside, Central and
Fife at Falkirk.
Central Region
Falkirk District.

Allanfearn, Inverness; Grampian,
Highland and Islands at Inverness.
Highland Region
Inverness District.

Allanton, Duns, Berwickshire;
Lothian and Borders at Duns.
Borders Region
Berwickshire District.

Allasdale, Castlebay, Isle of Barra;
Grampian, Highland and Islands at
Lochmaddy.
Western Isles Islands Council.

Alligin, Achnasheen, Ross-shire;
Grampian, Highland and Islands at
Dingwall.
Highland Region
Ross and Cromarty District.

Alloa, Clackmannanshire; Tayside,
Central and Fife at Alloa.
Central Region
Clackmannan District.

Alloway, Ayr; South Strathclyde,
Dumfries and Galloway at Ayr.
Strathclyde Region
Kyle and Carrick District.

Almondbank, Perth; Tayside,
Central and Fife at Perth.
Tayside Region
Perth and Kinross District.

Alness, Ross-shire; Grampian,
Highland and Islands at Tain.
Highland Region
Ross and Cromarty District.

Altass, Lairg, Sutherland;
Grampian, Highland and Islands at
Dornoch.
Highland Region
Sutherland District.

Altnabreac, Halkirk, Caithness;
Grampian, Highland and Islands at
Wick.
Highland Region
Caithness District.

Altnahara, Lairg, Sutherland;
Grampian, Highland and Islands at
Dornoch.
Highland Region
Sutherland District.

Altyre, Forres, Morayshire;
Grampian, Highland and Islands at
Elgin.
Grampian Region
Moray District.

Alva, Clackmannanshire; Tayside,
Central and Fife at Alloa.
Central Region
Clackmannan District.

Alvah, Banff; Grampian, Highland
and Islands at Banff.
Grampian Region
Banff and Buchan District.

Alves, Elgin, Morayshire;
Grampian, Highland and Islands at
Elgin.
Grampian Region
Moray District.

Alvie, Kingussie, Inverness-shire;
Grampian, Highland and Islands at
Inverness.
Highland Region
Badenoch and Strathspey District.

Alyth, Perthshire; Tayside, Central
and Fife at Perth.
Tayside Region
Perth and Kinross District.

Amhuinnsuidh, Isle of Harris;
Grampian, Highland and Islands at
Stornoway.
Western Isles Islands Council.

Amisfield, Dumfries; South
Strathclyde, Dumfries and
Galloway at Dumfries.
Dumfries and Galloway Region
Nithsdale District.

Amulree, Dunkeld, Perthshire;
Tayside, Central and Fife at Perth.
Tayside Region
Perth and Kinross District.

Ancrum, Jedburgh, Roxburghshire;
Lothian and Borders at Jedburgh.
Borders Region
Roxburgh District.

Annan, Dumfriesshire; South
Strathclyde, Dumfries and
Galloway at Dumfries.
Dumfries and Galloway Region
Annandale and Eskdale District.

Annathill, Coatbridge, Lanarkshire;
South Strathclyde, Dumfries and
Galloway at Airdrie.
Strathclyde Region
Monklands District.

Annbank, Ayr; South Strathclyde,
Dumfries and Galloway at Ayr.
Strathclyde Region
Kyle and Carrick District.

Anstruther, Fife; Tayside, Central
and Fife at Cupar.
Fife Region
North East Fife District.

Appin, Ballachulish, Argyll; North
Strathclyde at Oban.
Strathclyde Region
Argyll and Bute District.

Applecross, Lochcarron, Ross-
shire; Grampian, Highland and
Islands at Dingwall.
Highland Region
Ross and Cromarty District.

Applegarth, Lockerbie,
Dumfriesshire; South Strathclyde,
Dumfries and Galloway at
Dumfries.
Dumfries and Galloway Region
Annandale and Eskdale District.

Arabella, Tain, Ross-shire;
Grampian, Highland and Islands at
Tain.
Highland Region
Ross and Cromarty District.

Arbeg, Port Ellon, Isle of Islay;
North Strathclyde at
Campbeltown.
Strathclyde Region
Argyll and Bute District.

Arbilot, Arbroath, Angus; Tayside,
Central and Fife at Arbroath.
Tayside Region
Angus District.

Arbroath, Angus; Tayside, Central
and Fife at Arbroath.
Tayside Region
Angus District.

Arbuthnott, Laurencekirk,
Kincardineshire; Grampian,
Highland and Islands at
Stonehaven.
Grampian Region
Kincardine and Deeside District.

Archattan, Connel, Argyll; North
Strathclyde at Oban.
Strathclyde Region
Argyll and Bute District.

Archiestown, Carron, Morayshire;
Grampian, Highland and Islands at
Elgin.
Grampian Region
Moray District.

Ardallie, Peterhead,
Aberdeenshire; Grampian,
Highland and Islands at
Peterhead.
Grampian Region
Banff and Buchan District.

Ardbeg, Rothesay, Isle of Bute;
North Strathclyde at Rothesay.
Strathclyde Region
Argyll and Bute District.

Ardbrecknish, Dalmally, Argyll;
North Strathclyde at Oban.
Strathclyde Region
Argyll and Bute District.

Ardchung, Isle of Benbecula;
Grampian, Highland and Islands at
Lochmaddy.
Western Isles Islands Council.

Ardchyle, Crianlarich, Perthshire;
Tayside, Central and Fife at
Stirling.
Central Region
Stirling District.

Ardeer, Stevenson, Ayrshire; North
Strathclyde at Kilmarnock.
Strathclyde Region
Kilmarnock and Louden District.

Ardelve, Kyle, Ross-shire;
Grampian, Highland and Islands at
Dingwall.
Highland Region
Skye and Lochalsh District.

Arden, Alexandria, Dunbartonshire;
North Strathclyde at Dumbarton.
Strathclyde Region
Dumbarton District.

Ardentellen, Oban, Argyll; North
Strathclyde at Oban.
Strathclyde Region
Argyll and Bute District.

Ardentinny, Dunoon, Argyll; North
Strathclyde at Dunoon.
Strathclyde Region
Argyll and Bute District.

Ardeonaig, Killin, Perthshire;
Tayside, Central and Fife at
Stirling.
Central Region
Stirling District.

Ardersier, Inverness; Grampian,
Highland and Islands at Inverness.
Highland Region
Inverness District.

Ardfenaig, Isle of Mull; North Strathclyde at Oban.
Strathclyde Region
Argyll and Bute District.

Ardfern, Lochgilphead, Argyll; North Strathclyde at Dunoon.
Strathclyde Region
Argyll and Bute District.

Ardgour, Fort William, Inverness-shire; Grampian, Highland and Islands at Fort William.
Highland Region
Lochaber District.

Ardhasaig, Isle of Harris; Grampian, Highland and Islands at Stornoway.
Western Isles Islands Council.

Ardheisker, Lochmaddy, Isle of North Uist; Grampian, Highland and Islands at Lochmaddy.
Western Isles Islands Council.

Ardheslaig, Strathcarron, Ross-shire; Grampian, Highland and Islands at Dingwall.
Highland Region
Ross and Cromarty District.

Ardinashaig, Scalpay, Isle of Skye; Grampian, Highland and Islands at Portree.
Highland Region
Skye and Lochalsh District.

Ardindrean, Garve, Ross-shire; Grampian, Highland and Islands at Dingwall.
Highland Region
Ross and Cromarty District.

Ardineaskan, Lochcarron, Ross-shire; Grampian, Highland and Islands at Dingwall.
Highland Region
Ross and Cromarty District.

Ardivachar, Lochboisdale, Isle of South Uist; Grampian, Highland and Islands at Lochmaddy.
Western Isles Islands Council.

Ardler, Meigle, Perthshire; Tayside, Central and Fife at Perth.
Tayside Region
Perth and Kinross District.

Ardlui, Arrochar, Dunbartonshire; North Strathclyde at Dumbarton.
Strathclyde Region
Dumbarton District.

Ardlussa, Craighouse, Isle of Jura; North Strathclyde at Campbeltown.
Strathclyde Region
Argyll and Bute District.

Ardmaddy, Oban, Argyll; North Strathclyde at Oban.
Strathclyde Region
Argyll and Bute District.

Ardmhor, Castlebay, Isle of Barra; Grampian, Highland and Islands at Lochmaddy.
Western Isles Islands Council.

Ardminish, Isle of Gigha; North Strathclyde at Campbeltown.
Strathclyde Region
Argyll and Bute District.

Ardmore, Lochboisdale, Isle of South Uist; Grampian, Highland and Islands at Lochmaddy.
Western Isles Islands Council.

Ardnakille, Scalpay, Isle of Skye; Grampian, Highland and Islands at Portree.
Highland Region
Skye and Lochalsh District.

Ardnamonie, Lochboisdale, Isle of South Uist; Grampian, Highland and Islands at Lochmaddy.
Western Isles Islands Council.

Ardnastruban, Lochmaddy, Isle of North Uist; Grampian, Highland and Islands at Lochmaddy.
Western Isles Islands Council.

Ardnave, Isle of Islay; North Strathclyde at Campbeltown.
Strathclyde Region
Argyll and Bute District.

Ardochrig, East Kilbride, Glasgow; South Strathclyde, Dumfries and Galloway at Hamilton.
Strathclyde Region
Hamilton District.

Ardoe, Aberdeenshire; Grampian, Highland and Islands at Stonehaven.
Grampian Region
Kincardine and Deeside District.

Ardpatrick, Tarbert, Argyll; North Strathclyde at Campbeltown.
Strathclyde Region
Argyll and Bute District.

Ardrishaig, Lochgilphead, Argyll; North Strathclyde at Dunoon.
Strathclyde Region
Argyll and Bute District.

Ardroil, Isle of Lewis; Grampian, Highland and Islands at Stornoway.
Western Isles Islands Council.

Ardross, Alness, Ross-shire; Grampian, Highland and Islands at Tain.
Highland Region
Ross and Cromarty District.

Ardrossan, Ayrshire; North Strathclyde at Kilmarnock.
Strathclyde Region
Kilmarnock and Louden District.

Ardslave, Isle of Harris; Grampian, Highland and Islands at Stornoway.
Western Isles Islands Council.

Ardtalnaig, Aberfeldy, Perthshire; Tayside, Central and Fife at Perth.
Tayside Region
Perth and Kinross District.

Ardtoe, Acharacle, Argyll; Grampian, Highland and Islands at Fort William.
Highland Region
Lochaber District.

Ardtornish, Morvern, Argyll; Grampian, Highland and Islands at Fort William.
Highland Region
Lochaber District.

Ardtun, Bunessan, Isle of Mull; North Strathclyde at Oban.
Strathclyde Region
Argyll and Bute District.

Arduaine, Oban, Argyll; North Strathclyde at Oban.
Strathclyde Region
Argyll and Bute District.

Ardvassar, Armadale, Isle of Skye; Grampian, Highland and Islands at Portree.
Highland Region
Skye and Lochalsh District.

Ardveenish, Castlebay, Isle of Barra; Grampian, Highland and Islands at Lochmaddy.
Western Isles Islands Council.

Ardvey, Finsbay, Isle of Harris; Grampian, Highland and Islands at Stornoway.
Western Isles Islands Council.

Ardvey, Stockinish, Isle of Harris; Grampian, Highland and Islands at Stornoway.
Western Isles Islands Council.

Ardvourlie, Isle of Harris; Grampian, Highland and Islands at Stornoway.
Western Isles Islands Council.

Ardwell, Stranraer, Wigtownshire; South Strathclyde, Dumfries and Galloway at Stranraer.
Dumfries and Galloway Region
Wigtown District.

Argaty, Doune, Perthshire; Tayside, Central and Fife at Stirling.
Central Region
Stirling District.

Argday, Ross-shire; Grampian, Highland and Islands at Dornoch.
Highland Region
Sutherland District.

Arinagour, Isle of Coll; North Strathclyde at Oban.
Strathclyde Region
Argyll and Bute District.

Arisaig, Mallaig, Inverness-shire; Grampian, Highland and Islands at Fort William.
Highland Region
Lochaber District.

Arivegaig, Acharacle, Argyll; Grampian, Highland and Islands at Fort William.
Highland Region
Lochaber District.

Arivruaich, Isle of Lewis; Grampian, Highland and Islands at Stornoway.
Western Isles Islands Council.

Armadale, Bathgate, West Lothian; Lothian and Borders at Linlithgow.
Lothian Region
West Lothian District.

Armadale, Melvich, Thurso, Caithness; Grampian, Highland and Islands at Dornoch.
Highland Region
Sutherland District.

Armadale, Sleat, Isle of Skye; Grampian, Highland and Islands at Portree.
Highland Region
Skye and Lochalsh District.

Arnage, Ellon, Aberdeenshire; Grampian, Highland and Islands at Aberdeen.
Grampian Region
Gordon District.

Arncroach, Anstruther, Fife;
Tayside, Central and Fife at
Cupar.
Fife Region
North East Fife District.

Arnisdale, Kyle, Ross-shire;
Grampian, Highland and Islands at
Dingwall.
Highland Region
Skye and Lochalsh District.

Arnisort, Portree, Isle of Skye;
Grampian, Highland and Islands at
Portree.
Highland Region
Skye and Lochalsh District.

Arnol, Isle of Lewis; Grampian,
Highland and Islands at
Stornoway.
Western Isles Islands Council.

Arnprior, Stirling; Tayside, Central
and Fife at Stirling.
Central Region
Stirling District.

Aros, Tobermory, Isle of Mull; North
Strathclyde at Oban.
Strathclyde Region
Argyll and Bute District.

Arrina, Strathcarron, Ross-shire;
Grampian, Highland and Islands at
Dingwall.
Highland Region
Ross and Cromarty District.

Arrochar, Dunbartonshire; North
Strathclyde at Dumbarton.
Strathclyde Region
Dumbarton District.

Artafallie, North Kessock, Ross-
shire; Grampian, Highland and
Islands at Dingwall.
Highland Region
Ross and Cromarty District.

Arthrath, Ellon, Aberdeenshire;
Grampian, Highland and Islands at
Aberdeen.
Grampian Region
Gordon District.

Ascog, Rothesay, Isle of Bute;
North Strathclyde at Rothesay.
Strathclyde Region
Argyll and Bute District.

Ashkirk, Selkirk; Lothian and
Borders at Selkirk.
Borders Region
Ettrick and Lauderdale District.

Askernish, Lochboisdale, Isle of
South Uist; Grampian, Highland
and Islands at Lochmaddy.
Western Isles Islands Council.

Assynt, Lairg, Sutherland;
Grampian, Highland and Islands at
Dornoch.
Highland Region
Sutherland District.

Athelstaneford, North Berwick,
East Lothian; Lothian and Borders
at Haddington.
Lothian Region
East Lothian District.

Auchaleek, Campbeltown, Argyll;
North Strathclyde at
Campbeltown.
Strathclyde Region
Argyll and Bute District.

Auchenairn, Bishopbriggs,
Glasgow; Glasgow and
Strathkelvin at Glasgow.
Strathclyde Region
City of Glasgow District.

Auchenblae, Laurencekirk,
Kincardineshire; Grampian,
Highland and Islands at
Stonehaven.
Grampian Region
Kincardine and Deeside District.

Auchenblae, Stonehaven,
Kincardineshire; Grampian,
Highland and Islands at
Stonehaven.
Grampian Region
Kincardine and Deeside District.

Auchenbowie, Stirling; Tayside,
Central and Fife at Stirling.
Central Region
Stirling District.

Auchencairn, Castle Douglas,
Kirkcudbrightshire; South
Strathclyde, Dumfries and
Galloway at Kirkcudbright.
Dumfries and Galloway Region
Stewartry District.

Auchencoir, Rhynie, Huntly,
Aberdeenshire; Grampian,
Highland and Islands at Aberdeen.
Grampian Region
Gordon District.

Auchencrow, Eyemouth,
Berwickshire; Lothian and Borders
at Duns.
Borders Region
Berwickshire District.

Auchencruive, Ayr; South
Strathclyde, Dumfries and
Galloway at Ayr.
Strathclyde Region
Kyle and Carrick District.

Auchendinny, Penicuik,
Midlothian; Lothian and Borders at
Edinburgh.
Lothian Region
Midlothian District.

Auchengate, Irvine, Ayrshire; North
Strathclyde at Kilmarnock.
Strathclyde Region
Kilmarnock and Louden District.

Auchengray, Carnwath, Lanark;
South Strathclyde, Dumfries and
Galloway at Lanark.
Strathclyde Region
Clydesdale District.

Auchenhalrig, Spey Bay,
Fochabers, Morayshire; Grampian,
Highland and Islands at Elgin.
Grampian Region
Moray District.

Auchenheath, Lanark; South
Strathclyde, Dumfries and
Galloway at Lanark.
Strathclyde Region
Clydesdale District.

Auchenlay, Dunblane, Perthshire;
Tayside, Central and Fife at
Stirling.
Central Region
Stirling District.

Auchenmalg, Glenluce,
Wigtownshire; South Strathclyde,
Dumfries and Galloway at
Stranraer.
Dumfries and Galloway Region
Wigtown District.

Auchentiber, Dunlop, Ayrshire; North Strathclyde at Kilmarnock.
Strathclyde Region
Kilmarnock and Louden District.

Auchindoun, Dufftown, Keith, Banffshire; Grampian, Highland and Islands at Elgin.
Grampian Region
Moray District.

Auchinleck, Cumnock, Ayrshire; South Strathclyde, Dumfries and Galloway at Ayr.
Strathclyde Region
Cumnock and Doon Valley District.

Auchinloch, Kirkintilloch, Glasgow; Glasgow and Strathkelvin at Glasgow.
Strathclyde Region
Strathkelvin District.

Auchleuchries, Ellon, Aberdeenshire; Grampian, Highland and Islands at Aberdeen.
Grampian Region
Gordon District.

Auchleven, Insch, Aberdeenshire; Grampian, Highland and Islands at Aberdeen.
Grampian Region
Gordon District.

Auchmacoy, Ellon, Aberdeenshire; Grampian, Highland and Islands at Aberdeen.
Grampian Region
Gordon District.

Auchmithie, Arbroath, Angus; Tayside, Central and Fife at Arbroath.
Tayside Region
Angus District.

Auchmuirbridge, Glenrothes, Fife; Tayside, Central and Fife at Kirkcaldy.
Fife Region
Kirkcaldy District.

Auchnagatt, Ellon, Aberdeenshire; Grampian, Highland and Islands at Aberdeen.
Grampian Region
Gordon District.

Auchnarrow, Ballindalloch, Banffshire; Grampian, Highland and Islands at Elgin.
Grampian Region
Moray District.

Auchterarder, Perthshire; Tayside, Central and Fife at Perth.
Tayside Region
Perth and Kinross District.

Auchterawe, Fort Augustus, Inverness-shire; Grampian, Highland and Islands at Inverness.
Highland Region
Inverness District.

Auchterderran, Lochgelly, Fife; Tayside, Central and Fife at Dunfermline.
Fife Region
Dunfermline District.

Auchterhouse, Dundee; Tayside, Central and Fife at Dundee.
Tayside Region
City of Dundee District.

Auchterless, Turriff, Banffshire;
Grampian, Highland and Islands at
Banff.
Grampian Region
Banff and Buchan District.

Auchtermuchty, Cupar, Fife;
Tayside, Central and Fife at
Cupar.
Fife Region
North East Fife District.

Auchtertool, Kirkcaldy, Fife;
Tayside, Central and Fife at
Kirkcaldy.
Fife Region
Kirkcaldy District.

Auchtertyre, Dornie, Ross-shire;
Grampian, Highland and Islands at
Dingwall.
Highland Region
Skye and Lochalsh District.

Auchtoo, Lochearnhead,
Perthshire; Tayside, Central and
Fife at Stirling.
Central Region
Stirling District.

Aukengill, Keiss, Wick, Caithness;
Grampian, Highland and Islands at
Wick.
Highland Region
Caithness District.

Auldearn, Nairn; Grampian,
Highland and Islands at Inverness.
Highland Region
Nairn District.

Auldgirth, Dumfries; South
Strathclyde, Dumfries and
Galloway at Dumfries.
Dumfries and Galloway Region
Nithsdale District.

Auldhouse, East Kilbride,
Glasgow; South Strathclyde,
Dumfries and Galloway at
Hamilton.
Strathclyde Region
Hamilton District.

Aultbea, Gairloch, Ross-shire;
Grampian, Highland and Islands at
Dingwall.
Highland Region
Ross and Cromarty District.

Aultguish, Garve, Ross-shire;
Grampian, Highland and Islands at
Dingwall.
Highland Region
Ross and Cromarty District

Aultguish Inn, Garve, Ross-shire;
Grampian, Highland and Islands at
Dingwall.
Highland Region
Ross and Cromarty District.

Aultnamain Inn, Edderton, Tain,
Ross-shire; Grampian, Highland
and Islands at Tain.
Highland Region
Ross and Cromarty District.

Aviemore, Inverness-shire;
Grampian, Highland and Islands at
Inverness.
Highland Region
Badenoch and Strathspey District.

Avoch, Fortrose, Ross-shire;
Grampian, Highland and Islands at
Dingwall.
Highland Region
Ross and Cromarty District.

Avonbridge, Falkirk, Stirlingshire; Tayside, Central and Fife at Falkirk.
Central Region
Falkirk District.

Ayr; South Strathclyde, Dumfries and Galloway at Ayr.
Strathclyde Region
Cumnock and Doon Valley District.

Ayton, Eyemouth, Berwickshire; Lothian and Borders at Duns.
Borders Region
Berwickshire District.

Aywick, East Yell, Shetland; Grampian, Highland and Islands at Lerwick.
Shetland Islands Council.

Back, Isle of Lewis; Grampian, Highland and Islands at Stornoway.
Western Isles Islands Council.

Backaland, Eday, Orkney; Grampian, Highland and Islands at Kirkwall.
Orkney Islands Council.

Backhill, Berneray, Isle of North Uist; Grampian, Highland and Islands at Lochmaddy.
Western Isles Islands Council.

Backmuir of Liff, Dundee; Tayside, Central and Fife at Dundee.
Tayside Region
City of Dundee District.

Badachro, Gairloch, Ross-shire; Grampian, Highland and Islands at Dingwall.
Highland Region
Ross and Cromarty District.

Badcaul, Kyle of Lochalsh, Ross-shire; Grampian, Highland and Islands at Dingwall.
Highland Region
Skye and Lochalsh District.

Badenscoth, Inverurie, Aberdeenshire; Grampian, Highland and Islands at Aberdeen.
Grampian Region
Gordon District.

Badluachrach, Garve, Ross-shire; Grampian, Highland and Islands at Dingwall.
Highland Region
Ross and Cromarty District.

Baila, Uyesound, Unst, Shetland; Grampian, Highland and Islands at Lerwick.
Shetland Islands Council.

Baillieston, Glasgow; Glasgow and Strathkelvin at Glasgow.
Strathclyde Region
City of Glasgow District.

Bainsford, Falkirk, Stirlingshire; Tayside, Central and Fife at Falkirk.
Central Region
Falkirk District.

Balado, Kinross, Perthshire; Tayside, Central and Fife at Perth.
Tayside Region
Perth and Kinross District.

Balallan, Isle of Lewis; Grampian, Highland and Islands at Stornoway.
Western Isles Islands Council.

Balblair, Conon Bridge, Ross-shire; Grampian, Highland and Islands at Dingwall.
Highland Region
Ross and Cromarty District.

Balchrik, Lairg, Sutherland; Grampian, Highland and Islands at Dornoch.
Highland Region
Sutherland District.

Balchraggan, Invergordon, Ross-shire; Grampian, Highland and Islands at Dingwall.
Highland Region
Ross and Cromarty District.

Balcurvie, Leven, Fife; Tayside, Central and Fife at Kirkcaldy.
Fife Region
Kirkcaldy District.

Baldernock, Milngavie, Glasgow; North Strathclyde at Dumbarton.
Strathclyde Region
Bearsden and Milngavie District.

Baleloch, Lochmaddy, Isle of North Uist; Grampian, Highland and Islands at Lochmaddy.
Western Isles Islands Council.

Balemore, Lochmaddy, Isle of North Uist; Grampian, Highland and Islands at Lochmaddy.
Western Isles Islands Council.

Balephetrish, Scarinish, Isle of Tiree; North Strathclyde at Oban.
Strathclyde Region
Argyll and Bute District.

Balephuill, Scarinish, Isle of Tiree; North Strathclyde at Oban.
Strathclyde Region
Argyll and Bute District.

Balerno, Midlothian; Lothian and Borders at Edinburgh.
Lothian Region
Midlothian District.

Baleshare, Lochmaddy, Isle of North Uist; Grampian, Highland and Islands at Lochmaddy.
Western Isles Islands Council.

Balevullin, Scarinish, Isle of Tiree; North Strathclyde at Oban.
Strathclyde Region
Argyll and Bute District.

Balfour, Orkney; Grampian, Highland and Islands at Kirkwall.
Orkney Islands Council.

Balfron, Glasgow; Tayside, Central and Fife at Stirling.
Central Region
Stirling District.

Balgaveny, Huntly, Aberdeenshire; Grampian, Highland and Islands at Aberdeen.
Grampian Region
Gordon District.

Balgownie, Bridge of Don, Aberdeenshire; Grampian, Highland and Islands at Aberdeen.
Grampian Region
City of Aberdeen District.

Balintore, Fearn, Ross-shire; Grampian, Highland and Islands at Tain.
Highland Region
Ross and Cromarty District.

Balishare, Lochmaddy, Isle of
North Uist; Grampian, Highland
and Islands at Lochmaddy.
Western Isles Islands Council.

Balivanich, Isle of Benbecula;
Grampian, Highland and Islands at
Lochmaddy.
Western Isles Islands Council.

Balla, Eriskay, Isle of South Uist;
Grampian, Highland and Islands at
Lochmaddy.
Western Isles Islands Council.

Ballachulish, Kinlochleven, Fort
William; Grampian, Highland and
Islands at Fort William.
Highland Region
Lochaber District.

Ballanoch, Lochgilphead, Argyll;
North Strathclyde at Dunoon.
Strathclyde Region
Argyll and Bute District.

Ballantrae, Girvan, Ayrshire; South
Strathclyde, Dumfries and
Galloway at Ayr.
Strathclyde Region
Cumnock and Doon Valley District.

Ballantrushal, Isle of Lewis;
Grampian, Highland and Islands at
Stornoway.
Western Isles Islands Council.

Ballater, Kincardineshire;
Grampian, Highland and Islands at
Stonehaven.
Grampian Region
Kincardine and Deeside District.

Ballindalloch, Banffshire;
Grampian, Highland and Islands at
Elgin.
Grampian Region
Banff and Buchan District.

Ballingry, Lochgelly, Fife; Tayside,
Central and Fife at Dunfermline.
Fife Region
Dunfermline District.

Ballinluig, Pitlochry, Perthshire;
Tayside, Central and Fife at Perth.
Tayside Region
Perth and Kinross District.

Ballintuim, Blairgowrie, Perthshire;
Tayside, Central and Fife at Perth.
Tayside Region
Perth and Kinross District.

Balloch, Alexandria,
Dunbartonshire; North Strathclyde
at Dumbarton.
Strathclyde Region
Dumbarton District.

Balloch, Inverness; Grampian,
Highland and Islands at Inverness.
Highland Region
Inverness District.

Ballochry, Tarbert, Argyll; North
Strathclyde at Campbeltown.
Strathclyde Region
Argyll and Bute District.

Ballogie, Aboyne, Kincardineshire;
Grampian, Highland and Islands at
Stonehaven.
Grampian Region
Kincardine and Deeside District.

Ballumbie, Dundee; Tayside, Central and Fife at Dundee.
Tayside Region
City of Dundee District.

Ballygown, Ulva Ferry, Isle of Mull; North Strathclyde at Oban.
Strathclyde Region
Argyll and Bute District.

Ballygrant, Isle of Islay; North Strathclyde at Campbeltown.
Strathclyde Region
Argyll and Bute District.

Balmacara, Kyle of Lochalsh, Ross-shire; Grampian, Highland and Islands at Dingwall.
Highland Region
Skye and Lochalsh District.

Balmaclellan, Castle Douglas, Kirkcudbrightshire; South Strathclyde, Dumfries and Galloway at Kirkcudbright.
Dumfries and Galloway Region
Stewartry District.

Balmaghie, Castle Douglas, Kirkcudbrightshire; South Strathclyde, Dumfries and Galloway at Kirkcudbright.
Dumfries and Galloway Region
Stewartry District.

Balmaha, Glasgow; Tayside, Central and Fife at Stirling.
Central Region
Stirling District.

Balmalcolm, Cupar, Fife; Tayside, Central and Fife at Cupar.
Fife Region
North East Fife District.

Balmaqueen, Portree, Isle of Skye; Grampian, Highland and Islands at Portree.
Highland Region
Skye and Lochalsh District.

Balmartin, Lochmaddy, Isle of North Uist; Grampian, Highland and Islands at Lochmaddy.
Western Isles Islands Council.

Balmartine, Scarinish, Isle of Tiree; North Strathclyde at Oban.
Strathclyde Region
Argyll and Bute District.

Balmedie, Aberdeen; Grampian, Highland and Islands at Aberdeen.
Highland Region
City of Aberdeen District.

Balmerino, Newport-on-Tay, Fife; Tayside, Central and Fife at Cupar.
Fife Region
North East Fife District.

Balmoral, Ballater, Kincardineshire; Grampian, Highland and Islands at Stonehaven.
Grampian Region
Kincardine and Deeside District.

Balmore, Torrance, Glasgow; Glasgow and Strathkelvin at Glasgow.
Strathclyde Region
City of Glasgow District.

Balmullo, St Andrews, Fife; Tayside, Central and Fife at Cupar.
Fife Region
North East Fife District.

Balnabeen, Conon Bridge, Ross-
shire; Grampian, Highland and
Islands at Dingwall.
Highland Region
Ross and Cromarty District.

Balnabodach, Castlebay, Isle of
Barra; Grampian, Highland and
Islands at Lochmaddy.
Western Isles Islands Council.

Balnaguard, Strathtay, Perthshire;
Tayside, Central and Fife at Perth.
Tayside Region
Perth and Kinross District.

Balnaha, Callander, Stirlingshire;
Tayside, Central and Fife at
Stirling.
Central Region
Stirling District.

Balnaha, Fearn, Ross-shire;
Grampian, Highland and Islands at
Tain.
Highland Region
Ross and Cromarty District.

Balnain, Inverness; Grampian,
Highland and Islands at Inverness.
Highland Region
Inverness District.

Balquhidder, Lochearnhead,
Stirlingshire; Tayside, Central and
Fife at Stirling.
Central Region
Stirling District.

Balranald, Lochmaddy, Isle of
North Uist; Grampian, Highland
and Islands at Lochmaddy.
Western Isles Islands Council.

Baltasound, Unst, Shetland;
Grampian, Highland and Islands at
Lerwick.
Shetland Islands Council.

Balvicar, Oban, Argyll; North
Strathclyde at Oban.
Strathclyde Region
Argyll and Bute District.

Banavie, Fort William, Inverness-
shire; Grampian, Highland and
Islands at Fort William.
Highland Region
Lochaber District.

Banchory, Devenick,
Kincardineshire; Grampian,
Highland and Islands at
Stonehaven.
Grampian Region
Kincardine and Deeside District.

Banff, Grampian, Highland and
Islands at Banff.
Grampian Region
Banff and Buchan District.

Bankend, Dumfries; South
Strathclyde, Dumfries and
Galloway at Dumfries.
Dumfries and Galloway Region
Nithsdale District.

Bankfoot, Perth; Tayside, Central
and Fife at Perth.
Tayside Region
Perth and Kinross District.

Bankhead, Bucksburn, Aberdeen;
Grampian, Highland and Islands at
Aberdeen.
Grampian Region
City of Aberdeen District.

Banknock, Bonnybridge, Stirling;
Tayside, Central and Fife at
Stirling.
Central Region
Stirling District.

Bankshill, Lockerbie,
Dumfriesshire; South Strathclyde,
Dumfries and Galloway at
Dumfries.
Dumfries and Galloway Region
Annandale and Eskdale District.

Bannockburn, Stirling; Tayside,
Central and Fife at Stirling.
Central Region
Stirling District.

Banton, Kilsyth, Glasgow; South
Strathclyde, Dumfries and
Galloway at Airdrie.
Strathclyde Region
Cumbernauld and Kilsyth District.

Barassie, Troon, Ayrshire; South
Strathclyde, Dumfries and
Galloway at Ayr.
Strathclyde Region
Kyle and Carrick District.

Barbaraville, Invergordon, Ross-
shire; Grampian, Highland and
Islands at Tain.
Highland Region
Ross and Cromarty District.

Barbreck, Lochgilphead, Argyll;
North Strathclyde at Dunoon.
Strathclyde Region
Argyll and Bute District.

Barcaldine, Connel, Argyll; North
Strathclyde at Oban.
Strathclyde Region
Argyll and Bute District.

Bardister, Gluss, Ollaberry,
Shetland; Grampian, Highland and
Islands at Lerwick.
Shetland Islands Council.

Bardowie, Milngavie, Glasgow;
North Strathclyde at Dumbarton.
Strathclyde Region
Bearsden and Milngavie District.

Bargeddie, Baillieston, Glasgow;
South Strathclyde, Dumfries and
Galloway at Airdrie.
Strathclyde Region
Monklands District.

Bargrennan, Newton Stewart,
Wigtownshire; South Strathclyde,
Dumfries and Galloway at
Stranraer.
Dumfries and Galloway Region
Wigtown District.

Barnhill, Broughty Ferry, Dundee;
Tayside, Central and Fife at
Dundee.
Tayside Region
City of Dundee District.

Barnhill, Forres, Morayshire;
Grampian, Highland and Islands at
Elgin.
Grampian Region
Moray District.

Barns of Wedderburn, Dundee;
Tayside, Central and Fife at
Dundee.
Tayside Region
City of Dundee District.

Barnton, Edinburgh; Lothian and
Borders at Edinburgh.
Lothian Region
City of Edinburgh District.

Barr, Girvan, Ayrshire; South
Strathclyde, Dumfries and
Galloway at Ayr.
Strathclyde Region
Kyle and Carrick District.

Barrachan, Mochrum, Newton
Stewart, Wigtownshire; South
Strathclyde, Dumfries and
Galloway at Stranraer.
Dumfries and Galloway Region
Wigtown District.

Barrapoll, Scarinish, Isle of Tiree;
North Strathclyde at Oban.
Strathclyde Region
Argyll and Bute District.

Barrhead, Glasgow; North
Strathclyde at Paisley.
Strathclyde Region
Renfrew District.

Barrhill, Girvan, Ayrshire; South
Strathclyde, Dumfries and
Galloway at Ayr.
Strathclyde Region
Kyle and Carrick District.

Barrock, Thurso, Caithness;
Grampian, Highland and Islands at
Wick.
Highland Region
Caithness District.

Barry, Carnoustie, Angus; Tayside,
Central and Fife at Arbroath.
Tayside Region
Angus District.

Barthol Chapel, Inverurie,
Aberdeenshire; Grampian,
Highland and Islands at Aberdeen.
Grampian Region
Gordon District.

Barvas, Isle of Lewis; Grampian,
Highland and Islands at
Stornoway.
Western Isles Islands Council.

Bathgate, West Lothian; Lothian
and Borders at Linlithgow.
Lothian Region
West Lothian District.

Baugh, Scarinish, Isle of Tiree;
North Strathclyde at Oban.
Strathclyde Region
Argyll and Bute District.

Bayble, Isle of Lewis; Grampian,
Highland and Islands at
Stornoway.
Western Isles Islands Council.

Bayhead, Isle of Scalpay, Harris;
Grampian, Highland and Islands at
Stornoway.
Western Isles Islands Council.

Bayhead, Lochmaddy, Isle of North
Uist; Grampian, Highland and
Islands at Lochmaddy.
Western Isles Islands Council.

Bayherivagh, Castlebay, Isle of
Barra; Grampian, Highland and
Islands at Lochmaddy.
Western Isles Islands Council.

Baymore, Lochmaddy, Isle of North
Uist; Grampian, Highland and
Islands at Lochmaddy.
Western Isles Islands Council.

Bearsden, Glasgow; North
Strathclyde at Dumbarton.
Strathclyde Region
Bearsden and Milngavie District.

41

Beattock, Moffat, Dumfriesshire; South Strathclyde, Dumfries and Galloway at Dumfries.
Dumfries and Galloway Region
Annandale and Eskdale District.

Beauly, Inverness-shire; Grampian, Highland and Islands at Inverness.
Highland Region
Inverness District.

Beckrivig, Isle of Harris; Grampian, Highland and Islands at Stornoway.
Western Isles Islands Council.

Bedersaig, Isle of Harris; Grampian, Highland and Islands at Stornoway.
Western Isles Islands Council.

Beeswing, Dalbeattie, Kirkcudbrightshire; South Strathclyde, Dumfries and Galloway at Kirkcudbright.
Dumfries and Galloway Region
Stewartry District.

Beith, Ayrshire; North Strathclyde at Kilmarnock.
Strathclyde Region
Kilmarnock and Louden District.

Belhaven, Dunbar, East Lothian; Lothian and Borders at Haddington.
Lothian Region
East Lothian District.

Belhelvie, Aberdeen; Grampian, Highland and Islands at Aberdeen.
Grampian Region
City of Aberdeen District.

Bellie, Fochabers, Morayshire; Grampian, Highland and Islands at Elgin.
Grampian Region
Moray District.

Bellochantuy, Campbeltown, Argyll; North Strathclyde at Campbeltown.
Strathclyde Region
Argyll and Bute District.

Bellshill, Lanarkshire; South Strathclyde, Dumfries and Galloway at Hamilton.
Strathclyde Region
Hamilton District.

Bellsquarry, Livingston, West Lothian; Lothian and Borders at Linlithgow.
Lothian Region
West Lothian District.

Belmont, Unst, Shetland; Grampian, Highland and Islands at Lerwick.
Shetland Islands Council.

Benbecula, Isle of South Uist; Grampian, Highland and Islands at Lockmaddy.
Western Isles Islands Council.

Benderloch, Connel, Argyll; North Strathclyde at Oban.
Strathclyde Region
Argyll and Bute District.

Benholm, Montrose, Angus; Tayside, Central and Fife at Arbroath.
Tayside Region
Angus District.

Benmore, Dunoon, Argyll; North
Strathclyde at Dunoon.
Strathclyde Region
Argyll and Bute District.

Bentangaval, Castlebay, Isle of
Barra; Grampian, Highland and
Islands at Lochmaddy.
Western Isles Islands Council.

Bentpath, Langholm,
Dumfriesshire; South Strath-
clyde, Dumfries and Galloway at
Dumfries.
Dumfries and Galloway Region
Annandale and Eskdale District.

Bernera, Isle of Lewis; Grampian,
Highland and Islands at
Stornoway.
Western Isles Islands Council.

Berneray, Lochmaddy, Isle of North
Uist; Grampian, Highland and
Islands at Lochmaddy.
Western Isles Islands Council.

Bernisdale, Portree, Isle of Skye;
Grampian, Highland and Islands at
Portree.
Highland Region
Skye and Lochalsh District

Berriedale, Caithness; Grampian,
Highland and Islands at Wick.
Highland Region
Caithness District.

Bettyhill, Thurso, Caithness;
Grampian, Highland and Islands at
Dornoch.
Highland Region
Sutherland District.

Bieldside, Aberdeen; Grampian,
Highland and Islands at Aberdeen.
Grampian Region
City of Aberdeen District.

Biggar, Lanarkshire; South
Strathclyde, Dumfries and
Galloway at Lanark.
Strathclyde Region
Clydesdale District.

Bigton, Shetland; Grampian,
Highland and Islands at Lerwick.
Shetland Islands Council.

Bilbster, Wick, Caithness;
Grampian, Highland and Islands at
Wick.
Highland Region
Caithness District.

Bilston, Roslin, Midlothian; Lothian
and Borders at Edinburgh.
Lothian Region
Midlothian District.

Birkhill, Dundee; Tayside, Central
and Fife at Dundee.
Tayside Region
City of Dundee District.

Birnam, Dunkeld, Perthshire;
Tayside, Central and Fife at Perth.
Tayside Region
Perth and Kinross District.

Birness, Ellon, Aberdeenshire;
Grampian, Highland and Islands at
Aberdeen.
Grampian Region
Gordon District.

Birnie, Elgin, Morayshire;
Grampian, Highland and Islands at
Elgin.
Grampian Region
Moray District.

Birsay, Orkney; Grampian,
Highland and Islands at Kirkwall.
Orkney Islands Council.

Bishopbriggs, Glasgow; Glasgow
and Strathkelvin at Glasgow.
Strathclyde Region
City of Glasgow District.

Bishopmill, Elgin, Morayshire;
Grampian, Highland and Islands at
Elgin.
Grampian Region
Moray District.

Bishopton, Renfrewshire; North
Strathclyde at Paisley.
Strathclyde Region
Renfrew District.

Bixter, Shetland; Grampian,
Highland and Islands at Lerwick.
Shetland Islands Council.

Blackburn, Aberdeen; Grampian,
Highland and Islands at Aberdeen.
Grampian Region
City of Aberdeen District.

Blackburn, Bathgate, West
Lothian; Lothian and Borders at
Linlithgow.
Lothian Region
West Lothian District.

Blackcraig, Newton Stewart,
Wigtownshire; South Strathclyde,
Dumfries and Galloway at
Stranraer.
Dumfries and Galloway Region
Wigtown District.

Blackford, Auchterarder,
Perthshire; Tayside, Central and
Fife at Perth.
Tayside Region
Perth and Kinross District.

Blackhall, Edinburgh; Lothian and
Borders at Edinburgh.
Lothian Region
City of Edinburgh District.

Blackhills, Peterhead,
Aberdeenshire; Grampian,
Highland and Islands at
Peterhead.
Grampian Region
Banff and Buchan District.

Blacklaw, Aberchirder, Banffshire;
Grampian, Highland and Islands at
Banff.
Grampian Region
Banff and Buchan District.

Blacklunans, Blairgowrie
Perthshire; Tayside, Central and
Fife at Perth.
Tayside Region
Perth and Kinross District.

Blackness, Linlithgow, West
Lothian; Tayside, Central and Fife
at Linlithgow.
Lothian Region
West Lothian District.

Blackpart, Dumfries; South
Strathclyde, Dumfries and
Galloway at Dumfries.
Dumfries and Galloway Region
Nithsdale District.

Blackrock, Isle of Islay; North
Strathclyde at Campbeltown.
Strathclyde Region
Argyll and Bute District.

Blacksboat, Ballindalloch,
Morayshire; Grampian, Highland
and Islands at Elgin.
Grampian Region
Moray District.

Blackshiels, Pathhead, Midlothian;
Lothian and Borders at Edinburgh.
Lothian Region
Midlothian District.

Blackwaterfoot, Brodick, Isle of
Arran; North Strathclyde at
Kilmarnock.
Strathclyde Region
Cunninghame District.

Blackwood, Lanark; South
Strathclyde, Dumfries and
Galloway at Lanark.
Strathclyde Region
Clydesdale District.

Bladnoch, Newton Stewart,
Wigtownshire; South Strathclyde,
Dumfries and Galloway at
Stranraer.
Dumfries and Galloway Region
Wigtown District.

Blaich, Fort William, Inverness-
shire; Grampian, Highland and
Islands at Fort William.
Highland Region
Lochaber District.

Blainslie, Galashiels, Selkirkshire;
Lothian and Borders at Selkirk.
Borders Region
Ettrick and Lauderdale District.

Blair Atholl, Pitlochry, Perthshire;
Tayside, Central and Fife at Perth.
Tayside Region
Perth and Kinross District.

Blair Drummond, Stirling; Tayside,
Central and Fife at Stirling.
Central Region
Stirling District.

Blairadam, Kelty, Fife; Tayside,
Central and Fife at Dunfermline.
Fife Region
Dunfermline District.

Blairdaff, Inverurie, Aberdeenshire;
Grampian, Highland and Islands at
Aberdeen.
Grampian Region
Gordon District.

Blairgowrie, Perthshire; Tayside,
Central and Fife at Perth.
Tayside Region
Perth and Kinross District.

Blairhall, Dunfermline, Fife;
Tayside, Central and Fife at
Dunfermline.
Fife Region
Dunfermline District.

Blairingone, Dollar,
Clackmannanshire; Tayside,
Central and Fife at Alloa.
Central Region
Clackmannan District.

Blairlogie, Stirling; Tayside, Central
and Fife at Stirling.
Central Region
Stirling District.

Blairmore, Dunoon, Argyll; North
Strathclyde at Dunoon.
Strathclyde Region
Argyll and Bute District.

Blairs, Aberdeen; Grampian,
Highland and Islands at Aberdeen.
Grampian Region
City of Aberdeen District.

Blanefield, Glasgow; Tayside,
Central and Fife at Stirling.
Central Region
Stirling District.

Blantyre, Glasgow; South
Strathclyde, Dumfries and
Galloway at Hamilton.
Strathclyde Region
Hamilton District.

Blashaval, Lochmaddy, Isle of
North Uist; Grampian, Highland
and Islands at Lochmaddy.
Western Isles Islands Council.

Blebo Craigs, Cupar, Fife; Tayside,
Central and Fife at Cupar.
Fife Region
North East Fife District.

Blyth Bridge, West Linton,
Peeblesshire; Lothian and Borders
at Peebles.
Borders Region
Tweeddale District.

Bo'ness, Grangemouth, Falkirk;
Tayside, Central and Fife at
Falkirk.
Central Region
Falkirk District.

Boarhills, St Andrews, Fife;
Tayside, Central and Fife at
Cupar.
Fife Region
North East Fife District.

Boat of Garten, Aviemore,
Inverness-shire; Grampian,
Highland and Islands at Inverness.
Highland Region
Badenoch and Strathspey District.

Boath, Alness, Ross-shire;
Grampian, Highland and Islands at
Tain.
Highland Region
Ross and Cromarty District.

Boddam, Peterhead,
Aberdeenshire; Grampian,
Highland and Islands at
Peterhead.
Grampian Region
Banff and Buchan District.

Bodesbeck, Moffat, Dumfriesshire;
South Strathclyde, Dumfries and
Galloway at Dumfries.
Dumfries and Galloway Region.
Annandale and Eskdale District.

Bogach, Castlebay, Isle of Barra;
Grampian, Highland and Islands at
Lochmaddy.
Western Isles Islands Council.

Bogend, Duns, Berwickshire;
Lothian and Borders at Duns.
Borders Region
Berwickshire District.

Boghead, Lesmahagow,
Lanarkshire; South Strathclyde,
Dumfries and Galloway at Lanark.
Strathclyde Region
Clydesdale District.

Bogmoor, Spey Bay, Fochabers
Morayshire; Grampian, Highland
and Islands at Elgin.
Grampian Region
Moray District.

Bogmuchais, Fordyce, Portsoy,
Banffshire; Grampian, Highland
and Islands at Banff.
Grampian Region
Banff and Buchan District.

Bogroy, Kirkhill, Inverness-shire;
Grampian, Highland and Islands at
Inverness.
Highland Region
Inverness.

Bogside, Irvine, Ayrshire; North
Strathclyde at Kilmarnock.
Strathclyde Region
Cunninghame District.

Bogside Station, Alloa,
Clackmannanshire; Tayside,
Central and Fife at Alloa.
Central Region
Clackmannan District.

Bogston, Greenock, Renfrewshire;
North Strathclyde at Greenock.
Strathclyde Region
Inverclyde District.

Bonahaven, Port Askaig, Isle of
Islay; North Strathclyde at
Campbeltown.
Strathclyde Region
Argyll and Bute District.

Bonar Bridge, Ardgay, Ross-shire;
Grampian, Highland and Islands at
Dornoch.
Highland Region
Sutherland District.

Bonawe, Connel, Argyll; North
Strathclyde at Oban.
Strathclyde Region
Argyll and Bute District.

Bonchester Bridge, Hawick,
Roxburghshire; Lothian and
Borders at Jedburgh.
Borders Region
Roxburgh District.

Bonhill, Alexandria,
Dunbartonshire; North Strathclyde
at Dumbarton.
Strathclyde Region
Dumbarton District.

Bonjedward, Jedburgh,
Roxburghshire; Lothian and
Borders at Jedburgh.
Borders Region
Roxburgh District.

Bonkyl, Duns, Berwickshire;
Lothian and Borders at Duns.
Borders Region
Berwickshire District.

Bonnybank, Leven, Fife; Tayside,
Central and Fife at Kirkcaldy.
Fife Region
Kirkcaldy District.

Bonnybridge, Falkirk; Tayside,
Central and Fife at Falkirk.
Central Region
Falkirk District.

Bonnykelly, Fraserburgh,
Aberdeenshire; Grampian,
Highland and Islands at Banff.
Grampian Region
Banff and Buchan District.

Bonnyrigg, Midlothian; Lothian and
Borders at Edinburgh.
Lothian Region
Midlothian District.

Boqhan, Stirling; Tayside, Central
and Fife at Stirling.
Central Region
Stirling District.

Boreland, Lockerbie,
Dumfriesshire; South Strath-
clyde, Dumfries and Galloway at
Dumfries.
Dumfries and Galloway Region
Annandale and Eskdale District.

Borgie, Skerray, Thurso,
Caithness; Grampian, Highland
and Islands at Dornoch.
Highland Region
Sutherland District.

Borgue, Kirkcudbright; South
Strathclyde, Dumfries and
Galloway at Kirkcudbright.
Dumfries and Galloway Region
Stewartry District.

Bornish, Lochboisdale, Isle of
South Uist; Grampian, Highland
and Islands at Lochmaddy.
Western Isles Islands Council.

Borreraig, Portree, Isle of Skye;
Grampian, Highland and Islands at
Portree.
Highland Region
Skye and Lochalsh District.

Borrisdale, Leverburgh, Isle of
Harris; Grampian, Highland and
Islands at Stornoway.
Western Isles Islands Council.

Borrowston, Isle of Lewis;
Grampian, Highland and Islands at
Stornoway.
Western Isles Islands Council.

Borsam, Isle of Harris; Grampian,
Highlands and Islands at
Stornoway.
Western Isles Islands Council.

Borthwickbrae, Hawick,
Roxburghshire; Lothian and
Borders at Jedburgh.
Borders Region
Roxburgh District.

Borve, Castlebay, Isle of Barra;
Grampian, Highland and Islands at
Lochmaddy.
Western Isles Islands Council.

Borve, Isle of Harris; Grampian,
Highland and Islands at
Stornoway.
Western Isles Islands Council.

Borve, Isle of Lewis; Grampian,
Highland and Islands at
Stornoway.
Western Isles Islands Council.

Borve, Portree, Isle of Skye;
Grampian, Highland and Islands at
Portree.
Highland Region
Skye and Lochalsh District.

Bothkennar, Falkirk, Stirlingshire; Tayside, Central and Fife at Falkirk.
Central Region
Falkirk District.

Bothwell, Glasgow; South Strathclyde, Dumfries and Galloway at Hamilton.
Strathclyde Region
Hamilton District.

Botriphnie, Keith, Banffshire; Grampian, Highland and Islands at Elgin.
Grampian Region
Moray District.

Bourtie, Inverurie, Aberdeenshire; Grampian, Highland and Islands at Aberdeen.
Grampian Region
Gordon District.

Bourtreehill, Irvine, Ayrshire; North Strathclyde at Kilmarnock.
Strathclyde Region
Cunninghame District.

Bow of Fife, Cupar, Fife; Tayside, Central and Fife at Cupar.
Fife Region
North East Fife District.

Bowden, Melrose, Roxburghshire; Lothian and Borders at Selkirk.
Borders Region
Ettrick and Lauderdale District.

Bower, Wick, Caithness; Grampian, Highland and Islands at Wick.
Highland Region
Caithness District.

Bowglass, Isle of Harris; Grampian, Highland and Islands at Stornoway.
Western Isles Islands Council.

Bowland, Galashiels, Selkirkshire; Lothian and Borders at Selkirk.
Borders Region
Ettrick and Lauderdale District.

Bowling, Dumbarton; North Strathclyde at Dumbarton.
Strathclyde Region
Dumbarton District.

Bowmore, Isle of Islay; North Strathclyde at Campbeltown.
Strathclyde Region
Argyll and Bute District.

Bowtrees, Grangemouth, Stirlingshire; Tayside, Central and Fife at Falkirk.
Central Region
Falkirk District.

Boyndie, Banff; Grampian, Highland and Islands at Banff.
Grampian Region
Banff and Buchan District.

Boyndlie, Fraserburgh, Banffshire; Grampian, Highland and Islands at Banff.
Grampian Region
Banff and Buchan District.

Bracadale, Portree, Isle of Skye; Grampian, Highland and Islands at Portree.
Highland Region
Skye and Lochalsh District.

Braco, Dunblane, Stirlingshire;
Tayside, Central and Fife at
Stirling.
Central Region
Stirling District.

Bracora, Morar, Mallaig, Inverness-
shire; Grampian, Highland and
Islands at Fort William.
Highland Region
Lochaber District.

Brae, Shetland; Grampian,
Highland and Islands at Lerwick.
Shetland Islands Council.

Braehead, Forth, Lanark; South
Strathclyde, Dumfries and
Galloway at Lanark.
Strathclyde Region
Clydesdale District.

Braemar, Kincardineshire;
Grampian, Highland and Islands at
Stonehaven.
Strathclyde Region
Kincardine and Deeside District.

Braemore, Dunbeath, Caithness;
Grampian, Highland and Islands at
Wick.
Highland Region
Caithness District.

Braemore Lodge, Garve, Ross-
shire; Grampian, Highland and
Islands at Dingwall.
Highland Region
Ross and Cromarty District.

Braes, Portree, Isle of Skye;
Grampian, Highland and Islands at
Portree.
Highland Region
Skye and Lochalsh District.

Braes of Coull, Kirriemuir, Angus;
Tayside, Central and Fife at
Forfar.
Tayside Region
Angus District.

Braeswick, Sanday, Orkney;
Grampian, Highland and Islands at
Kirkwall.
Orkney Islands Council.

Bragar, Isle of Lewis; Grampian,
Highland and Islands at
Stornoway.
Western Isles Islands Council.

Brahan, Conon Bridge, Ross-shire;
Grampian, Highland and Islands at
Dingwall.
Highland Region
Ross and Cromarty District.

Braidhills, Midlothian; Lothian and
Borders at Edinburgh.
Lothian Region
Midlothian District.

Braidwood, Carluke, Lanarkshire;
South Strathclyde, Dumfries and
Galloway at Lanark.
Strathclyde Region
Clydesdale District.

Branahuie, Isle of Lewis;
Grampian, Highland and Islands at
Stornoway.
Western Isles Islands Council.

Brasswell, Dumfries; South
Strathclyde, Dumfries and
Galloway at Dumfries.
Dumfries and Galloway Region
Nithsdale District.

Breaclete, Bernera, Isle of Lewis; Grampian, Highland and Islands at Stornoway.
Western Isles Islands Council.

Breakish, Isle of Skye; Grampian, Highland and Islands at Portree.
Highland Region
Skye and Lochalsh District.

Breanish, Isle of Lewis; Grampian, Highland and Islands at Stornoway.
Western Isles Islands Council.

Breasclete, Isle of Lewis; Grampian, Highland and Islands at Stornoway.
Western Isles Islands Council.

Brechin, Angus; Tayside, Central and Fife at Forfar.
Tayside Region
Angus District.

Breich, West Calder, West Lothian; Lothian and Borders at Linlithgow.
Lothian Region
West Lothian District.

Bressay, Shetland; Grampian, Highland and Islands at Lerwick.
Shetland Islands Council.

Brettabister, Shetland; Grampian, Highland and Islands at Lerwick.
Shetland Islands Council.

Brevig, Castlebay, Isle of Barra; Grampian, Highland and Islands at Lochmaddy.
Western Isles Islands Council.

Bridge of Alford, Alford, Aberdeenshire; Grampian, Highland and Islands at Aberdeen.
Grampian Region
Gordon District.

Bridge of Allan, Stirling; Tayside, Central and Fife at Stirling.
Central Region
Stirling District.

Bridge of Balgie, Aberfeldy, Perthshire; Tayside, Central and Fife at Perth.
Tayside Region
Perth and Kinross District.

Bridge of Cally, Blairgowrie, Perthshire; Tayside, Central and Fife at Perth.
Tayside Region
Perth and Kinross District.

Bridge of Canny, Banchory, Kincardineshire; Grampian, Highland and Islands at Stonehaven.
Grampian Region
Kincardine and Deeside District.

Bridge of Dee, Castle Douglas, Kirkcudbright; South Strathclyde, Dumfries and Galloway at Kirkcudbright.
Dumfries and Galloway Region
Stewartry District.

Bridge of Dee, Kincardineshire; Grampian, Highland and Islands at Stonehaven.
Grampian Region
Kincardine and Deeside District.

Bridge of Don, Aberdeenshire;
Grampian, Highland and Islands at
Aberdeen.
Grampian Region
Gordon District.

Bridge of Dun, Montrose, Angus;
Tayside, Central and Fife at
Arbroath.
Tayside Region
Angus District.

Bridge of Dye, Kincardineshire;
Grampian, Highland and Islands at
Stonehaven.
Grampian Region
Kincardine and Deeside District.

Bridge of Earn, Perth; Tayside,
Central and Fife at Perth.
Tayside Region
Perth and Kinross District.

Bridge of Feugh, Banchory,
Kincardineshire; Grampian,
Highland and Islands at
Stonehaven.
Grampian Region
Kincardine and Deeside District.

Bridge of Fiddich, Dufftown,
Morayshire; Grampian, Highland
and Islands at Elgin.
Grampian Region
Moray District.

Bridge of Gairn, Ballater,
Kincardineshire; Grampian,
Highland and Islands at
Stonehaven.
Grampian Region
Kincardine and Deeside District.

Bridge of Gaur, Rannoch Station,
Perthshire; Tayside, Central and
Fife at Perth.
Tayside Region
Perth and Kinross District.

Bridge of Marnoch, Huntly,
Aberdeenshire; Grampian,
Highland and Islands at Aberdeen.
Grampian Region
Gordon District.

Bridge of Orchy, Oban, Argyll;
North Strathclyde at Oban.
Strathclyde Region
Argyll and Bute District.

Bridge of Urr, Castle Douglas,
Kirkcudbright; South Strathclyde,
Dumfries and Galloway at
Kirkcudbright.
Dumfries and Galloway Region
Stewartry District.

Bridge of Walls, Shetland;
Grampian, Highland and Islands at
Lerwick.
Shetland Islands Council.

Bridge of Weir, Johnstone,
Renfrewshire; North Strathclyde at
Paisley.
Strathclyde Region
Renfrew District.

Bridgefoot, Dundee; Tayside,
Central and Fife at Dundee.
Tayside Region
City of Dundee District.

Bridgend, Dumbarton; North
Strathclyde at Dumbarton.
Strathclyde Region
Dumbarton District.

Bridgend, Isle of Islay; North Strathclyde at Campbeltown.
Strathclyde Region
Argyll and Bute District.

Bridgend, Linlithgow, West Lothian; Lothian and Borders at Linlithgow.
Lothian Region
West Lothian District.

Bridgend, Shetland; Grampian, Highland and Islands at Lerwick.
Shetland Islands Council.

Bridgeton, Glasgow; Glasgow and Strathkelvin at Glasgow.
Strathclyde Region
City of Glasgow District.

Brig O'Turk, Callander, Stirlingshire; Tayside, Central and Fife at Stirling.
Central Region
Stirling District.

Brightons, Falkirk, Stirlingshire; Tayside, Central and Fife at Falkirk.
Central Region
Falkirk District.

Brighty, Dundee; Tayside, Central and Fife at Dundee.
Tayside Region
City of Dundee District.

Broadford, Isle of Skye; Grampian, Highland and Islands at Portree.
Highland Region
Skye and Lochalsh District.

Broadsea, Fraserburgh, Banffshire; Grampian, Highland and Islands at Banff.
Grampian Region
Banff and Buchan District.

Brodick, Isle of Arran; North Strathclyde at Kilmarnock.
Strathclyde Region
Cunninghame District.

Brodie, Forres, Morayshire; Grampian, Highland and Islands at Elgin.
Grampian Region
Moray District.

Brodiesord, Cornhill, Banffshire; Grampian, Highland and Islands at Banff.
Grampian Region
Banff and Buchan District.

Broker, Isle of Lewis; Grampian, Highland and Islands at Stornoway.
Western Isles Islands Council.

Brookfield, Johnstone, Renfrewshire; North Strathclyde at Paisley.
Strathclyde Region
Renfrew District.

Broomhouse, Uddingston, Glasgow; South Strathclyde, Dumfries and Galloway at Hamilton.
Strathclyde Region
Hamilton District.

Brora, Sutherland; Grampian, Highland and Islands at Dornoch.
Highland Region
Sutherland District.

Brough, Thurso, Caithness; Grampian, Highland and Islands at Wick.
Highland Region
Caithness District.

Brough, Whalsay, Shetland; Grampian, Highland and Islands at Lerwick.
Shetland Islands Council.

Broughton, Biggar, Lanarkshire; Lothian and Borders at Peebles.
Borders Region
Tweeddale District.

Broughty Ferry, Dundee; Tayside, Central and Fife at Dundee.
Tayside Region
City of Dundee District.

Broxburn, West Lothian; Lothian and Borders at Linlithgow.
Lothian Region
West Lothian District.

Brucehill, Arnprior, Stirling; Tayside, Central and Fife at Stirling.
Central Region
Stirling District.

Brucklay, Peterhead, Aberdeenshire; Grampian, Highland and Islands at Peterhead.
Grampian Region
Banff and Buchan District.

Brue, Isle of Lewis; Grampian, Highland and Islands at Stornoway.
Western Isles Islands Council.

Bruernish, Castlebay, Isle of Barra; Grampian, Highland and Islands at Lochmaddy.
Western Isles Islands Council.

Bruichdu, Port Charlotte, Isle of Islay; North Strathclyde at Campbeltown.
Strathclyde Region
Argyll and Bute District.

Bruichladdich, Isle of Islay; North Strathclyde at Campbeltown.
Strathclyde Region
Argyll and Bute District.

Brunton, Cupar, Fife; Tayside, Central and Fife at Cupar.
Fife Region
North East Fife District.

Brusta, Berneray, Isle of North Uist; Grampian, Highland and Islands at Lochmaddy.
Western Isles Islands Council.

Brydekirk, Annan, Dumfriesshire; South Strathclyde, Dumfries and Galloway at Dumfries.
Dumfries and Galloway Region
Annandale and Eskdale District.

Bualdudh, Lochboisdale, Isle of South Uist; Grampian, Highland and Islands at Lochmaddy.
Western Isles Islands Council.

Buchanhaven, Peterhead, Aberdeenshire; Grampian, Highland and Islands at Peterhead.
Grampian Region
Banff and Buchan District.

Buchany, Doune, Perthshire; Tayside, Central and Fife at Stirling.
Central Region
Stirling District.

Buchlyvie, Stirling; Tayside, Central and Fife at Stirling.
Central Region
Stirling District.

Buckhaven, Leven, Fife; Tayside, Central and Fife at Kirkcaldy.
Fife Region
Kirkcaldy District.

Buckie, Banffshire; Grampian, Highland and Islands at Elgin.
Grampian Region
Moray District.

Buckpool, Buckie, Banffshire; Grampian, Highland and Islands at Elgin.
Grampian Region
Moray District.

Bucksburn, Aberdeen; Grampian, Highland and Islands at Aberdeen.
Grampian Region
City of Aberdeen District.

Bun-a-Mhullin, Eriskay, Isle of South Uist; Grampian, Highland and Islands at Lochmaddy.
Western Isles Islands Council.

Bunanuisg, Bowmore, Isle of Islay; North Strathclyde at Campbeltown.
Strathclyde Region
Argyll and Bute District.

Bunavoneader, Isle of Harris; Grampian, Highland and Islands at Lochmaddy.
Western Isles Islands Council.

Bunchrew, Inverness; Grampian, Highland and Islands at Inverness.
Highland Region
Inverness District.

Bunessan, Isle of Mull; North Strathclyde at Oban.
Strathclyde Region
Argyll and Bute District.

Bunnahabhainn, Isle of Islay; North Strathclyde at Campbeltown.
Strathclyde Region
Argyll and Bute District.

Burghead, Elgin, Morayshire; Grampian, Highland and Islands at Elgin.
Grampian Region
Moray District.

Burgie, Forres, Morayshire; Grampian, Highland and Islands at Elgin.
Grampian Region
Moray District.

Burn of Cambus, Doune, Stirlingshire; Tayside, Central and Fife at Stirling.
Central Region
Stirling District.

Burnbank, Hamilton, Lanarkshire; South Strathclyde, Dumfries and Galloway at Hamilton.
Strathclyde Region
Hamilton District.

Burnbrae, Alexandria, Dunbartonshire; North Strathclyde at Dumbarton.
Strathclyde Region
Dumbarton District.

Burnfoot, Lesmahagow, Lanarkshire; South Strathclyde, Dumfries and Galloway at Lanark.
Strathclyde Region
Clydesdale District.

Burnhaven, Peterhead,
Aberdeenshire; Grampian,
Highland and Islands at
Peterhead.
Grampian Region
Banff and Buchan District.

Burnhead, Thornhill,
Dumfriesshire; South Strath-
clyde, Dumfries and Galloway at
Dumfries.
Dumfries and Galloway Region
Nithsdale District.

Burnhervie, Inverurie,
Aberdeenshire; Grampian,
Highland and Islands at Aberdeen.
Grampian Region
Gordon District.

Burnhouse, Beith, Ayrshire; North
Strathclyde at Kilmarnock.
Strathclyde Region
Cunninghame District.

Burnmouth, Eyemouth,
Berwickshire; Lothian and Borders
at Duns.
Borders Region
Berwickshire District.

Burnside, Borve, Isle of Lewis;
Grampian, Highland and Islands at
Stornoway.
Western Isles Islands Council.

Burnside, Forfar, Angus; Tayside,
Central and Fife at Forfar.
Tayside Region
Angus District.

Burnside, Rutherglen, Glasgow;
Glasgow and Strathkelvin at
Glasgow.
Strathclyde Region
City of Glasgow District.

Burntisland, Fife; Tayside, Central
and Fife at Kirkcaldy.
Fife Region
Kirkcaldy District.

Burravoe, Yell, Shetland;
Grampian, Highland and Islands at
Lerwick.
Shetland Islands Council.

Burray, Orkney; Grampian,
Highland and Islands at Kirkwall.
Orkney Islands Council.

Burrelton, Blairgowrie, Perthshire;
Tayside, Central and Fife at Perth.
Tayside Region
Perth and Kinross District.

Burwick, Orkney; Grampian,
Highland and Islands at Kirkwall.
Orkney Islands Council.

Busby, Clarkston, Glasgow; North
Strathclyde at Paisley.
Strathclyde Region
Renfrew District.

Bush Estate, Penicuik, Midlothian;
Lothian and Borders at Edinburgh.
Lothian Region
Midlothian District.

Butterston, Dunkeld, Perthshire;
Tayside, Central and Fife at Perth.
Tayside Region
Perth and Kinross District.

Cabrach, Huntly, Morayshire;
Grampian, Highland and Islands at
Elgin.
Grampian Region
Moray District.

Caerlaverock, Dumfries; South Strathclyde, Dumfries and Galloway at Dumfries.
Dumfries and Galloway Region
Nithsdale District.

Cairnbaan, Lochgilphead, Argyll; North Strathclyde at Dunoon.
Strathclyde Region
Argyll and Bute District.

Cairnbulg, Fraserburgh, Aberdeenshire; Grampian, Highland and Islands at Banff.
Grampian Region
Banff and Buchan District.

Cairndow, Inverary, Argyll; North Strathclyde at Dunoon.
Strathclyde Region
Argyll and Bute District.

Cairness, Fraserburgh, Aberdeenshire; Grampian, Highland and Islands at Banff.
Grampian Region
Banff and Buchan District.

Cairneyhill, Dunfermline, Fife; Tayside, Central and Fife at Dunfermline.
Fife Region
Dunfermline District.

Cairnie, Huntly, Aberdeenshire; Grampian, Highland and Islands at Aberdeen.
Grampian Region
Gordon District.

Cairnorrie, Ellon, Aberdeenshire; Grampian, Highland and Islands at Aberdeen.
Grampian Region
Gordon District.

Cairnryan, Stranraer, Wigtownshire; South Strathclyde, Dumfries and Galloway at Stranraer.
Dumfries and Galloway Region
Wigtown District.

Calbost, Isle of Lewis; Grampian, Highland and Islands at Stornoway.
Western Isles Islands Council.

Calcots, Elgin, Morayshire; Grampian, Highland and Islands at Elgin.
Grampian Region
Moray District.

Caldarvan, Alexandria, Dunbartonshire; North Strathclyde at Dumbarton.
Strathclyde Region
Dumbarton District.

Calderbank, Airdrie, Lanarkshire; South Strathclyde, Dumfries and Galloway at Airdrie.
Strathclyde Region
Monklands District.

Caldercruix, Airdrie, Lanarkshire; South Strathclyde, Dumfries and Galloway at Airdrie.
Strathclyde Region
Monklands District.

Caldermill, Strathaven, Lanarkshire; South Strathclyde, Dumfries and Galloway at Hamilton.
Strathclyde Region
Hamilton District.

Caldwell, Uplawmoor, Glasgow;
North Strathclyde at Paisley.
Strathclyde Region
Renfrew District.

Calfsound, Eday, Orkney;
Grampian, Highland and Islands at
Kirkwall.
Orkney Islands Council.

Calgary, Ardvassar, Isle of Skye;
Grampian, Highland and Islands at
Portree.
Highland Region
Skye and Lochalsh District.

Calgary, Tobermory, Isle of Mull;
North Strathclyde at Oban.
Strathclyde Region
Argyll and Bute District.

California, Falkirk, Stirlingshire;
Tayside, Central and Fife at
Falkirk.
Central Region
Falkirk District.

Callander, Stirlingshire; Tayside,
Central and Fife at Stirling.
Central Region
Stirling District.

Callanish, Isle of Lewis; Grampian,
Highland and Islands at
Stornoway.
Western Isles Islands Council.

Calvine, Pitlochry, Perthshire;
Tayside, Central and Fife at Perth.
Tayside Region
Perth and Kinross District.

Camasnacroise, Strontian,
Inverness-shire; Grampian,
Highland and Islands at Fort
William.
Highland Region
Lochaber District.

Camb, Yell, Shetland; Grampian,
Highland and Islands at Lerwick.
Shetland Islands Council.

Cambroe, Coatbridge, Lanarkshire;
South Strathclyde, Dumfries and
Galloway at Airdrie.
Strathclyde Region
Monklands District.

Cambus O'May, Ballater,
Kincardineshire; Grampian,
Highland and Islands at
Stonehaven.
Grampian Region
Kincardine and Deeside District.

Cambusbarron, Stirling; Tayside,
Central and Fife at Stirling.
Central Region
Stirling District.

Cambuslang, Glasgow; Glasgow
and Strathkelvin at Glasgow.
Strathclyde Region
City of Glasgow District.

Cambusmore, Callander,
Stirlingshire; Tayside, Central and
Fife at Stirling.
Central Region
Stirling District.

Camelon, Falkirk, Stirlingshire;
Tayside, Central and Fife at
Falkirk.
Central Region
Falkirk District.

Cammachmore, Stonehaven,
Kincardineshire; Grampian,
Highland and Islands at
Stonehaven.
Grampian Region
Kincardine and Deeside District.

Campbeltown, Argyll; North
Strathclyde at Campbeltown.
Strathclyde Region
Argyll and Bute District.

Campfield, Glassel,
Aberdeenshire; Grampian,
Highland and Islands at Aberdeen.
Grampian Region
City of Aberdeen District.

Cample, Thornhill, Dumfriesshire;
South Strathclyde, Dumfries and
Galloway at Dumfries.
Dumfries and Galloway Region
Nithsdale District.

Camserney, Aberfeldy, Perthshire;
Tayside, Central and Fife at Perth.
Tayside Region
Perth and Kinross District.

Camuscross, Isle Ornsay, Isle of
Skye; Grampian, Highland and
Islands at Portree.
Highland Region
Skye and Lochalsh District.

Camustianivaig, Portree, Isle of
Skye; Grampian, Highland and
Islands at Portree.
Highland Region
Skye and Lochalsh District.

Canisbay, John o' Groats, Wick,
Caithness; Grampian, Highland
and Islands at Wick.
Highland Region
Caithness District.

Cannich, Beauly, Inverness-shire;
Grampian, Highland and Islands at
Inverness.
Highland Region
Inverness District.

Canonbie, Annan, Dumfriesshire;
South Strathclyde, Dumfries and
Galloway at Dumfries.
Dumfries and Galloway Region
Annandale and Eskdale District.

Caol, Fort William, Inverness-shire;
Grampian, Highland and Islands at
Fort William.
Highland Region
Lochaber District.

Caolila, Port Askaig, Isle of Islay;
North Strathclyde at
Campbeltown.
Strathclyde Region
Argyll and Bute District.

Caolis, Scarinish, Isle of Tiree;
North Strathclyde at Oban.
Strathclyde Region
Argyll and Bute District.

Caolis, Vatersay, Castlebay, Isle of
Barra; Grampian, Highland and
Islands at Lochmaddy.
Western Isles Islands Council.

Cappercleuch, Selkirk; Lothian and
Borders at Selkirk.
Borders Region
Ettrick and Lauderdale District.

Caputh, Perth; Tayside, Central
and Fife at Perth.
Tayside Region
Perth and Kinross District.

Carberry, Musselburgh, East Lothian; Lothian and Borders at Haddington.
Lothian Region
East Lothian District.

Carbost, Sligachan, Portree, Isle of Skye; Grampian, Highland and Islands at Portree.
Highland Region
Skye and Lochalsh District.

Cardenden, Lochgelly, Fife; Tayside, Central and Fife at Kirkcaldy.
Fife Region
Kirkcaldy District.

Cardonald, Glasgow; Glasgow and Strathkelvin at Glasgow.
Strathclyde Region
City of Glasgow District.

Cardross, Dumbarton; North Strathclyde at Dumbarton.
Strathclyde Region
Dumbarton District.

Careston, Brechin, Angus; Tayside, Central and Fife at Forfar.
Tayside Region
Angus District.

Carfin, Lanarkshire; South Strathclyde, Dumfries and Galloway at Hamilton.
Strathclyde Region
Hamilton District.

Carfraemill, Lauder, Berwickshire; Lothian and Borders at Selkirk.
Borders Region
Ettrick and Lauderdale District.

Cargenbridge, Dumfries; South Strathclyde, Dumfries and Galloway at Dumfries.
Dumfries and Galloway Region
Nithsdale District.

Cargill, Perth; Tayside, Central and Fife at Perth.
Tayside Region
Perth and Kinross District.

Carinish, Lochmaddy, Isle of North Uist; Grampian, Highland and Islands at Lochmaddy.
Western Isles Islands Council.

Carishader, Uig, Isle of Lewis; Grampian, Highland and Islands at Stornoway.
Western Isles Islands Council.

Carlops, West Linton, Peeblesshire; Lothian and Borders at Peebles.
Borders Region
Tweeddale District.

Carloway, Isle of Lewis; Grampian, Highland and Islands at Stornoway.
Western Isles Islands Council.

Carluke, Lanarkshire; South Strathclyde, Dumfries and Galloway at Lanark.
Strathclyde Region
Clydesdale District.

Carmichael, Biggar, Lanarkshire; South Strathclyde, Dumfries and Galloway at Lanark.
Strathclyde Region
Clydesdale District.

Carmont, Stonehaven, Kincardineshire; Grampian, Highland and Islands at Stonehaven.
Grampian Region
Kincardine and Deeside District.

Carmunnock, Clarkston, Glasgow; Glasgow and Strathkelvin at Glasgow.
Strathclyde Region
City of Glasgow District.

Carmyle, Glasgow; Glasgow and Strathkelvin at Glasgow.
Strathclyde Region
City of Glasgow District.

Carmyllie, Arbroath, Angus; Tayside, Central and Fife at Arbroath.
Tayside Region
Angus District.

Carnan Eochar, Lochboisdale, Isle of South Uist; Grampian, Highland and Islands at Lochmaddy.
Western Isles Islands Council.

Carnbee, Anstruther, Fife; Tayside, Central and Fife at Cupar.
Fife Region
North East Fife District.

Carnbo, Kinross; Tayside, Central and Fife at Perth.
Tayside Region
Perth and Kinross District.

Carnish, Uig, Isle of Lewis; Grampian, Highland and Islands at Stornoway.
Western Isles Islands Council.

Carnock, Dunfermline, Fife; Tayside, Central and Fife at Dunfermline.
Fife Region
Dunfermline District.

Carnoustie, Angus; Tayside, Central and Fife at Arbroath.
Tayside Region
Angus District.

Carnwath, Lanark; South Strathclyde, Dumfries and Galloway at Lanark.
Strathclyde Region
Clydesdale District.

Caros, Cromore, Isle of Lewis; Grampian, Highland and Islands at Stornoway.
Western Isles Islands Council.

Carradale, Campbeltown, Argyll; North Strathclyde at Campbeltown.
Strathclyde Region
Argyll and Bute District.

Carrbridge, Inverness-shire; Grampian, Highland and Islands at Inverness.
Highland Region
Badenoch and Strathspey District.

Carrick, Lochgoilhead, Argyll; North Strathclyde at Dunoon.
Strathclyde Region
Argyll and Bute District.

Carriden, Bo'ness, Grangemouth, Stirlingshire; Tayside, Central and Fife at Falkirk.
Central Region
Falkirk District.

Carriegreich, Isle of Harris;
Grampian, Highland and Islands at
Stornoway.
Western Isles Islands Council.

Carrington, Gorebridge,
Midlothian; Lothian and Borders at
Edinburgh.
Lothian Region
Midlothian District.

Carron, Falkirk, Stirlingshire;
Tayside, Central and Fife at
Falkirk.
Central Region
Falkirk District.

Carron, Rothes, Morayshire;
Grampian, Highland and Islands at
Elgin.
Grampian Region
Moray District.

Carronbridge, Thornhill,
Dumfriesshire; South Strath-
clyde, Dumfries and Galloway at
Dumfries.
Dumfries and Galloway Region
Nithsdale District.

Carrutherstown, Dumfries:
South Strathclyde, Dumfries and
Galloway at Dumfries.
Dumfries and Galloway Region
Nithsdale District.

Carse, Tarbert, Argyll; North
Strathclyde at Campbeltown.
Strathclyde Region
Argyll and Bute District.

Carsethorn, Dumfries; South
Strathclyde, Dumfries and
Galloway at Dumfries.
Dumfries and Galloway Region
Nithsdale District.

Carskiey, Campbeltown, Argyll;
North Strathclyde at
Campbeltown.
Strathclyde Region
Argyll and Bute District.

Carsluith, Newton Stewart,
Wigtownshire; South Strathclyde,
Dumfries and Galloway at
Stranraer.
Dumfries and Galloway Region
Wigtown District.

Carsphairn, Castle Douglas,
Kirkcudbrightshire; South
Strathclyde, Dumfries and
Galloway at Kirkcudbright.
Dumfries and Galloway Region
Stewartry District.

Carstairs, Lanark; South
Strathclyde, Dumfries and
Galloway at Lanark.
Strathclyde Region
Clydesdale District.

Carter Bar, Jedburgh,
Roxburghshire; Lothian and
Borders at Jedburgh.
Borders Region
Roxburgh District.

Cartland, Lanark; South
Strathclyde, Dumfries and
Galloway at Lanark.
Strathclyde Region
Clydesdale District.

Cassilis Station, Maybole,
Ayrshire; South Strathclyde,
Dumfries and Galloway at Ayr.
Strathclyde Region
Kyle and Carrick District.

Castle Douglas,
Kirkcudbrightshire; South
Strathclyde, Dumfries and
Galloway at Kirkcudbright.
Dumfries and Galloway Region
Stewartry District.

Castle Fraser, Inverurie,
Aberdeenshire; Grampian,
Highland and Islands at Aberdeen.
Grampian Region
Gordon District.

Castle Kennedy, Stranraer,
Wigtownshire; South Strathclyde,
Dumfries and Galloway at
Stranraer.
Dumfries and Galloway Region
Wigtown District.

Castlebay, Isle of Barra; Grampian,
Highland and Islands at
Lochmaddy.
Western Isles Islands Council.

Castlecary, Bonnybridge, Falkirk;
Tayside, Central and Fife at
Falkirk.
Central Region
Falkirk District.

Castleton, Lochgilphead, Argyll;
North Strathclyde at Dunoon.
Strathclyde Region
Argyll and Bute District.

Castletown, Thurso, Caithness;
Grampian, Highland and Islands at
Wick.
Highland Region
Caithness District.

Catacol, Lochranza, Isle of Arran;
North Strathclyde at Kilmarnock.
Strathclyde Region
Cunninghame District.

Catfirth, Skellister, Shetland;
Grampian, Highland and Islands at
Lerwick.
Shetland Islands Council.

Cathcart (except odd nos. Cathcart
Rd), Glasgow; North Strathclyde at
Paisley.
Strathclyde Region
Renfrew District.

Cathcart (odd nos. only Cathcart
Rd), Glasgow; Glasgow and
Strathkelvin at Glasgow.
Strathclyde Region
City of Glasgow District.

Catrine, Mauchline, Ayrshire; South
Strathclyde, Dumfries and
Galloway at Ayr.
Strathclyde Region
Kyle and Carrick District.

Catterline, Stonehaven,
Kincardineshire; Grampian,
Highland and Islands at
Stonehaven.
Strathclyde Region
Kincardine and Deeside District.

Cauldhame, Kippen, Stirling;
Tayside, Central and Fife at
Stirling.
Central Region
Stirling District.

Causewayhead, Stirling; Tayside,
Central and Fife at Stirling.
Central Region
Stirling District.

Caw, Isle of Scalpay, Isle of Harris;
Grampian, Highland and Islands at
Stornoway.
Western Isles Islands Council.

Cawder, Nairn; Grampian, Highland
and Islands at Inverness.
Highland Region
Nairn District.

Cellardyke, Anstruther, Fife;
Tayside, Central and Fife at
Cupar.
Fife Region
North East Fife District.

Ceres, Cupar, Fife; Tayside,
Central and Fife at Cupar.
Fife Region
North East Fife District.

Chance Inn, Cupar, Fife; Tayside,
Central and Fife at Cupar.
Fife Region
North East Fife District.

Chapel, Kirkcaldy, Fife; Tayside,
Central and Fife at Kirkcaldy.
Fife Region
Kirkcaldy District.

Chapel of Garioch, Inverurie,
Aberdeenshire; Grampian,
Highland and Islands at Aberdeen.
Grampian Region
Gordon District.

Chapelcross, Annan,
Dumfriesshire; South Strath-
clyde, Dumfries and Galloway at
Dumfries.
Dumfries and Galloway Region
Annandale and Eskdale District.

Chapelhall, Airdrie, Lanarkshire;
South Strathclyde, Dumfries and
Galloway at Airdrie.
Strathclyde Region
Monklands District.

Chapelknowe, Canonbie,
Dumfriesshire; South Strathclyde,
Dumfries and Galloway at
Dumfries.
Dumfries and Galloway Region
Annandale and Eskdale District.

Chapelton, Arbroath, Angus;
Tayside, Central and Fife at
Arbroath.
Tayside Region
Angus District.

Chapelton, Strathaven,
Lanarkshire; South Strathclyde,
Dumfries and Galloway at
Hamilton.
Strathclyde Region.
Hamilton District.

Chapeltown, Ballindalloch,
Banffshire; Grampian, Highland
and Islands at Elgin.
Grampian Region
Moray District.

Charleston, Forfar, Angus;
Tayside, Central and Fife at
Forfar.
Tayside Region
Angus District.

Charlestown, Dunfermline, Fife;
Tayside, Central and Fife at
Dunfermline.
Fife Region
Dunfermline District.

Charterhall, Duns, Berwickshire;
Lothian and Borders at Duns.
Borders Region
Berwickshire District.

Chartershall, Stirling; Tayside, Central and Fife at Stirling.
Central Region
Stirling District.

Cheesebay, Lochmaddy, Isle of North Uist; Grampian, Highland and Islands at Lochmaddy.
Western Isles Islands Council.

Chesters, Hawick, Roxburghshire; Lothian and Borders at Jedburgh.
Borders Region
Roxburgh District.

Chirnside, Duns, Berwickshire; Lothian and Borders at Duns.
Borders Region
Berwickshire District.

Chryston, Glasgow; Glasgow and Strathkelvin at Glasgow.
Strathclyde Region
City of Glasgow District.

Clabhach, Isle of Coll; North Strathclyde at Oban.
Strathclyde Region
Argyll and Bute District.

Clachaig, Dunoon, Argyll; North Strathclyde at Dunoon.
Strathclyde Region
Argyll and Bute District.

Clachaig, Killin, Stirlingshire; Tayside, Central and Fife at Stirling.
Central Region
Stirling District.

Clachan, Eochar, Isle of South Uist; Grampian, Highland and Islands at Lochmaddy.
Western Isles Islands Council.

Clachan, Tarbert, Argyll; North Strathclyde at Campbeltown.
Strathclyde Region
Argyll and Bute District.

Clachan Locheport, Isle of North Uist; Grampian, Highland and Islands at Lochmaddy.
Western Isles Islands Council.

Clachan Seil, Oban, Argyll; North Strathclyde at Oban.
Strathclyde Region
Argyll and Bute District.

Clachnaharry, Inverness; Grampian, Highland and Islands at Inverness.
Highland Region
Inverness District.

Clackmannan; Tayside, Central and Fife at Alloa.
Central Region
Clackmannan District.

Claddach, Lochmaddy, Isle of North Uist; Grampian, Highland and Islands at Lochmaddy.
Western Isles Islands Council.

Cladich, Dalmally, Argyll; North Strathclyde at Oban.
Strathclyde Region
Argyll and Bute District.

Claonaig, Tarbert, Argyll; North Strathclyde at Campbeltown.
Strathclyde Region
Argyll and Bute District.

Clarebrand, Castle Douglas, Kirkcudbrightshire; South Strathclyde, Dumfries and Galloway at Kirkcudbright.
Dumfries and Galloway Region
Stewartry District.

Claredon, Thurso, Caithness; Grampian, Highland and Islands at Wick.
Highland Region
Caithness District.

Clarencefield, Dumfries; South Strathclyde, Dumfries and Galloway at Dumfries.
Dumfries and Galloway Region
Nithsdale District.

Clarkston, Glasgow; North Strathclyde at Paisley.
Strathclyde Region
Renfrew District.

Clashmore, Dornoch, Sutherland; Grampian, Highland and Islands at Dornoch.
Highland Region
Sutherland District.

Clashnessie, Lairg, Sutherland; Grampian, Highland and Islands at Dornoch.
Highland Region
Sutherland District.

Clathy, Crieff, Perthshire; Tayside, Central and Fife at Perth.
Tayside Region
Perth and Kinross District.

Clatt, Huntly, Aberdeenshire; Grampian, Highland and Islands at Aberdeen.
Grampian Region
Gordon District.

Claygate, Canonbie, Dumfriesshire; South Strathclyde, Dumfries and Galloway at Dumfries.
Dumfries and Galloway Region
Annandale and Eskdale District.

Cleat, Castlebay, Isle of Barra; Grampian, Highland and Islands at Lochmaddy.
Western Isles Islands Council.

Cleghorn, Lanark; South Strathclyde, Dumfries and Galloway at Lanark.
Strathclyde Region
Clydesdale District.

Cleish, Kinross; Tayside, Central and Fife at Perth.
Tayside Region
Perth and Kinross District.

Cleithaugh, Jedburgh, Roxburghshire; Lothian and Borders at Jedburgh.
Borders Region
Roxburgh District.

Cleland, Motherwell, Lanarkshire; South Strathclyde, Dumfries and Galloway at Hamilton.
Strathclyde Region
Hamilton District.

Clephanton, Nairn; Grampian, Highland and Islands at Inverness.
Highland Region
Nairn District.

Cliasmol, Isle of Harris; Grampian, Highland and Islands at Stornoway.
Western Isles Islands Council.

Cliff, Uig, Isle of Lewis; Grampian, Highland and Islands at Stornoway.
Western Isles Islands Council.

Clifton, Crianlarich, Stirlingshire; Tayside, Central and Fife at Stirling.
Central Region
Stirling District.

Clintmains, Newtown St. Boswells, Roxburghshire; Lothian and Borders at Selkirk.
Borders Region
Ettrick and Lauderdale District.

Clochan, Buckie, Banffshire; Grampian, Highland and Islands at Elgin.
Grampian Region
Moray District.

Clola, Peterhead, Aberdeenshire; Grampian, Highland and Islands at Peterhead.
Grampian Region
Banff and Buchan District.

Closeburn, Thornhill, Dumfriesshire; South Strathclyde, Dumfries and Galloway at Dumfries.
Dumfries and Galloway Region
Nithsdale District.

Clova, Kirriemuir, Angus; Tayside, Central and Fife at Forfar.
Tayside Region
Angus District.

Clovenfords, Galashiels, Selkirkshire; Lothian and Borders at Selkirk.
Borders Region
Ettrick and Lauderdale District.

Cluanie, Sheil Bridge, Ross-shire; Grampian, Highland and Islands at Dingwall.
Highland Region
Ross and Cromarty District.

Clunas, Nairn; Grampian, Highland and Islands at Inverness.
Highland Region
Nairn District.

Clunie, Blairgowrie, Perthshire; Tayside, Central and Fife at Perth.
Tayside Region
Perth and Kinross District.

Cluny, Inverurie, Aberdeenshire; Grampian, Highland and Islands at Aberdeen.
Grampian Region
Gordon District.

Cluny, Kirkcaldy, Fife; Tayside, Central and Fife at Kirkcaldy.
Fife Region
Kirkcaldy District.

Clydebank, Dunbartonshire; North Strathclyde at Dumbarton.
Strathclyde Region
Dumbarton District.

Clynder, Helensburgh, Dunbartonshire; North Strathclyde at Dumbarton.
Strathclyde Region
Dumbarton District.

Coalburn, Lanarkshire; South Strathclyde, Dumfries and Galloway at Lanark.
Strathclyde Region
Clydesdale District.

Coalhall, Ayr; South Strathclyde, Dumfries and Galloway at Ayr.
Strathclyde Region
Kyle and Carrick District.

Coalsnaughton, Tillicoultry, Clackmannanshire; Tayside, Central and Fife at Alloa.
Central Region
Clackmannan District.

Coaltown of Burnturk, Cupar, Fife; Tayside, Central and Fife at Cupar.
Fife Region
North East Fife District.

Coaltown, East Wemyss, Kirkcaldy, Fife; Tayside, Central and Fife at Kirkcaldy.
Fife Region
Kirkcaldy District.

Coatbridge, Lanarkshire; South Strathclyde, Dumfries and Galloway at Airdrie.
Strathclyde Region
Monklands District.

Coatdyke, Coatbridge, Lanarkshire; South Strathclyde, Dumfries and Galloway at Airdrie.
Strathclyde Region
Monklands District.

Cock Bridge, Strathdon, Aberdeenshire; Grampian, Highland and Islands at Aberdeen.
Grampian Region
Gordon District.

Cockburnspath, Berwickshire; Lothian and Borders at Duns.
Borders Region
Berwickshire District.

Cockenzie, Prestonpans, East Lothian; Lothian and Borders at Haddington.
Lothian Region
East Lothian District.

Cockney, Stonehaven, Kincardineshire; Grampian, Highland and Islands at Stonehaven.
Grampian Region
Kincardine and Deeside District.

Coilleag, Eriskay, Isle of South Uist; Grampian, Highland and Islands at Lochmaddy.
Western Isles Islands Council.

Coldbackie, Tongue, Sutherland; Grampian, Highland and Islands at Dornoch.
Highland Region
Sutherland District.

Coldingham, Eyemouth, Berwickshire; Lothian and Borders at Duns.
Borders Region
Berwickshire District.

Coldstream, Berwickshire; Lothian and Borders at Duns.
Borders Region
Berwickshire District.

Colinsburgh, Elie, Fife; Tayside, Central and Fife at Cupar.
Fife Region
North East Fife District.

Colinton, Edinburgh; Lothian and Borders at Edinburgh.
Lothian Region
City of Edinburgh District.

Colintraive, Argyll; North
Strathclyde at Dunoon.
Strathclyde Region
Argyll and Bute District.

Collace, Perth; Tayside, Central
and Fife at Perth.
Tayside Region
Perth and Kinross District.

Collessie, Cupar, Fife; Tayside,
Central and Fife at Cupar.
Fife Region
North East Fife District.

Collieston, Ellon, Aberdeenshire;
Grampian, Highland and Islands at
Aberdeen.
Grampian Region
Gordon District.

Collin, Dumfries; South
Strathclyde, Dumfries and
Galloway at Dumfries.
Dumfries and Galloway Region
Nithsdale District.

Colliston, Arbroath, Angus;
Tayside, Central and Fife at
Arbroath.
Tayside Region
Angus District.

Colmonell, Girvan, Ayrshire; South
Strathclyde, Dumfries and
Galloway at Ayr.
Strathclyde Region
Kyle and Carrick District.

Colpy, Insch, Aberdeenshire;
Grampian, Highland and Islands at
Aberdeen.
Grampian Region
Gordon District.

Coltfield, Alves, Elgin, Morayshire;
Grampian, Highland and Islands at
Elgin.
Grampian Region
Moray District.

Colvend, Dalbeattie,
Kirkcudbrightshire; South
Strathclyde, Dumfries and
Galloway at Kirkcudbright.
Dumfries and Galloway Region
Stewartry District.

Comrie, Crieff, Perthshire; Tayside,
Central and Fife at Perth.
Tayside Region
Perth and Kinross District.

Comrie, Dunfermline, Fife; Tayside,
Central and Fife at Dunfermline.
Fife Region
Dunfermline District.

Condorrat, Cumbernauld,
Glasgow; South Strathclyde,
Dumfries and Galloway at Airdrie.
Strathclyde Region
Cumbernauld and Kilsyth District.

Conicavel, Forres, Morayshire;
Grampian, Highland and Islands at
Elgin.
Grampian Region
Moray District.

Conista, Portree, Isle of Skye;
Grampian, Highland and Islands at
Portree.
Highland Region
Skye and Lochalsh District.

Connel, Argyll; North Strathclyde at
Oban.
Strathclyde Region
Argyll and Bute District.

Conon Bridge, Dingwall, Ross-shire; Grampian, Highland and Islands at Dingwall.
Highland Region
Ross and Cromarty District.

Contin, Strathpeffer, Dingwall, Ross-shire; Grampian, Highland and Islands at Dingwall.
Highland Region
Ross and Cromarty District.

Corgarff, Strathdon, Aberdeenshire; Grampian, Highland and Islands at Aberdeen.
Grampian Region
Gordon District.

Cormiston, Biggar, Lanarkshire; South Strathclyde, Dumfries and Galloway at Lanark.
Strathclyde Region
Clydesdale District.

Cornaigbeg, Scarinish, Isle of Tiree; North Strathclyde at Oban.
Strathclyde Region
Argyll and Bute District.

Cornhill, Banff; Grampian, Highland and Islands at Banff.
Grampian Region
Banff and Buchan District.

Corpach, Fort William, Inverness-shire; Grampian, Highland and Islands at Fort William.
Highland Region
Lochaber District.

Corrie, Brodick, Isle of Arran; North Strathclyde at Kilmarnock.
Strathclyde Region
Cunninghame District.

Corrie, Lockerbie, Dumfriesshire; South Strathclyde, Dumfries and Galloway at Dumfries.
Dumfries and Galloway Region
Annandale and Eskdale District.

Corriegills, Brodick, Isle of Arran; North Strathclyde at Kilmarnock.
Strathclyde Region
Cunninghame District.

Corrour, Roybridge, Glen Spean, Inverness-shire; Grampian, Highland and Islands at Fort William.
Highland Region
Lochaber District.

Corse, Huntly, Aberdeenshire; Grampian, Highland and Islands at Aberdeen.
Grampian Region
Gordon District.

Corsock, Castle Douglas, Kirkcudbrightshire; South Strathclyde, Dumfries and Galloway at Kirkcudbright.
Dumfries and Galloway Region
Stewartry District.

Corstorphine, Edinburgh; Lothian and Borders at Edinburgh.
Lothian Region
City of Edinburgh District.

Cortachy, Kirriemuir, Angus; Tayside, Central and Fife at Forfar.
Tayside Region
Angus District.

Coshieville, Pitlochry, Perthshire;
Tayside, Central and Fife at Perth.
Tayside Region
Perth and Kinross District.

Cothal, Aberdeen; Grampian,
Highland and Islands at Aberdeen.
Grampian Region
Gordon District.

Coull, Aboyne, Kincardineshire;
Grampian, Highland and Islands at
Stonehaven.
Grampian Region
Kincardine and Deeside District.

Coulport, Cove, Helensburgh,
Dunbartonshire; North Strathclyde
at Dumbarton.
Strathclyde Region
Dumbarton District.

Coulregrein, Stornoway, Isle of
Lewis; Grampian, Highland and
Islands at Stornoway.
Western Isles Islands Council.

Coulter, Biggar, Lanarkshire; South
Strathclyde, Dumfries and
Galloway at Lanark.
Strathclyde Region
Clydesdale District.

Counterswell, Aberdeen;
Grampian, Highland and Islands at
Aberdeen.
Grampian Region
City of Aberdeen District.

Coupar Angus, Blairgowrie,
Perthshire; Tayside, Central and
Fife at Perth.
Tayside Region
Perth and Kinross District.

Courance, Lockerbie,
Dumfriesshire; South Strath-
clyde, Dumfries and Galloway at
Dumfries.
Dumfries and Galloway Region
Annandale and Eskdale District.

Cousland, Dalkeith, Midlothian;
Lothian and Borders at Edinburgh.
Lothian Region
City of Edinburgh District.

Cove, Cockburnspath,
Berwickshire; Lothian and Borders
at Duns.
Borders Region
Berwickshire District.

Cove, Helensburgh,
Dunbartonshire; North Strathclyde
at Dumbarton.
Strathclyde Region
Dumbarton District.

Cove Bay, Aberdeen; Grampian,
Highland and Islands at Aberdeen.
Grampian Region
City of Aberdeen District.

Covington, Thankerton, Biggar,
Lanarkshire; South Strathclyde,
Dumfries and Galloway at Lanark.
Strathclyde Region
Clydesdale District.

Cowdenbeath, Fife; Tayside,
Central and Fife at Dunfermline.
Fife Region
Dunfermline District.

Cowie, Stirling; Tayside, Central
and Fife at Stirling.
Central Region
Stirling District.

Cowie, Stonehaven, Kincardineshire; Grampian, Highland and Islands at Stonehaven.
Grampian Region
Kincardine and Deeside District.

Coylton, Ayr; South Strathclyde, Dumfries and Galloway at Ayr.
Strathclyde Region
Kyle and Carrick District.

Coylumbridge, Aviemore, Inverness-shire; Grampian, Highland and Islands at Inverness.
Highland Region
Badenoch and Strathspey District.

Cradlehall, Culloden, Inverness; Grampian, Highland and Islands at Inverness.
Highland Region
Inverness District.

Craggan, Lochearnhead, Stirlingshire; Tayside, Central and Fife at Stirling.
Central Region
Stirling District.

Craichie, Forfar, Angus; Tayside, Central and Fife at Forfar.
Tayside Region
Angus District.

Craig, Plockton, Wester Ross; Grampian, Highland and Islands at Dingwall.
Highland Region
Ross and Cromarty District.

Craigellachie, Banffshire; Grampian, Highland and Islands at Elgin.
Grampian Region
Moray District.

Craigend, Perth; Tayside, Central and Fife at Perth.
Tayside Region
Perth and Kinross District.

Craigesk, Dalkeith, Midlothian; Lothian and Borders at Edinburgh.
Lothian Region
City of Edinburgh District.

Craigforth, Stirling; Tayside, Central and Fife at Stirling.
Central Region
Stirling District.

Craighall, Ellon, Aberdeenshire; Grampian, Highland and Islands at Aberdeen.
Grampian Region
Gordon District.

Craighouse, Isle of Jura; North Strathclyde at Campbeltown.
Strathclyde Region
Argyll and Bute District.

Craigie, Kilmarnock, Ayrshire; North Strathclyde at Kilmarnock.
Strathclyde Region
Kilmarnock and Louden District.

Craigiehall, South Queensferry, West Lothian; Lothian and Borders at Edinburgh.
Lothian Region
City of Edinburgh District.

Craigievar, Alford, Aberdeenshire;
Grampian, Highland and Islands at
Aberdeen.
Grampian Region
Gordon District.

Craigmill, Stirling; Tayside, Central
and Fife at Stirling.
Central Region
Stirling District.

Craigmillar, Edinburgh; Lothian
and Borders at Edinburgh.
Lothian Region
City of Edinburgh District.

Craigmore, Rothesay, Isle of Bute;
North Strathclyde at Rothesay.
Strathclyde Region
Argyll and Bute District.

Craigmure, Isle of Mull; North
Strathclyde at Oban.
Strathclyde Region
Argyll and Bute District.

Craigneuk, Airdrie, Lanarkshire;
South Strathclyde, Dumfries and
Galloway at Airdrie.
Strathclyde Region
Monklands District.

Craigneuk, Motherwell,
Lanarkshire; South Strathclyde,
Dumfries and Galloway at
Hamilton.
Strathclyde Region
Motherwell District.

Craignish, Lochgilphead, Argyll;
North Strathclyde at Oban.
Strathclyde Region
Argyll and Bute District.

Craigo, Montrose, Angus; Tayside,
Central and Fife at Arbroath.
Tayside Region
Angus District.

Craigrothie, Cupar, Fife; Tayside,
Central and Fife at Cupar.
Fife Region
North East Fife District.

Craigston, Castlebay, Isle of Barra;
Grampian, Highland and Islands at
Lochmaddy.
Western Isles Islands Council.

Craigstrome, Isle of Benbecula;
Grampian, Highland and Islands at
Lochmaddy.
Western Isles Islands Council.

Craigton, Kirriemuir, Angus;
Tayside, Central and Fife at
Forfar.
Tayside Region
Angus District.

Crail, Anstruther, Fife; Tayside,
Central and Fife at Cupar.
Fife Region
North East Fife District.

Crailing, Jedburgh, Roxburghshire;
Lothian and Borders at Jedburgh.
Borders Region
Roxburgh District.

Cramond, Edinburgh; Lothian and
Borders at Edinburgh.
Lothian Region
City of Edinburgh District.

Cranshaws, Duns, Berwickshire;
Lothian and Borders at Duns.
Borders Region
Berwickshire District.

Crarae, Furnace, Inveraray, Argyll;
North Strathclyde at Dunoon.
Strathclyde Region
Argyll and Bute District.

Crathes, Banchory,
Kincardineshire; Grampian,
Highland and Islands at
Stonehaven.
Grampian Region
Kincardine and Deeside District.

Crathie, Ballater, Kincardineshire;
Grampian, Highland and Islands at
Stonehaven.
Grampian Region
Kincardine and Deeside District.

Crawford, Biggar, Lanarkshire;
South Strathclyde, Dumfries and
Galloway at Lanark.
Strathclyde Region
Clydesdale District.

Crawfordjohn, Biggar, Lanarkshire;
South Strathclyde, Dumfries and
Galloway at Lanark.
Strathclyde Region
Clydesdale District.

Crawick, Sanquhar, Dumfriesshire;
South Strathclyde, Dumfries and
Galloway at Dumfries.
Dumfries and Galloway Region
Nithsdale District.

Creagan, Callander, Stirlingshire;
Tayside, Central and Fife at
Stirling.
Central Region
Stirling District.

Creagorry, Isle of Benbecula;
Grampian, Highland and Islands at
Lochmaddy.
Western Isles Islands Council.

Creetown, Newton Stewart,
Wigtownshire; South Strathclyde,
Dumfries and Galloway at
Stranraer.
Dumfries and Galloway Region
Wigtown District.

Crianlarich, Stirlingshire; Tayside,
Central and Fife at Stirling.
Central Region
Stirling District.

Crieff, Perthshire; Tayside, Central
and Fife at Perth.
Tayside Region
Perth and Kinross District.

Crimond, Fraserburgh,
Aberdeenshire; Grampian,
Highland and Islands at
Peterhead.
Grampian Region
Banff and Buchan District.

Crinan, Lochgilphead, Argyll; North
Strathclyde at Dunoon.
Strathclyde Region
Argyll and Bute District.

Crocketford, Dalbeattie,
Kirkcudbrightshire; South
Strathclyde, Dumfries and
Galloway at Kirkcudbright.
Dumfries and Galloway Region
Stewartry District.

Croftamie, Tayside, Central and
Fife at Stirling.
Central Region
Stirling District.

Croggan, Isle of Mull; North
Strathclyde at Oban.
Strathclyde Region
Argyll and Bute District.

Croir, Isle of Lewis; Grampian Highland and Islands at Stornoway.
Western Isles Islands Council.

Cromarty, Ross-shire; Grampian, Highland and Islands at Dingwall
Highland Region
Ross and Cromarty District.

Crombie, Dunfermline, Fife; Tayside, Central and Fife at Dunfermline.
Fife Region
Dunfermline District.

Cromdale, Grantown-on-Spey, Inverness-shire; Grampian, Highland and Islands at Inverness.
Highland Region
Badenoch and Strathspey District.

Cromlix, Dunblane, Stirlingshire; Tayside, Central and Fife at Stirling.
Central Region
Stirling District.

Cromore, Isle of Lewis; Grampian, Highland and Islands at Stornoway.
Western Isles Islands Council.

Cronberry, Cumnock, Ayrshire; South Strathclyde, Dumfries and Galloway at Ayr.
Strathclyde Region
Cumnock and Doon Valley District.

Crook of Devon, Kinross; Tayside, Central and Fife at Perth.
Tayside Region
Perth and Kinross District.

Crookedholm, Kilmarnock, Ayrshire; North Strathclyde at Kilmarnock.
Strathclyde Region
Kilmarnock and Louden District.

Cross, Isle of Lewis; Grampian, Highland and Islands at Stornoway.
Western Isles Islands Council.

Crossapool, Scarinish, Isle of Tiree; North Strathclyde at Oban.
Strathclyde Region
Argyll and Bute District.

Crossbost, Isle of Lewis; Grampian, Highland and Islands at Stornoway.
Western Isles Islands Council.

Crossford, Carluke, Lanarkshire; South Strathclyde, Dumfries and Galloway at Lanark.
Strathclyde Region
Clydesdale District.

Crossford, Dunfermline, Fife; Tayside, Central and Fife at Dunfermline.
Fife Region
Dunfermline District.

Crossgatehall, East Lothian; Lothian and Borders at Haddington.
Lothian Region
East Lothian District.

Crossgates, Cowdenbeath, Fife; Tayside, Central and Fife at Dunfermline.
Fife Region
Dunfermline District.

Crosshill, Glasgow; Glasgow and
Strathkelvin at Glasgow.
Strathclyde Region
City of Glasgow District.

Crosshill, Lochgelly, Fife; Tayside,
Central and Fife at Dunfermline.
Fife Region
Dunfermline District.

Crosshill, Maybole, Ayrshire; South
Strathclyde, Dumfries and
Galloway at Ayr.
Strathclyde Region
Kyle and Carrick District.

Crosshouse, Kilmarnock, Ayrshire;
North Strathclyde at Kilmarnock.
Strathclyde Region
Kilmarnock and Louden District.

Crosslee, Johnstone,
Renfrewshire; North Strathclyde at
Paisley.
Strathclyde Region
Renfrew District.

Crossmichael, Castle Douglas,
Kirkcudbrightshire; South
Strathclyde, Dumfries and
Galloway at Kirkcudbright.
Dumfries and Galloway Region
Stewartry District.

Crossroads, Keith, Morayshire;
Grampian, Highland and Islands at
Elgin.
Grampian Region
Moray District.

Crowlista, Isle of Lewis; Grampian,
Highland and Islands at
Stornoway.
Western Isles Islands Council.

Croy, Inverness; Grampian,
Highland and Islands at Inverness.
Highland Region
Inverness District.

Croy, Kilsyth, Glasgow; South
Strathclyde, Dumfries and
Galloway at Airdrie.
Strathclyde Region
Cumbernauld and Kilsyth District.

Croy, Maybole, Ayrshire; South
Strathclyde, Dumfries and
Galloway at Ayr.
Strathclyde Region
Kyle and Carrick District.

Cruard, Isle Ornsay, Isle of Skye;
Grampian, Highland and Islands at
Portree.
Highland Region
Skye and Lochalsh District.

Cruden Bay, Peterhead,
Aberdeenshire; Grampian,
Highland and Islands at
Peterhead.
Grampian Region
Banff and Buchan District.

Crudie, Turriff, Banffshire;
Grampian, Highland and Islands at
Banff.
Grampian Region
Banff and Buchan District.

Crulivig, Isle of Lewis; Grampian,
Highland and Islands at
Stornoway.
Western Isles Islands Council.

Cuan Ferry, Oban, Argyll; North
Strathclyde at Oban.
Strathclyde Region
Argyll and Bute District.

Cuddy Point, Isle of Scalpay, Isle of Harris; Grampian, Highland and Islands at Stornoway.
Western Isles Islands Council.

Culbokie, Conon Bridge, Ross-shire; Grampian, Highland and Islands at Dingwall.
Grampian Region
Ross and Cromarty District.

Culcabock, Inverness; Grampian, Highland and Islands at Inverness.
Highland Region
Inverness District.

Culkein, Lairg, Sutherland; Grampian, Highland and Islands at Dornoch.
Highland Region
Sutherland District.

Cullen, Buckie, Morayshire; Grampian, Highland and Islands at Elgin.
Grampian Region
Moray District.

Cullerie, Skene, Aberdeenshire; Grampian, Highland and Islands at Aberdeen.
Grampian Region
City of Aberdeen District.

Culliecudden, Conon Bridge, Ross-shire; Grampian, Highland and Islands at Dingwall.
Highland Region
Ross and Cromarty District.

Cullipool, Oban, Argyll; North Strathclyde at Oban.
Strathclyde Region
Argyll and Bute District.

Cullivoe, Shetland; Grampian, Highland and Islands at Lerwick.
Shetland Islands Council.

Culloden, Inverness; Grampian, Highland and Islands at Inverness.
Highland Region
Inverness District.

Culnacnock, Portree, Isle of Skye; Grampian, Highland and Islands at Portree.
Highland Region
Skye and Lochalsh District.

Culrain, Ardgay, Ross-shire; Grampian, Highland and Islands at Dornoch.
Highland Region
Sutherland District.

Culross, Dunfermline, Fife; Tayside, Central and Fife at Dunfermline.
Fife Region
Dunfermline District.

Culsalmond, Insch, Aberdeenshire; Grampian, Highland and Islands at Aberdeen.
Grampian Region
Gordon District.

Culter, Peterculter, Aberdeenshire; Grampian, Highland and Islands at Aberdeen.
Grampian Region
City of Aberdeen District.

Cultercullen, Udny, Aberdeenshire; Grampian, Highland and Islands at Aberdeen.
Grampian Region
City of Aberdeen District.

Cults, Aberdeen; Grampian, Highland and Islands at Aberdeen.
Grampian Region
City of Aberdeen District.

Culvie, Aberchirder, Banffshire; Grampian, Highland and Islands at Banff.
Grampian Region
Banff and Buchan District.

Culzean, Maybole, Ayrshire; South Strathclyde, Dumfries and Galloway at Ayr.
Strathclyde Region
Kyle and Carrick District.

Cumbernauld, Glasgow; South Strathclyde, Dumfries and Galloway at Airdrie.
Strathclyde Region
Cumbernauld and Kilsyth District.

Cuminestown, Turriff, Banffshire; Grampian, Highland and Islands at Banff.
Grampian Region
Banff and Buchan District.

Cummertrees, Annan, Dumfriesshire; South Strathclyde, Dumfries and Galloway at Dumfries.
Dumfries and Galloway Region
Annandale and Eskdale District.

Cummingston, Burghead, Elgin, Morayshire; Grampian, Highland and Islands at Elgin.
Grampian Region
Moray District.

Cumnock, Ayrshire; South Strathclyde, Dumfries and Galloway at Ayr.
Strathclyde Region
Cumnock and Doon Valley District.

Cunninghamhead, Kilmarnock, Ayrshire; North Strathclyde at Kilmarnock.
Strathclyde Region
Cunninghame District.

Cunningsburgh, Shetland; Grampian, Highland and Islands at Lerwick.
Shetland Islands Council.

Cupar, Fife; Tayside, Central and Fife at Cupar.
Fife Region
North East Fife District.

Currie, Midlothian; Lothian and Borders at Edinburgh.
Lothian Region
Midlothian District.

Cushnie, Alford, Aberdeenshire; Grampian, Highland and Islands at Aberdeen.
Grampian Region
Gordon District.

Dailly, Girvan, Ayrshire; South Strathclyde, Dumfries and Galloway at Ayr.
Strathclyde Region
Kyle and Carrick District.

Dairsie, Cupar, Fife; Tayside, Central and Fife at Cupar.
Fife Region
North East Fife District.

Dalavich, Taynuilt, Argyll; North
Strathclyde at Oban.
Strathclyde Region
Argyll and Bute District.

Dalbeattie, Kirkcudbrightshire;
South Strathclyde, Dumfries and
Galloway at Kircudbright.
Dumfries and Galloway Region
Stewartry District.

Dalbeg, Isle of Lewis; Grampian,
Highland and Islands at
Stornoway.
Western Isles Islands Council.

Dalchalm, Brora, Sutherland;
Grampian, Highland and Islands at
Dornoch.
Highland Region
Sutherland District.

Dalchreichart, Glenmoriston,
Inverness-shire; Grampian,
Highland and Islands at Inverness.
Highland Region
Inverness District.

Dalcross, Inverness; Grampian,
Highland and Islands at Inverness.
Highland Region
Inverness District.

Dalelia, Fort William, Inverness-
shire; Grampian, Highland and
Islands at Fort William.
Highland Region
Lochaber District.

Dalgetty Bay, Dunfermline, Fife;
Tayside, Central and Fife at
Dunfermline.
Fife Region
Dunfermline District.

Dalguise, Dunkeld, Perthshire;
Tayside, Central and Fife at Perth.
Tayside Region
Perth and Kinross District.

Dalhalvaig, Forsinard, Lairg,
Sutherland; Grampian, Highland
and Islands at Dornoch.
Highland Region
Sutherland District.

Daliburgh, Lochboisdale, Isle of
South Uist; Grampian, Highland
and Islands at Lochmaddy.
Western Isles Islands Council.

Daljarroch, Girvan, Ayrshire; South
Strathclyde, Dumfries and
Galloway at Ayr.
Strathclyde Region
Kyle and Carrick District.

Dalkeith, Midlothian; Lothian and
Borders at Edinburgh.
Lothian Region
Midlothian District.

Dallachy, Spey Bay, Fochabers,
Morayshire; Grampian, Highland
and Islands at Elgin.
Grampian Region
Moray District.

Dallas, Forres, Morayshire;
Grampian, Highland and Islands at
Elgin.
Grampian Region
Moray District.

Dalleagles, Cumnock, Ayrshire;
South Strathclyde, Dumfries and
Galloway at Ayr.
Strathclyde Region
Cumnock and Doon Valley District.

Dalmally, Oban, Argyll; North
Strathclyde at Oban.
Strathclyde Region
Argyll and Bute District.

Dalmellington, Ayr; South
Strathclyde, Dumfries and
Galloway at Ayr.
Strathclyde Region
Kyle and Carrick District.

Dalmeny, South Queensferry,
Edinburgh; Lothian and Borders at
Edinburgh.
Lothian Region
City of Edinburgh District.

Dalmore, Isle of Lewis; Grampian,
Highland and Islands at
Stornoway.
Western Isles Islands Council.

Dalmuir, Clydebank,
Dunbartonshire; North Strathclyde
at Dumbarton.
Strathclyde Region
Dumbarton District.

Dalnaspidal, Blair Atholl,
Perthshire; Tayside, Central and
Fife at Perth.
Tayside Region
Perth and Kinross District.

Dalry, Ayrshire; North Strathclyde
at Kilmarnock.
Strathclyde Region
Cunninghame District.

Dalry, Castle Douglas,
Kirkcudbrightshire; South
Strathclyde, Dumfries and
Galloway at Kirkcudbright.
Dumfries and Galloway Region
Stewartry District.

Dalrymple, Ayr; South Strathclyde,
Dumfries and Galloway at Ayr.
Strathclyde Region
Kyle and Carrick District.

Dalserf, Larkhall, Lanarkshire;
South Strathclyde, Dumfries and
Galloway at Hamilton.
Strathclyde Region
Hamilton District.

Dalsetter, Yell, Shetland;
Grampian, Highland and Islands at
Lerwick.
Shetland Islands Council.

Dalswinton, Dumfries; South
Strathclyde, Dumfries and
Galloway at Dumfries.
Dumfries and Galloway Region
Nithsdale District.

Dalton, Lockerbie, Dumfriesshire;
South Strathclyde, Dumfries and
Galloway at Dumfries.
Dumfries and Galloway Region
Annandale and Eskdale District.

Dalwhinnie, Newtonmore,
Inverness-shire; Grampian,
Highland and Islands at Inverness.
Highland Region
Badenoch and Strathspey District.

Danderhall, Dalkeith, Midlothian;
Lothian and Borders at Edinburgh.
Lothian Region
Midlothian District.

Darnaway, Forres, Morayshire;
Grampian, Highland and Islands at
Elgin.
Grampian Region
Moray District.

Darnick, Melrose, Roxburghshire;
Lothian and Borders at Selkirk.
Borders Region
Roxburgh District.

Darvel, Ayrshire; North Strathclyde
at Kilmarnock.
Strathclyde Region
Kilmarnock and Louden District.

Davidson's Mains, Edinburgh;
Lothian and Borders at Edinburgh.
Lothian Region
City of Edinburgh District.

Daviot, Inverness; Grampian,
Highland and Islands at Inverness.
Highland Region
Inverness District.

Daviot, Inverurie, Aberdeenshire;
Grampian, Highland and Islands at
Aberdeen.
Grampian Region
Gordon District.

Deans, Livingston, West Lothian;
Lothian and Borders at Linlithgow.
Lothian Region
West Lothian District.

Deanston, Doune, Perthshire;
Tayside, Central and Fife at
Stirling.
Central Region
Stirling District.

Dechmont, Broxburn, West
Lothian; Lothian and Borders at
Linlithgow.
Lothian Region
West Lothian District.

Deerness, Orkney; Grampian,
Highland and Islands at Kirkwall.
Orkney Islands Council.

Deiraclete, Harris; Grampian,
Highland and Islands at
Stornoway.
Western Isles Islands Council.

Delmore, Inverness; Grampian,
Highland and Islands at Inverness.
Highland Region
Inverness District.

Delny, Tain, Ross-shire; Grampian,
Highland and Islands at Tain.
Highland Region
Ross and Cromarty District.

Den of Lindores, Newburgh, Fife;
Tayside, Central and Fife at
Cupar.
Fife Region
North East Fife District.

Denhead, St Andrews, Fife;
Tayside, Central and Fife at
Cupar.
Fife Region
North East Fife District.

Denholm, Hawick, Roxburghshire;
Lothian and Borders at Jedburgh.
Borders Region
Roxburgh District.

Dennistoun, Glasgow; North
Strathclyde at Glasgow.
Strathclyde Region
City of Glasgow District.

Denny, Stirlingshire; Tayside,
Central and Fife at Falkirk.
Central Region
Falkirk District.

Dennyloanhead, Bonnybridge, Stirlingshire; Tayside, Central and Fife at Falkirk.
Central Region
Falkirk District.

Dervaig, Tobermory, Isle of Mull; North Strathclyde at Oban.
Strathclyde Region
Argyll and Bute District.

Deskford, Cullen, Buckie, Morayshire; Grampian, Highland and Islands at Elgin.
Grampian Region
Moray District.

Dess, Aboyne, Aberdeenshire; Grampian, Highland and Islands at Stonehaven.
Grampian Region
Kincardine and Deeside District.

Devonside, Tillicoultry, Clackmannanshire; Tayside, Central and Fife at Alloa.
Central Region
Clackmannan District.

Dewarton, Gorebridge, Midlothian; Lothian and Borders at Edinburgh.
Lothian Region
Midlothian District.

Dingwall, Ross-shire; Grampian, Highland and Islands at Dingwall.
Highland Region
Ross and Cromarty District.

Dinwoodie, Lockerbie, Dumfriesshire; South Strath-clyde, Dumfries and Galloway at Dumfries.
Dumfries and Galloway Region
Annandale and Eskdale District.

Dippe, Campbeltown, Argyll; North Strathclyde at Campbeltown.
Strathclyde Region
Argyll and Bute District.

Dippin, Brodick, Isle of Arran; North Strathclyde at Kilmarnock.
Strathclyde Region
Cunninghame District.

Dirleton, North Berwick, East Lothian; Lothian and Borders at Haddington.
Lothian Region
East Lothian District.

Disblair, New Machar, Aberdeenshire; Grampian, Highland and Islands at Aberdeen.
Grampian Region
City of Aberdeen District.

Dochfour, Inverness; Grampian, Highland and Islands at Inverness.
Highland Region
Inverness District.

Dochgarroch, Inverness; Grampian, Highland and Islands at Inverness.
Highland Region
Inverness District.

Dollar, Clackmannanshire; Tayside, Central and Fife at Alloa.
Central Region
Clackmannan District.

Dolphinton, West Linton, Peeblesshire; South Strathclyde, Dumfries and Galloway at Lanark.
Strathclyde Region
Clydesdale District.

Donibristle, Dunfermline, Fife;
Tayside, Central and Fife at
Dunfermline.
Fife Region
Dunfermline District.

Dores, Inverness; Grampian,
Highland and Islands at Inverness.
Highland Region
Inverness District.

Dornie, Kyle of Lochalsh, Ross-
shire; Grampian, Highland and
Islands at Dingwall.
Highland Region
Skye and Lochalsh District.

Dornoch, Sutherland; Grampian,
Highland and Islands at Dornoch.
Highland Region
Sutherland District.

Dornock, Annan, Dumfriesshire;
South Strathclyde, Dumfries and
Galloway at Dumfries.
Dumfries and Galloway Region
Annandale and Eskdale District.

Douglas, Lanark; South
Strathclyde, Dumfries and
Galloway at Lanark.
Strathclyde Region
Clydesdale District.

Douglas Pier, Lochgoilhead, Argyll;
North Strathclyde at Dunoon.
Strathclyde Region
Argyll and Bute District.

Douglas Water, Lanark; South
Strathclyde, Dumfries and
Galloway at Lanark.
Strathclyde Region
Clydesdale District.

Douglas West, Lanark; South
Strathclyde, Dumfries and
Galloway at Lanark.
Strathclyde Region
Clydesdale District.

Douglastown, Forfar, Angus;
Tayside, Central and Fife at
Forfar.
Tayside Region
Angus District.

Dounby, Orkney; Grampian,
Highland and Islands at Kirkwall.
Orkney Islands Council.

Doune, Carloway, Isle of Lewis;
Grampian, Highland and Islands at
Stornoway.
Western Isles Islands Council.

Doune, Perthshire; Tayside,
Central and Fife at Stirling.
Central Region
Stirling District.

Dounreay, Thurso, Caithness;
Grampian, Highland and Islands at
Wick.
Highland Region
Caithness District.

Dowally, Aberfeldy, Perthshire;
Tayside, Central and Fife at Perth.
Tayside Region
Perth and Kinross District.

Downies, Portlethen, Aberdeen;
Grampian, Highland and Islands at
Stonehaven.
Grampian Region
Kincardine and Deeside District.

Drainie, Lossiemouth, Morayshire; Grampian, Highland and Islands at Elgin.
Grampian Region
Moray District.

Dreghorn, Irvine, Ayrshire; North Strathclyde at Kilmarnock.
Strathclyde Region
Cunninghame District.

Drem, North Berwick, East Lothian; Lothian and Borders at Haddington.
Lothian Region
East Lothian District.

Drimin, Lochaline, Strontian, Inverness-shire; Grampian, Highland and Islands at Fort William.
Highland Region
Lochaber District.

Drimisdale, Lochboisdale, Isle of South Uist; Grampian, Highland and Islands at Lochmaddy.
Western Isles Islands Council.

Drinnishader, Harris; Grampian, Highland and Islands at Stornoway.
Western Isles Islands Council.

Drip Bridge, Stirling; Tayside, Central and Fife at Stirling.
Central Region
Stirling District.

Drongan, Ayr; South Strathclyde, Dumfries and Galloway at Ayr.
Strathclyde Region
Kyle and Carrick District.

Dronley, Dundee; Tayside, Central and Fife at Dundee.
Tayside Region
City of Dundee District.

Drum, Banchory, Kincardineshire; Grampian, Highland and Islands at Stonehaven.
Grampian Region
Kincardine and Deeside District.

Drumbeg, Lairg, Sutherland; Grampian, Highland and Islands at Dornoch.
Highland Region
Sutherland District.

Drumblade, Huntly, Aberdeenshire; Grampian, Highland and Islands at Aberdeen.
Grampian Region
Gordon District.

Drumbuie, Kyle of Lochalsh, Ross-shire; Grampian, Highland and Islands at Dingwall.
Highland Region
Ross and Cromarty District.

Drumchapel, Glasgow; Glasgow and Strathkelvin at Glasgow.
Strathclyde Region
City of Glasgow District.

Drumchardine, Kirkhill, Inverness; Grampian, Highland and Islands at Inverness.
Highland Region
Inverness District.

Drumclog, Strathaven, Lanarkshire; South Strathclyde, Dumfries and Galloway at Hamilton.
Strathclyde Region.
Hamilton District.

Drumelzier, Biggar, Lanarkshire;
South Strathclyde, Dumfries and
Galloway at Lanark.
Strathclyde Region
Clydesdale District.

Drumemble, Campbeltown, Argyll;
North Strathclyde at
Campbeltown.
Strathclyde Region
Argyll and Bute District.

Drumfearn, Isle Ornsay, Isle of
Skye; Grampian, Highland and
Islands at Portree.
Highland Region
Skye and Lochalsh District.

Drumgoyne, Glasgow; North
Strathclyde at Glasgow.
Strathclyde Region
City of Glasgow District.

Drumlithie, Stonehaven,
Kincardineshire; Grampian,
Highland and Islands at
Stonehaven.
Grampian Region
Kincardine and Deeside District.

Drummore, Stranraer,
Wigtownshire; South Strathclyde,
Dumfries and Galloway at
Stranraer.
Dumfries and Galloway Region
Wigtown District.

Drummuir, Keith, Banffshire;
Grampian, Highland and Islands at
Elgin.
Grampian Region
Moray District.

Drumnadrochit, Inverness;
Grampian, Highland and Islands at
Inverness.
Highland Region
Inverness District.

Drumoak, Banchory,
Kincardineshire; Grampian,
Highland and Islands at
Stonehaven.
Grampian Region
Kincardine and Deeside District.

Drumoyne, Glasgow; Glasgow and
Strathkelvin at Glasgow.
Strathclyde Region
City of Glasgow District.

Drumry, Glasgow; Glasgow and
Strathkelvin at Glasgow.
Strathclyde Region
City of Glasgow District.

Drumsleet, Dumfries; South
Strathclyde, Dumfries and
Galloway at Dumfries.
Dumfries and Galloway Region
Nithsdale District.

Drumuie, Portree, Isle of Skye;
Grampian, Highland and Islands at
Portree.
Highland Region
Skye and Lochalsh District.

Drumvaich, Callander, Perthshire;
Tayside, Central and Fife at
Stirling.
Central Region
Stirling District.

Drybridge, Buckie, Morayshire;
Grampian, Highland and Islands at
Elgin.
Grampian Region
Moray District.

Drybridge, Irvine, Ayrshire; North
Strathclyde at Kilmarnock.
Strathclyde Region
Cunninghame District.

Drylaw, Edinburgh; Lothian and
Borders at Edinburgh.
Lothian Region
City of Edinburgh District.

Drymen, Glasgow; Tayside, Central
and Fife at Stirling.
Central Region
Stirling District.

Drynoch, Carbost, Isle of Skye;
Grampian, Highland and Islands at
Portree.
Highland Region
Skye and Lochalsh District.

Dubford, Banff; Grampian,
Highland and Islands at Banff.
Grampian Region
Banff and Buchan District.

Dufftown, Keith, Morayshire;
Grampian, Highland and Islands at
Elgin.
Grampian Region
Moray District.

Duffus, Elgin; Grampian, Highland
and Islands at Elgin.
Grampian Region
Moray District.

Duirinish, Kyle of Lochalsh, Ross-
shire; Grampian, Highland and
Islands at Dingwall.
Highland Region
Skye and Lochalsh District.

Duisdale Beag, Isle Ornsay, Isle of
Skye; Grampian, Highland and
Islands at Portree.
Highland Region
Skye and Lochalsh District.

Duisdale Mhor, Isle Ornsay, Isle of
Skye; Grampian, Highland and
Islands at Portree.
Highland Region
Skye and Lochalsh District.

Dull, Aberfeldy, Perthshire;
Tayside, Central and Fife at Perth.
Tayside Region
Perth and Kinross District.

Dulnain Bridge, Grantown-on-
Spey, Inverness-shire; Grampian,
Highland and Islands at Inverness.
Highland Region
Badenoch and Strathspey District.

Dumbarton; North Strathclyde at
Dumbarton.
Strathclyde Region
Dumbarton District.

Dumfries; South Strathclyde,
Dumfries and Galloway at
Dumfries.
Dumfries and Galloway Region
Nithsdale District.

Dunach, Oban, Argyll; North
Strathclyde at Oban.
Strathclyde Region
Argyll and Bute District.

Dunalistair, Pitlochry, Perthshire;
Tayside, Central and Fife at Perth.
Tayside Region
Perth and Kinross District.

Dunan, Broadford, Isle of Skye; Grampian, Highland and Islands at Portree.
Highland Region
Skye and Lochalsh District.

Dunbar, East Lothian; Lothian and Borders at Haddington.
Lothian Region
East Lothian District.

Dunbeath, Caithness; Grampian, Highland and Islands at Wick.
Highland Region
Caithness District.

Dunbeg, Connel, Argyll; North Strathclyde at Oban.
Strathclyde Region
Argyll and Bute District.

Dunblane, Stirlingshire; Tayside, Central and Fife at Stirling.
Central Region
Stirling District.

Duncanston, Conon Bridge, Ross-shire; Grampian, Highland and Islands at Dingwall.
Highland Region
Ross and Cromarty District.

Duncanston, Insch, Aberdeenshire; Grampian, Highland and Islands at Aberdeen.
Grampian Region
Gordon District.

Duncow, Dumfries; South Strathclyde, Dumfries and Galloway at Dumfries.
Dumfries and Galloway Region
Nithsdale District.

Duncreive, Glenfarg, Perth; Tayside, Central and Fife at Perth.
Tayside Region
Perth and Kinross District.

Dundee; Tayside, Central and Fife at Dundee.
Tayside Region
City of Dundee District.

Dundonald, Kilmarnock, Ayrshire; South Strathclyde, Dumfries and Galloway at Ayr.
Strathclyde Region
Kyle and Carrick District.

Dundonnel, Garve, Ross-shire; Grampian, Highland and Islands at Dingwall.
Highland Region
Ross and Cromarty District.

Dundrennan, Kirkcudbright; South Strathclyde, Dumfries and Galloway at Kirkcudbright.
Dumfries and Galloway Region
Stewartry District.

Dunecht, Skene, Aberdeenshire; Grampian, Highland and Islands at Aberdeen.
Grampian Region
City of Aberdeen District.

Dunfermline, Fife; Tayside, Central and Fife at Dunfermline.
Fife Region
Dunfermline District.

Dunganachy, Isle of Benbecula; Grampian, Highland and Islands at Lochmaddy.
Western Isles Islands Council.

Dungavel, Strathaven, Lanarkshire;
South Strathclyde, Dumfries and
Galloway at Hamilton.
Strathclyde Region
Hamilton District.

Dunino, St Andrews, Fife; Tayside,
Central and Fife at Cupar.
Fife Region
North East Fife District.

Dunipace, Denny, Stirlingshire;
Tayside, Central and Fife at
Falkirk.
Central Region
Falkirk District.

Dunira, Comrie, Crieff, Perthshire;
Tayside, Central and Fife at Perth.
Tayside Region
Perth and Kinross District.

Dunkeld, Perthshire; Tayside,
Central and Fife at Perth.
Tayside Region
Perth and Kinross District.

Dunlop, Kilmarnock, Ayrshire;
North Strathclyde at Kilmarnock.
Strathclyde Region
Kilmarnock and Louden District.

Dunlugas, Turiff, Banffshire;
Grampian, Highland and Islands at
Banff.
Grampian Region
Banff and Buchan District.

Dunmore, Falkirk; Tayside, Central
and Fife at Falkirk.
Central Region
Falkirk District.

Dunmore, Tarbert, Argyll; North
Strathclyde at Campbeltown.
Strathclyde Region
Argyll and Bute District.

Dunnet, Castletown, Caithness;
Grampian, Highland and Islands at
Wick.
Highland Region
Caithness District.

Dunnichen, Forfar, Angus;
Tayside, Central and Fife at
Forfar.
Tayside Region
Angus District.

Dunning, Perth; Tayside, Central
and Fife at Perth.
Tayside Region
Perth and Kinross District.

Dunning Glen, Dollar,
Clackmannanshire; Tayside,
Central and Fife at Alloa.
Central Region
Clackmannan District.

Dunnottar, Stonehaven,
Kincardineshire; Grampian,
Highland and Islands at
Stonehaven.
Grampian Region
Kincardine and Deeside District.

Dunoon, Argyll; North Strathclyde
at Dunoon.
Strathclyde Region
Argyll and Bute District.

Dunphail, Forres, Morayshire;
Grampian, Highland and Islands at
Elgin.
Grampian Region
Moray District.

Dunragit, Stranraer, Wigtownshire;
South Strathclyde, Dumfries and
Galloway at Stranraer.
Dumfries and Galloway Region
Wigtown District.

Dunrobin Castle, Golspie,
Sutherland; Grampian, Highland
and Islands at Dornoch.
Highland Region
Sutherland District.

Dunrossness, Shetland;
Grampian, Highland and Islands at
Lerwick.
Shetland Islands Council.

Duns, Berwickshire; Lothian and
Borders at Duns.
Borders Region
Berwickshire District.

Dunscore, Dumfries; South
Strathclyde, Dumfries and
Galloway at Dumfries.
Dumfries and Galloway Region
Nithsdale District.

Dunshalt, Cupar, Fife; Tayside,
Central and Fife at Cupar.
Fife Region
North East Fife District.

Dunsyre, Carnwath, Lanarkshire;
South Strathclyde, Dumfries and
Galloway at Lanark.
Strathclyde Region
Clydesdale District.

Duntocher, Clydebank,
Dunbartonshire; North Strathclyde
at Dumbarton.
Strathclyde Region
Dumbarton District.

Duntrune, Dundee; Tayside,
Central and Fife at Dundee.
Tayside Region
City of Dundee District.

Duntulm, Uig, Isle of Skye;
Grampian, Highland and Islands at
Portree.
Highland Region
Skye and Lochalsh District.

Dunure, Ayr; South Strathclyde,
Dumfries and Galloway at Ayr.
Strathclyde Region
Kyle and Carrick District.

Dunvegan, Isle of Skye; Grampian,
Highland and Islands at Portree.
Highland Region
Skye and Lochalsh District.

Dura Den, Cupar, Fife; Tayside,
Central and Fife at Cupar.
Tayside Region
North East Fife District.

Durisdeer, Thornhill,
Dumfriesshire; South Strath-
clyde, Dumfries and Galloway at
Dumfries.
Dumfries and Galloway Region
Nithsdale District.

Durness, Lairg, Sutherland;
Grampian, Highland and Islands at
Dornoch.
Highland Region
Sutherland District.

Durno, Inverurie, Aberdeenshire;
Grampian, Highland and Islands at
Aberdeen.
Grampian Region
Gordon District.

Duror, Appin, Argyll; Grampian, Highland and Islands at Fort William.
Highland Region
Lochaber District.

Durris, Banchory, Kincardineshire; Grampian, Highland and Islands at Stonehaven.
Grampian Region
Kincardine and Deeside District.

Dyce, Aberdeen; Grampian, Highland and Islands at Aberdeen.
Grampian Region
City of Aberdeen District.

Dyke, Forres, Morayshire; Grampian, Highland and Islands at Elgin.
Grampian Region
Moray District.

Dysart, Kirkcaldy, Fife; Tayside, Central and Fife at Kirkcaldy.
Fife Region
Kirkcaldy District.

Eaglesfield, Lockerbie, Dumfriesshire; South Strathclyde, Dumfries and Galloway at Dumfries.
Dumfries and Galloway Region
Annandale and Eskdale District.

Eaglesham, Glasgow; North Strathclyde at Paisley,
Strathclyde Region
Renfrew District.

Eagleton, Bayble, Isle of Lewis; Grampian, Highland and Islands at Stornoway.
Western Isles Islands Council.

Earlish, Portree, Isle of Skye; Grampian, Highland and Islands at Portree.
Highland Region
Skye and Lochalsh District.

Earlsferry, Leven, Fife; Tayside, Central and Fife at Cupar.
Fife Region
North East Fife District.

Earlston, Berwickshire; Lothian and Borders at Selkirk.
Borders Region
Ettrick and Lauderdale District.

Earsary, Castlebay, Isle of Barra; Grampian, Highland and Islands at Lochmaddy.
Western Isles Islands Council.

Earshader, Isle of Lewis; Grampian, Highland and Islands at Stornoway.
Western Isles Islands Council.

Easdale, Oban, Argyll; North Strathclyde at Oban.
Strathclyde Region
Argyll and Bute District.

Easdale Island, Oban, Argyll; North Strathclyde at Oban.
Strathclyde Region
Argyll and Bute District.

Eassie, Forfar, Angus; Tayside, Central and Fife at Forfar.
Tayside Region
Angus District.

East Calder, Livingstone, West Lothian; Lothian and Borders at Linlithgow.
Lothian Region
West Lothian District.

East Cluden, Dumfries; South Strathclyde, Dumfries and Galloway at Dumfries.
Dumfries and Galloway Region
Nithsdale District.

East Clyne, Brora, Sutherland; Grampian, Highland and Islands at Dornoch.
Highland Region
Sutherland District.

East Fortune, North Berwick, East Lothian; Lothian and Borders at Haddington.
Lothian Region
East Lothian District.

East Gerinish, Lochboisdale, Isle of South Uist; Grampian, Highland and Islands at Lochmaddy.
Western Isles Islands Council.

East Kilbride, Glasgow; South Strathclyde, Dumfries and Galloway at Hamilton.
Strathclyde Region
Hamilton District.

East Kilbride, Lochboisdale, Isle of South Uist; Grampian, Highland and Islands at Lochmaddy.
Western Isles Islands Council.

East Linton, East Lothian; Lothian and Borders at Haddington.
Lothian Region
East Lothian District.

East Saltoun, Pencaitland, East Lothian; Lothian and Borders at Haddington.
Lothian Region
East Lothian District.

East Tarbert, Isle of Harris; Grampian, Highland and Islands at Stornoway.
Western Isles Islands Council.

East Wemyss, Kirkcaldy, Fife; Tayside, Central and Fife at Kirkcaldy.
Fife Region
Kirkcaldy District.

East Whitburn, Broxburn, West Lothian; Lothian and Borders at Linlithgow.
Lothian Region
West Lothian District.

East Yell, Shetland; Grampian, Highland and Islands at Lerwick.
Shetland Islands Council.

Easter Balgeddie, Kinross; Tayside, Central and Fife at Perth.
Tayside Region
Perth and Kinross District.

Easter Howgate, Penicuik, Midlothian; Lothian and Borders at Edinburgh.
Lothian Region
Midlothian District.

Easterhouse, Glasgow; Glasgow and Strathkelvin at Glasgow.
Strathclyde Region
City of Glasgow District.

Eastfield, Shotts, Lanarkshire; South Strathclyde, Dumfries and Galloway at Hamilton.
Strathclyde Region
Hamilton District.

Easthouses, Dalkeith, Midlothian;
Lothian and Borders at Edinburgh.
Lothian Region
Midlothian District.

Eastriggs, Annan, Dumfriesshire;
South Strathclyde, Dumfries and
Galloway at Dumfries.
Dumfries and Galloway Region
Annandale and Eskdale District.

Ebost, Portree, Isle of Skye;
Grampian, Highland and Islands at
Portree.
Highland Region
Skye and Lochalsh District.

Ecclefechan, Lockerbie,
Dumfriesshire; South Strath-
clyde, Dumfries and Galloway at
Dumfries.
Dumfries and Galloway Region
Annandale and Eskdale District.

Eccles, Coldstream, Berwickshire;
Lothian and Borders at Duns.
Borders Region
Berwickshire District.

Ecclesmachan, Broxburn, West
Lothian; Lothian and Borders at
Linlithgow.
Lothian Region
West Lothian District.

Echt, Skene, Aberdeenshire;
Grampian, Highland and Islands at
Aberdeen.
Grampian Region
City of Aberdeen District.

Eckford, Jedburgh, Roxburgh;
Lothian and Borders at Jedburgh.
Borders Region
Roxburgh District.

Eday, Orkney; Grampian, Highland
and Islands at Kirkwall.
Orkney Islands Council.

Edderton, Tain, Ross-shire;
Grampian, Highland and Islands at
Tain.
Highland Region
Ross and Cromarty District.

Eddleston, Peebles; Lothian and
Borders at Peebles.
Borders Region
Tweeddale District.

Eden, Banff; Grampian, Highland
and Islands at Banff.
Grampian Region
Banff and Buchan District.

Edinbane, Portree, Isle of Skye;
Grampian, Highland and Islands at
Portree.
Highland Region
Skye and Lochalsh District.

Edinburgh, Lothian and Borders at
Edinburgh.
Lothian Region
City of Edinburgh District.

Edinchip, Lochearnhead,
Perthshire; Tayside, Central and
Fife at Stirling.
Central Region
Stirling District.

Edinkillie, Dunphail, Forres,
Morayshire; Grampian, Highland
and Islands at Elgin.
Grampian Region
Moray District.

Edinville, Aberlour, Morayshire;
Grampian, Highland and Islands at
Elgin.
Grampian Region
Moray District.

Ednam, Kelso, Roxburghshire;
Lothian and Borders at Duns.
Borders Region
Berwickshire District.

Edrom, Duns, Berwickshire;
Lothian and Borders at Duns.
Borders Region
Berwickshire District.

Edzell, Brechin, Angus; Tayside,
Central and Fife at Forfar.
Tayside Region
Angus District.

Egilsay, Orkney; Grampian,
Highland and Islands at Kirkwall.
Orkney Islands Council.

Eilean Shona, Acharacle,
Inverness-shire; Grampian,
Highland and Islands at Fort
William.
Highland Region
Lochaber District.

Eileanreach, Glenelg, Kyle, Ross-
shire; Grampian, Highland and
Islands at Portree.
Highland Region
Skye and Lochalsh District.

Eilian-Anabuich, Isle of Harris;
Grampian, Highland and Islands at
Stornoway.
Western Isles Islands Council.

Eishkin, Isle of Lewis; Grampian,
Highland and Islands at
Stornoway.
Western Isles Islands Council.

Elchies, Craigellachie, Morayshire;
Grampian, Highland and Islands at
Elgin.
Grampian Region
Moray District.

Elderslie, Johnstone,
Renfrewshire; North Strathclyde at
Paisley.
Strathclyde Region
Renfrew District.

Elgin, Morayshire; Grampian,
Highland and Islands at Elgin.
Grampian Region
Moray District.

Elgol, Broadford, Isle of Skye;
Grampian, Highland and Islands at
Portree.
Highland Region
Skye and Lochalsh District.

Elie, Leven, Fife; Tayside, Central
and Fife at Cupar.
Fife Region
North East Fife District.

Elliot, Arbroath, Angus; Tayside,
Central and Fife at Arbroath.
Tayside Region
Angus District.

Ellon, Aberdeenshire; Grampian,
Highland and Islands at Aberdeen.
Grampian Region
Gordon District.

Elphin, Ledmore, Lairg, Sutherland; Grampian, Highland and Islands at Dornoch.
Highland Region
Sutherland District.

Elphinstone, Tranent, East Lothian; Lothian and Borders at Haddington.
Lothian Region
East Lothian District.

Elrig, Newton Stewart, Wigtownshire; South Strathclyde, Dumfries and Galloway at Stranraer.
Dumfries and Galloway Region
Wigtown District.

Elsrickle, Biggar, Lanarkshire; South Strathclyde, Dumfries and Galloway at Lanark.
Strathclyde Region
Clydesdale District.

Elvanfoot, Biggar, Lanarkshire; South Strathclyde, Dumfries and Galloway at Lanark.
Strathclyde Region
Clydesdale District.

Embo, Dornoch, Sutherland; Grampian, Highland and Islands at Dornoch.
Highland Region
Sutherland District.

Emerivale, Port Ellen, Isle of Islay; North Strathclyde at Campbeltown.
Strathclyde Region
Argyll and Bute District.

Eneclate, Isle of Lewis; Grampian, Highland and Islands at Stornoway.
Western Isles Islands Council.

Enochdhu, Blairgowrie, Perthshire; Tayside, Central and Fife at Perth.
Tayside Region
Perth and Kinross District.

Enterkinfoot, Thornhill, Dumfriesshire; South Strathclyde, Dumfries and Galloway at Dumfries.
Dumfries and Galloway Region
Nithsdale District.

Enzie, Buckie, Morayshire; Grampian, Highland and Islands at Elgin.
Grampian Region
Moray District.

Eochar, Lochboisdale, Isle of South Uist; Grampian, Highland and Islands at Lochmaddy.
Western Isles Islands Council.

Eoligary, Castlebay, Isle of Barra; Grampian, Highland and Islands at Lochmaddy.
Western Isles Islands Council.

Eorodale, Isle of Lewis; Grampian, Highland and Islands at Stornoway.
Western Isles Islands Council.

Eoropie, Isle of Lewis; Grampian, Highland and Islands at Stornoway.
Western Isles Islands Council.

Erbusaig, Kyle of Lochalsh, Ross-shire; Grampian, Highland and Islands at Dingwall.
Highland Region
Skye and Lochalsh District.

Eredine, Dalmally, Argyll; North Strathclyde at Oban.
Strathclyde Region
Argyll and Bute District.

Errogie, Inverness; Grampian, Highland and Islands at Inverness.
Highland Region
Inverness District.

Errol, Perth; Tayside, Central and Fife at Perth.
Tayside Region
Perth and Kinross District.

Erskine, Renfrewshire; North Strathclyde at Paisley.
Strathclyde Region
Renfrew District.

Eshaness, Shetland; Grampian, Highland and Islands at Lerwick.
Shetland Islands Council.

Eskbank, Dalkeith, Midlothian; Lothian and Borders at Edinburgh.
Lothian Region
Midlothian District.

Eskdalemuir, Langholm, Dumfriesshire; South Strath-clyde, Dumfries and Galloway at Dumfries.
Dumfries and Galloway Region
Annandale and Eskdale District.

Esslemont, Ellon, Aberdeenshire; Grampian, Highland and Islands at Aberdeen.
Grampian Region
Gordon District.

Ettrick, Newton Stewart, Wigtownshire; South Strathclyde, Dumfries and Galloway at Stranraer.
Dumfries and Galloway Region
Wigtown District.

Ettrick, Selkirk; Lothian and Borders at Selkirk.
Borders Region
Ettrick and Lauderdale District.

Ettrick Bay, Rothesay, Isle of Bute; North Strathclyde at Rothesay.
Strathclyde Region
Argyll and Bute District.

Ettrick Valley, Selkirk; Lothian and Borders at Selkirk.
Borders Region
Ettrick and Lauderdale District.

Ettrickbridge, Selkirk; Lothian and Borders at Selkirk.
Borders Region
Ettrick and Lauderdale District.

Evanton, Ross-shire; Grampian, Highland and Islands at Dingwall.
Highland Region
Ross and Cromarty District.

Evelix, Dornoch, Sutherland; Grampian, Highland and Islands at Dornoch.
Highland Region
Sutherland District.

Evertown, Canonbie,
Dumfriesshire; South Strath-
clyde, Dumfries and Galloway at
Dumfries.
Dumfries and Galloway Region
Nithsdale District.

Evie, Orkney; Grampian, Highland
and Islands at Kirkwall.
Orkney Islands Council.

Ewes, Langholm, Dumfriesshire;
South Strathclyde, Dumfries and
Galloway at Dumfries.
Dumfries and Galloway Region
Annandale and Eskdale District.

Eyemouth, Berwickshire; Lothian
and Borders at Duns.
Borders Region
Berwickshire District.

Eynort, Carbost, Isle of Skye;
Grampian, Highland and Islands at
Portree.
Highland Region
Skye and Lochalsh District.

Fa'side, Musselburgh, Midlothian;
Lothian and Borders at Edinburgh.
Lothian Region
Midlothian District.

Failford, Mauchline, Ayrshire;
South Strathclyde, Dumfries and
Galloway at Ayr.
Strathclyde Region
Kyle and Carrick District.

Fair Isle, Orkney; Grampian,
Highland and Islands at Kirkwall.
Orkney Islands Council.

Fairlie, Largs, Ayrshire; North
Strathclyde at Kilmarnock.
Strathclyde Region
Cunninghame District.

Fairmilehead, Edinburgh; Lothian
and Borders at Edinburgh.
Lothian Region
City of Edinburgh District.

Fairy Bridge, Isle of Skye;
Grampian, Highland and Islands at
Portree.
Highland Region
Skye and Lochalsh District.

Fala Dam, Pathhead, Midlothian;
Lothian and Borders at Edinburgh.
Lothian Region
Midlothian District.

Fala Village, Pathhead, Midlothian;
Lothian and Borders at Edinburgh.
Lothian Region
Midlothian District.

Falkirk, Stirlingshire; Tayside,
Central and Fife at Falkirk.
Central Region
Falkirk District.

Falkland, Cupar, Fife; Tayside,
Central and Fife at Cupar.
Fife Region
North East Fife District.

Fallin, Stirling; Tayside, Central and
Fife at Stirling.
Central Region
Stirling District.

Fankerton, Denny, Stirlingshire;
Tayside, Central and Fife at
Falkirk.
Central Region
Falkirk District.

Farnell, Brechin, Angus; Tayside,
Central and Fife at Forfar.
Tayside Region
Angus District.

Farr, Inverness; Grampian,
Highland and Islands at Inverness.
Highland Region
Inverness District.

Faslane, Helensburgh,
Dunbartonshire; North Strathclyde
at Dumbarton.
Strathclyde Region
Dumbarton District.

Fasnacloich, Appin, Argyll; North
Strathclyde at Oban.
Strathclyde Region
Argyll and Bute District.

Faucheldean, Broxburn, West
Lothian; Lothian and Borders at
Linlithgow.
Lothian Region
West Lothian District.

Fauldhouse, Bathgate, West
Lothian; Lothian and Borders at
Linlithgow.
Lothian Region
West Lothian District.

Fearn, Tain, Ross-shire; Grampian,
Highland and Islands at Tain.
Highland Region
Ross and Cromarty District.

Fearnan, Aberfeldy, Perthshire;
Tayside, Central and Fife at Perth.
Tayside Region
Perth and Kinross District.

Feltar, Shetland; Grampian,
Highland and Islands at Lerwick.
Shetland Islands Council.

Fenwick, Kilmarnock, Ayrshire;
North Strathclyde at Kilmarnock.
Strathclyde Region
Cunninghame District.

Ferintosh, Conon Bridge, Ross-
shire; Grampian, Highland and
Islands at Dingwall.
Highland Region
Ross and Cromarty District.

Fern, Forfar, Angus; Tayside,
Central and Fife at Forfar.
Tayside Region
Angus District.

Ferness, Nairn; Grampian,
Highland and Islands at Inverness.
Highland Region
Nairn District.

Fernie, Cupar, Fife; Tayside,
Central and Fife at Cupar.
Fife Region
North East Fife District.

Fernilea, Carbost, Isle of Skye;
Grampian, Highland and Islands at
Portree.
Highland Region
Skye and Lochalsh District.

Ferrindonald, Teangue, Sleat, Isle
of Skye; Grampian, Highland and
Islands at Portree.
Highland Region
Skye and Lochalsh District.

Ferrinquarrie, Glendale,
Dunvegan, Isle of Skye;
Grampian, Highland and Islands at
Portree.
Highland Region
Skye and Lochalsh District.

Ferryden, Montrose, Angus;
Tayside, Central and Fife at
Arbroath.
Tayside Region
Angus District.

Feshie Bridge, Kingussie,
Inverness-shire; Grampian,
Highland and Islands at Inverness.
Highland Region
Badenoch and Strathspey District.

Fetterangus, Peterhead,
Aberdeenshire; Grampian,
Highland and Islands at
Peterhead.
Grampian Region
Banff and Buchan District.

Fettercairn, Laurencekirk,
Kincardineshire; Grampian,
Highland and Islands at
Stonehaven.
Grampian Region
Kincardine and Deeside District.

Fetteresso, Stonehaven,
Kincardineshire; Grampian,
Highland and Islands at
Stonehaven.
Grampian Region
Kincardine and Deeside District.

Fetternear, Inverurie,
Aberdeenshire; Grampian,
Highland and Islands at Aberdeen.
Grampian Region
Gordon District.

Feughside, Banchory,
Kincardineshire; Grampian,
Highland and Islands at
Stonehaven.
Grampian Region
Kincardine and Deeside District.

Fevig, Shawbost, Isle of Lewis;
Grampian, Highland and Islands at
Stornoway.
Western Isles Islands Council.

Fife Keith, Morayshire; Grampian,
Highland and Islands at Elgin.
Grampian Region
Moray District.

Finavon, Forfar, Angus; Tayside,
Central and Fife at Forfar.
Tayside Region
Angus District.

Fincastle, Pitlochry, Perthshire;
Tayside, Central and Fife at Perth.
Tayside Region
Perth and Kinross District.

Findhorn, Forres, Morayshire;
Grampian, Highland and Islands at
Elgin.
Grampian Region
Moray District.

Findo Gask, Perth; Tayside,
Central and Fife at Perth.
Tayside Region
Perth and Kinross District.

Findochty, Buckie, Morayshire;
Grampian, Highland and Islands at
Elgin.
Grampian Region
Moray District.

Findon, Portlethen, Aberdeen;
Grampian, Highland and Islands at
Stonehaven.
Grampian Region
Kincardine and Deeside District.

Finnart, Arrochar, Dunbartonshire;
North Strathclyde at Dumbarton.
Strathclyde Region
Dumbarton District.

Finsbay, Isle of Harris; Grampian,
Highland and Islands at
Stornoway.
Western Isles Islands Council.

Finstown, Orkney; Grampian,
Highland and Islands at Kirkwall.
Orkney Islands Council.

Fintry, Killearn, Stirlingshire;
Tayside, Central and Fife at
Stirling.
Central Region
Stirling District.

Fintry, Turriff, Banffshire;
Grampian, Highland and Islands at
Banff.
Grampian Region
Banff and Buchan District.

Finzean, Banchory,
Kincardineshire; Grampian,
Highland and Islands at
Stonehaven.
Grampian Region
Kincardine and Deeside District.

Fionnphort, Isle of Mull; North
Strathclyde at Oban.
Strathclyde Region
Argyll and Bute District.

Firth, Finstown, Orkney; Grampian,
Highland and Islands at Kirkwall.
Orkney Islands Council.

Fiscovaig, Carbost, Isle of Skye;
Grampian, Highland and Islands at
Portree.
Highland Region
Skye and Lochalsh District.

Fishcross, Alloa,
Clackmannanshire; Tayside,
Central and Fife at Alloa.
Central Region
Clackmannan District.

Fisherford, Inverurie,
Aberdeenshire; Grampian,
Highland and Islands at Aberdeen.
Grampian Region
Gordon District.

Fisherie, Turriff, Banffshire;
Grampian, Highland and Islands at
Banff.
Grampian Region
Banff and Buchan District.

Fisherton, Ayr; South Strathclyde,
Dumfries and Galloway at Ayr.
Strathclyde Region
Kyle and Carrick District.

Fivepenny, Port of Ness, Isle of
Lewis; Grampian, Highland and
Islands at Stornoway.
Western Isles Islands Council.

Fiveways, Hurlford, Kilmarnock,
Ayrshire; North Strathclyde at
Kilmarnock.
Strathclyde Region
Kilmarnock and Louden District.

Flesherin, Isle of Lewis; Grampian,
Highland and Islands at
Stornoway.
Western Isles Islands Council.

Flichity, Inverness; Grampian,
Highland and Islands at Inverness.
Highland Region
Inverness District.

Floda, Alyth, Perthshire; Tayside,
Central and Fife at Perth.
Tayside Region
Perth and Kinross District.

Flodabay, Harris; Grampian,
Highland and Islands at
Stornoway.
Western Isles Islands Council.

Flodigary, Portree, Isle of Skye;
Grampian, Highland and Islands at
Portree.
Highland Region
Skye and Lochalsh District.

Flotta, Stromness, Orkney;
Grampian, Highland and Islands at
Kirkwall.
Orkney Islands Council.

Fochabers, Morayshire; Grampian,
Highland and Islands at Elgin.
Grampian Region
Moray District.

Foelin Ferry, Isle of Jura; North
Strathclyde at Campbeltown.
Strathclyde Region
Argyll and Bute District.

Fogo, Duns, Berwickshire; Lothian
and Borders at Duns.
Borders Region
Berwickshire District.

Foindle, Lairg, Sutherland;
Grampian, Highland and Islands at
Dornoch.
Highland Region
Sutherland District.

Folla Rule, Rothienorman,
Banffshire; Grampian, Highland
and Islands at Banff.
Grampian Region
Banff and Buchan District.

Foodieash, Cupar, Fife; Tayside,
Central and Fife at Cupar.
Fife Region
North East Fife District.

Forbes, Alford, Aberdeenshire;
Grampian, Highland and Islands at
Aberdeen.
Grampian Region
Gordon District.

Ford, Lochgilphead, Argyll; North
Strathclyde at Oban.
Strathclyde Region
Argyll and Bute District.

Ford, Pathhead, Midlothian; Lothian
and Borders at Edinburgh.
Lothian Region
Midlothian District.

Fordoun, Laurencekirk,
Kincardineshire; Grampian,
Highland and Islands at
Stonehaven.
Grampian Region
Kincardine and Deeside District.

Fordyce, Banff; Grampian,
Highland and Islands at Banff.
Grampian Region
Banff and Buchan District.

Foreside, Forfar, Angus; Tayside,
Central and Fife at Forfar.
Tayside Region
Angus District.

Forfar, Angus; Tayside, Central
and Fife at Forfar.
Tayside Region
Angus District.

Forgandenny, Perth; Tayside,
Central and Fife at Perth.
Tayside Region
Perth and Kinross District.

Forglen, Turriff, Banffshire;
Grampian, Highland and Islands at
Banff.
Grampian Region
Banff and Buchan District.

Forgue, Huntly, Aberdeenshire;
Grampian, Highland and Islands at
Aberdeen.
Grampian Region
Gordon District.

Forneth, Blairgowrie, Perthshire;
Tayside, Central and Fife at Perth.
Tayside Region
Perth and Kinross District.

Forres, Morayshire; Grampian,
Highland and Islands at Elgin.
Grampian Region
Moray District.

Forrestfield, Caldercruix, Airdrie,
Lanarkshire; South Strathclyde,
Dumfries and Galloway at Airdrie.
Strathclyde Region
Monklands District.

Forrestmill, Alloa,
Clackmannanshire; Tayside,
Central and Fife at Alloa.
Central Region
Clackmannan District.

Forsinard, Sutherland; Grampian,
Highland and Islands at Dornoch.
Highland Region
Sutherland District.

Forss, Thurso, Caithness;
Grampian, Highland and Islands at
Wick.
Highland Region
Caithness District.

Fort Augustus, Inverness-shire;
Grampian, Highland and Islands at
Inverness.
Highland Region
Inverness District.

Fort George, Ardersier, Inverness;
Grampian, Highland and Islands at
Inverness.
Highland Region
Inverness District.

Fort Matilda, Greenock,
Renfrewshire; North Strathclyde at
Greenock.
Strathclyde Region
Inverclyde District.

Fort William, Inverness-shire;
Grampian, Highland and Islands at
Fort William.
Highland Region
Lochaber District.

Forteviot, Perth; Tayside, Central
and Fife at Perth.
Tayside Region
Perth and Kinross District.

Forth, Lanark; South Strathclyde,
Dumfries and Galloway at Lanark.
Strathclyde Region
Clydesdale District.

Fortingall, Aberfeldy, Perthshire;
Tayside, Central and Fife at Perth.
Tayside Region
Perth and Kinross District.

Fortrie, Turriff, Banffshire;
Grampian, Highland and Islands at
Banff.
Grampian Region
Banff and Buchan District.

Fortrose, Ross-shire; Grampian,
Highland and Islands at Dingwall.
Highland Region
Ross and Cromarty District.

Foss, Pitlochry, Perthshire;
Tayside, Central and Fife at Perth.
Tayside Region
Perth and Kinross District.

Fossoway, Kinross; Tayside,
Central and Fife at Perth.
Tayside Region
Perth and Kinross District.

Foula, Shetland; Grampian,
Highland and Islands at Lerwick.
Shetland Islands Council.

Fountainhall, Galashiels,
Selkirkshire; Lothian and Borders
at Selkirk.
Borders Region
Ettrick and Lauderdale District.

Foveran, Ellon, Aberdeenshire;
Grampian, Highland and Islands at
Aberdeen.
Grampian Region
Gordon District.

Fowlis, Dundee; Tayside, Central
and Fife at Dundee.
Tayside Region
City of Dundee District.

Fowlis Wester, Creiff, Perthshire;
Tayside, Central and Fife at Perth.
Tayside Region
Perth and Kinross District.

Foxbar, Paisley, Renfrewshire;
North Strathclyde at Paisley.
Strathclyde Region
Renfrew District.

Foxhole, Kiltarlity, Inverness-shire;
Grampian, Highland and Islands at
Inverness.
Highland Region
Inverness District.

Foyers, Inverness; Grampian,
Highland and Islands at Inverness.
Highland Region
Inverness District.

Fraserburgh, Aberdeenshire;
Grampian, Highland and Islands at
Banff.
Grampian Region
Banff and Buchan District.

Frenchie, Falkland, Cupar, Fife;
Tayside, Central and Fife at
Cupar.
Fife Region
North East Fife District.

Freswick, Wick, Caithness;
Grampian, Highland and Islands at
Wick.
Highland Region
Caithness District.

Freuchie, Cupar, Fife; Tayside,
Central and Fife at Cupar.
Fife Region
North East Fife District.

Friockhelm, Arbroath, Angus;
Tayside, Central and Fife at
Arbroath.
Tayside Region
Angus District.

Frobost, Lochboisdale, Isle of
South Uist; Grampian, Highland
and Islands at Lochmaddy.
Western Isles Islands Council.

Funzie, Fetlar, Shetland; Grampian,
Highland and Islands at Lerwick.
Shetland Islands Council.

Furnace, Inverary, Argyll; North
Strathclyde at Dunoon.
Strathclyde Region
Argyll and Bute District.

Fyvie, Turriff, Banffshire; Grampian,
Highland and Islands at Banff.
Grampian Region
Banff and Buchan District.

Gaihgenhouse, Craighouse, Isle of
Jura; North Strathclyde at
Campbeltown.
Strathclyde Region
Argyll and Bute District.

Gairloch, Ross-shire; Grampian,
Highland and Islands at Dingwall.
Highland Region
Ross and Cromarty District.

Gairlochy, Spean Bridge,
Inverness-shire; Grampian,
Highland and Islands at Fort
William.
Grampian Region
Lochaber District.

Gairnsheil, Ballater,
Kincardineshire; Grampian,
Highland and Islands at
Stonehaven.
Grampian Region
Kincardine and Deeside District.

Galashiels, Selkirkshire; Lothian
and Borders at Selkirk.
Borders Region
Ettrick and Lauderdale District.

Gallatown, Kirkcaldy, Fife; Tayside,
Central and Fife at Kirkcaldy.
Fife Region
Kirkcaldy District.

Galson, Borve, Isle of Lewis;
Grampian, Highland and Islands at
Stornoway.
Western Isles Islands Council.

Galston, Ayrshire; North
Strathclyde at Kilmarnock.
Strathclyde Region
Kilmarnock and Louden District.

Gamrie, Banffshire; Grampian,
Highland and Islands at Banff.
Grampian Region
Banff and Buchan District.

Gardenstown, Banffshire;
Grampian, Highland and Islands at
Banff.
Grampian Region
Banff and Buchan District.

Garderhouse, Shetland; Grampian,
Highland and Islands at Lerwick.
Shetland Islands Council.

Garelochhead, Helensburgh, Dunbartonshire; North Strathclyde at Dumbarton.
Strathclyde Region
Dumbarton District.

Garenin, Isle of Lewis; Grampian, Highland and Islands at Stornoway.
Western Isles Islands Council.

Gargunnock, Stirling; Tayside, Central and Fife at Stirling.
Central Region
Stirling District.

Garland, Turriff, Banffshire; Grampian, Highland and Islands at Banff.
Grampian Region
Banff and Buchan District.

Garlieston, Newton Stewart, Wigtownshire; South Strathclyde, Dumfries and Galloway at Stranraer.
Dumfries and Galloway Region
Wigtown District.

Garlogie, Skene, Aberdeenshire; Grampian, Highland and Islands at Aberdeen.
Grampian Region
City of Aberdeen District.

Garmouth, Fochabers, Morayshire; Grampian, Highland and Islands at Elgin.
Grampian Region
Moray District.

Garnkirk, Chryston, Glasgow; Glasgow and Strathkelvin at Glasgow.
Strathclyde Region
City of Glasgow District.

Garrabost, Point, Isle of Lewis; Grampian, Highland and Islands at Stornoway.
Western Isles Islands Council.

Garrygal, Castlebay, Isle of Barra; Grampian, Highland and Islands at Lochmaddy.
Western Isles Islands Council.

Garryheillie, Lochboisdale, Isle of South Uist; Grampian, Highland and Islands at Lochmaddy.
Western Isles Islands Council.

Garrynamonie, Lochboisdale, Isle of South Uist; Grampian, Highland and Islands at Lochmaddy.
Western Isles Islands Council.

Gartcosh, Glasgow; Glasgow and Strathkelvin at Glasgow.
Strathclyde Region
City of Glasgow District.

Gartly, Huntly, Aberdeenshire; Grampian, Highland and Islands at Aberdeen.
Grampian Region
Gordon District.

Gartmore, Stirling; Tayside, Central and Fife at Stirling.
Central Region
Stirling District.

Gartnatra, Bowmore, Isle of Islay; North Strathclyde at Campbeltown.
Strathclyde Region
Argyll and Bute District.

Gartocharn, Dunbartonshire; North Strathclyde at Dumbarton.
Strathclyde Region
Dumbarton District.

Gartymore, Helmsdale, Sutherland;
Grampian, Highland and Islands at
Dornoch.
Highland Region
Sutherland District.

Garvald, Haddington, East Lothian;
Lothian and Borders at
Haddington.
Lothian Region
East Lothian District.

Garve, Ross-shire; Grampian,
Highland and Islands at Dingwall.
Highland Region
Ross and Cromarty District.

Garynahine, Isle of Lewis;
Grampian, Highland and Islands at
Stornoway.
Western Isles Islands Council.

Garyvard, Isle of Lewis; Grampian,
Highland and Islands at
Stornoway.
Western Isles Islands Council.

Gask, Auchterarder, Perthshire;
Tayside, Central and Fife at Perth.
Tayside Region
Perth and Kinross District.

Gatehead, Kilmarnock, Ayrshire;
North Strathclyde at Kilmarnock.
Strathclyde Region
Kilmarnock and Louden District.

Gatehouse of Fleet, Castle
Douglas, Kirkcudbrightshire; South
Strathclyde, Dumfries and
Galloway at Kirkcudbright.
Dumfries and Galloway Region
Stewartry District.

Gatelawbridge, Thornhill,
Dumfriesshire; South Strath-
clyde, Dumfries and Galloway at
Dumfries.
Dumfries and Galloway Region
Nithsdale District.

Gateside, Beith, Ayrshire; North
Strathclyde at Kilmarnock.
Strathclyde Region
Cunninghame District.

Gateside, Cupar, Fife; Tayside,
Central and Fife at Cupar.
Fife Region
North East Fife District.

Gattonside, Melrose,
Roxburghshire; Lothian and
Borders at Selkirk.
Borders Region
Ettrick and Lauderdale District.

Gauldry, Newport-on-Tay, Fife;
Tayside, Central and Fife at
Cupar.
Fife Region
North East Fife District.

Gavinton, Duns, Berwickshire;
Lothian and Borders at Duns.
Borders Region
Berwickshire District.

Gaza, Fearn, Ross-shire;
Grampian, Highland and Islands at
Tain.
Highland Region
Ross and Cromarty District.

Geanies, Fearn, Ross-shire;
Grampian, Highland and Islands at
Tain.
Highland Region
Ross and Cromarty District.

Gearadhu, Lochmaddy, Isle of North Uist; Grampian, Highland and Islands at Lochmaddy. Western Isles Islands Council.

Geddes, Nairn; Grampian, Highland and Islands at Inverness. Highland Region Nairn District.

Gelston, Castle Douglas, Kirkcudbrightshire; South Strathclyde, Dumfries and Galloway at Kirkcudbright. Dumfries and Galloway Region Stewartry District.

Geocrab, Isle of Harris; Grampian, Highland and Islands at Stornoway. Western Isles Islands Council.

Georgemas Junction, Halkirk, Caithness; Grampian, Highland and Islands at Wick. Highland Region Caithness District.

Georgetown, Johnstone, Renfrewshire; North Strathclyde at Paisley. Strathclyde Region Renfrew District.

Geshader, Isle of Lewis; Grampian, Highland and Islands at Stornoway. Western Isles Islands Council.

Giffnock, Glasgow; North Strathclyde at Paisley. Strathclyde Region Renfrew District.

Gifford, Haddington, East Lothian; Lothian and Borders at Haddington. Lothian Region East Lothian District.

Giffordtown, Cupar, Fife; Tayside, Central and Fife at Cupar. Fife Region North East Fife District.

Gight, Ellon, Aberdeenshire; Grampian, Highland and Islands at Aberdeen. Grampian Region Gordon District.

Gillock, Halkirk, Caithness; Grampian, Highland and Islands at Wick. Highland Region Caithness District.

Gilmerton, Crieff, Perthshire; Tayside, Central and Fife at Perth. Tayside Region Perth and Kinross District.

Gilmerton, Edinburgh; Lothian and Borders at Edinburgh. Lothian Region City of Edinburgh District.

Gilmourton, Strathaven, Lanarkshire; South Strathclyde, Dumfries and Galloway at Hamilton. Strathclyde Region Hamilton District.

Gilnockie, Canonbie, Dumfriesshire; South Strathclyde, Dumfries and Galloway at Dumfries. Dumfries and Galloway Region Annandale and Eskdale District.

Girdle Toll, Irvine, Ayrshire; North
Strathclyde at Kilmarnock.
Strathclyde Region
Cunninghame District.

Girlsta, Lerwick, Shetland;
Grampian, Highland and Islands at
Lerwick.
Shetland Islands Council.

Girvan, Ayrshire; South
Strathclyde, Dumfries and
Galloway at Ayr.
Strathclyde Region
Kyle and Carrick District.

Gladsmuir, Tranent, East Lothian;
Lothian and Borders at
Haddington.
Lothian Region
East Lothian District.

Glamis, Forfar, Angus; Tayside,
Central and Fife at Forfar.
Tayside Region
Angus District.

Glasgow; Glasgow and
Strathkelvin at Glasgow.
Strathclyde Region
City of Glasgow District.

Glasgow Airport, Abbotsinch,
Renfrewshire; North Strathclyde at
Paisley.
Strathclyde Region
Renfrew District.

Glasnakille, Broadford, Isle of
Skye; Grampian, Highland and
Islands at Portree.
Highland Region
Skye and Lochalsh District.

Glass, Huntly, Aberdeenshire;
Grampian, Highland and Islands at
Aberdeen.
Grampian Region
Gordon District.

Glassard, Isle of Colonsay; North
Strathclyde at Oban.
Strathclyde Region
Argyll and Bute District.

Glassaugh, Portsoy, Banffshire;
Grampian, Highland and Islands at
Banff.
Grampian Region
Banff and Buchan District.

Glassel, Banchory,
Kincardineshire; Grampian,
Highland and Islands at
Stonehaven.
Grampian Region
Kincardine and Deeside District.

Glasserton, Whithorn, Newton
Stewart, Wigtownshire; South
Strathclyde, Dumfries and
Galloway at Stranraer.
Dumfries and Galloway Region
Wigtown District.

Glassford, Strathaven,
Lanarkshire; South Strathclyde,
Dumfries and Galloway at
Hamilton.
Strathclyde Region
Hamilton District.

Glassingall, Dunblane,
Stirlingshire; Tayside, Central and
Fife at Stirling.
Central Region
Stirling District.

Glasslie, Falkland, Fife; Tayside,
Central and Fife at Cupar.
Fife Region
North East Fife District.

Glen, Castlebay, Isle of Barra;
Grampian, Highland and Islands at
Lochmaddy.
Western Isles Islands Council.

Glen, Gravir, Isle of Lewis;
Grampian, Highland and Islands at
Stornoway.
Western Isles Islands Council.

Glencaple, Dumfries; South
Strathclyde, Dumfries and
Galloway at Dumfries.
Dumfries and Galloway Region
Nithsdale District.

Glen Caladh, Tighnabruaich,
Argyll; North Strathclyde at
Dunoon.
Strathclyde Region
Argyll and Bute District.

Glen Kyles, Leverburgh, Isle of
Harris; Grampian, Highland and
Islands at Stornoway.
Western Isles Islands Council.

Glen Masson, Dunoon, Argyll;
North Strathclyde at Dunoon.
Strathclyde Region
Argyll and Bute District.

Glen Village, Falkirk, Stirlingshire;
Tayside, Central and Fife at
Falkirk.
Central Region
Falkirk District.

Glenachulish, Ballachulish,
Inverness-shire; Grampian,
Highland and Islands at Fort
William.
Highland Region
Lochaber District.

Glenalmond, Perth; Tayside,
Central and Fife at Perth.
Tayside Region
Perth and Kinross District.

Glenbarr, Tarbert, Argyll; North
Strathclyde at Campbeltown.
Strathclyde Region
Argyll and Bute District.

Glenbarry, Banffshire; Grampian,
Highland and Islands at Banff.
Grampian Region
Banff and Buchan District.

Glenbervie, Stonehaven,
Kincardineshire; Grampian,
Highland and Islands at
Stonehaven.
Grampian Region
Kincardine and Deeside District.

Glenboig, Coatbridge, Lanarkshire;
South Strathclyde, Dumfries and
Galloway at Airdrie.
Strathclyde Region
Monklands District.

Glenborrodale, Acharacle,
Inverness-shire; Grampian,
Highland and Islands at Fort
William.
Highland Region
Lochaber District.

Glenbrittle, Carbost, Isle of Skye;
Grampian, Highland and Islands at
Portree.
Highland Region
Skye and Lochalsh District.

Glenbuchat, Strathdon,
Aberdeenshire; Grampian,
Highland and Islands at Aberdeen.
Grampian Region
Gordon District.

Glenbuck, Cumnock, Ayrshire;
South Strathclyde, Dumfries and
Galloway at Ayr.
Strathclyde Region
Kyle and Carrick District.

Glenburn, Paisley, Renfrewshire;
North Strathclyde at Paisley.
Strathclyde Region
Renfrew District.

Glencarse, Perth; Tayside, Central
and Fife at Perth.
Tayside Region
Perth and Kinross District.

Glenclova, Kirriemuir, Angus;
Tayside, Central and Fife at
Forfar.
Tayside Region
Angus District.

Glencoe, Ballachulish, Inverness-
shire; Grampian, Highland and
Islands at Fort William.
Highland Region
Lochaber District.

Glencraig, Lochgelly, Fife; Tayside,
Central and Fife at Dunfermline.
Fife Region
Dunfermline District.

Glencraigs, Campbeltown, Argyll;
North Strathclyde at
Campbeltown.
Strathclyde Region
Argyll and Bute District.

Glencruitton, Oban, Argyll; North
Strathclyde at Oban.
Strathclyde Region
Argyll and Bute District.

Glendale, Dunvegan, Isle of Skye;
Grampian, Highland and Islands at
Portree.
Highland Region
Skye and Lochalsh District.

Glendaruel, Colintraive, Argyll;
North Strathclyde at Dunoon.
Strathclyde Region
Argyll and Bute District.

Glendaveny, Peterhead,
Aberdeenshire; Grampian,
Highland and Islands at
Peterhead.
Grampian Region
Banff and Buchan District.

Glendevon, Dollar,
Clackmannanshire; Tayside,
Central and Fife at Perth.
Tayside Region
Perth and Kinross District.

Glendoich, Glencarse, Perthshire;
Tayside, Central and Fife at Perth.
Tayside Region
Perth and Kinross District.

Gleneagles, Auchterarder,
Perthshire; Tayside, Central and
Fife at Perth.
Tayside Region
Perth and Kinross District.

Glenegedale, Port Ellen, Islay;
North Strathclyde at
Campbeltown.
Strathclyde Region
Argyll and Bute District.

Glenelg, Kyle of Lochalsh, Ross-
shire; Grampian, Highland and
Islands at Portree.
Highland Region
Skye and Lochalsh District.

Glenetive, Ballachulish, Inverness-
shire; Grampian, Highland and
Islands at Fort William.
Highland Region
Lochaber District.

Glenfarg, Perthshire; Tayside,
Central and Fife at Perth.
Tayside Region
Perth and Kinross District.

Glenferness, Nairn; Grampian,
Highland and Islands at Inverness.
Highland Region
Nairn District.

Glenfinnan, Fort William,
Inverness-shire; Grampian,
Highland and Islands at Fort
William.
Highland Region
Lochaber District.

Glenforsa, Aros, Isle of Mull; North
Strathclyde at Oban.
Strathclyde Region
Argyll and Bute District.

Glengarnock, Beith, Ayrshire;
North Strathclyde at Kilmarnock.
Strathclyde Region
Cunninghame District.

Glengirnaig, Ballater,
Kincardineshire; Grampian,
Highland and Islands at
Stonehaven.
Grampian Region
Kincardine and Deeside District.

Glengorm, Tobermory, Isle of Mull;
North Strathclyde at Oban.
Strathclyde Region
Argyll and Bute District.

Glenisla, Alyth, Perthshire;
Tayside, Central and Fife at
Forfar.
Tayside Region
Angus District.

Glenkindle, Alford, Aberdeenshire;
Grampian, Highland and Islands at
Aberdeen.
Grampian Region
Gordon District.

Glenlivet, Ballindalloch,
Morayshire; Grampian, Highland
and Islands at Elgin.
Grampian Region
Moray District.

Glenloan, Oban, Argyll; North
Strathclyde at Oban.
Strathclyde Region
Argyll and Bute District.

Glenlochar, Castle Douglas,
Kirkcudbrightshire; South
Strathclyde, Dumfries and
Galloway at Kirkcudbright.
Dumfries and Galloway Region
Stewartry District.

Glenlochay, Killin, Stirlingshire;
Tayside, Central and Fife at
Stirling.
Central Region
Stirling District.

Glenluce, Newton Stewart,
Wigtownshire; South Strathclyde,
Dumfries and Galloway at
Stranraer.
Dumfries and Galloway Region
Wigtown District.

Glenlyon, Aberfeldy, Perthshire;
Tayside, Central and Fife at Perth.
Tayside Region
Perth and Kinross District.

Glenmavis, Airdrie, Lanarkshire;
South Strathclyde, Dumfries and
Galloway at Airdrie.
Strathclyde Region
Monklands District.

Glenmore, Aviemore, Inverness-
shire; Grampian, Highland and
Islands at Inverness.
Highland Region
Badenoch and Strathspey District.

Glenmore, Portree, Isle of Skye;
Grampian, Highland and Islands at
Portree.
Highland Region
Skye and Lochalsh District.

Glenmoriston, Inverness;
Grampian, Highland and Islands at
Inverness.
Highland Region
Inverness District.

Glenmoy, Kirriemuir, Angus;
Tayside, Central and Fife at
Forfar.
Tayside Region
Angus District.

Glenmuick, Ballater,
Kincardineshire; Grampian,
Highland and Islands at
Stonehaven.
Grampian Region
Kincardine and Deeside District.

Glenogil, Forfar, Angus; Tayside,
Central and Fife at Forfar.
Tayside Region
Angus District.

Glenogilvy, Forfar, Angus;
Tayside, Central and Fife at
Forfar.
Tayside Region
Angus District.

Glenogle, Lochearnhead,
Stirlingshire; Tayside, Central and
Fife at Stirling.
Central Region
Stirling District.

Glenprosen, Kirriemuir, Angus;
Tayside, Central and Fife at
Forfar.
Tayside Region
Angus District.

Glenquiech, Forfar, Angus;
Tayside, Central and Fife at
Forfar.
Tayside Region
Angus District.

Glenramskill, Campbeltown, Argyll;
North Strathclyde at
Campbeltown.
Strathclyde Region
Argyll and Bute District.

Glenrinnes, Dufftown, Morayshire;
Grampian, Highland and Islands at
Elgin.
Grampian Region
Moray District.

Glenrothes, Fife; Tayside, Central
and Fife at Kirkcaldy.
Fife Region
Kirkcaldy District.

Glensburgh, Grangemouth,
Stirlingshire; Tayside, Central and
Fife at Falkirk.
Central Region
Falkirk District.

Glenshee, Blairgowrie, Perthshire;
Tayside, Central and Fife at Perth.
Tayside Region
Perth and Kinross District.

Glensheil, Kyle of Lochalsh, Ross-
shire; Grampian, Highland and
Islands at Dingwall.
Highland Region
Skye and Lochalsh District.

Glenside, Maybole, Ayrshire; South
Strathclyde, Dumfries and
Galloway at Ayr.
Strathclyde Region
Kyle and Carrick District.

Glentanar, Aboyne,
Kincardineshire; Grampian,
Highland and Islands at
Stonehaven.
Grampian Region
Kincardine and Deeside District.

Glentrool, Newton Stewart,
Wigtownshire; South Strathclyde,
Dumfries and Galloway at
Stranraer.
Dumfries and Galloway Region
Wigtown District.

Glenuig, Lochailort, Fort William,
Inverness-shire; Grampian,
Highland and Islands at Fort
William.
Highland Region
Lochaber District.

Glespin, Lanark; South Strathclyde,
Dumfries and Galloway at Lanark.
Strathclyde Region
Clydesdale District.

Gletness, Shetland; Grampian,
Highland and Islands at Lerwick.
Shetland Islands Council.

Gluss, Ollabery, Shetland;
Grampian, Highland and Islands at
Lerwick.
Shetland Islands Council.

Gogar, Midlothian; Lothian and
Borders at Edinburgh.
Lothian Region
Midlothian District.

Goldenacre, Edinburgh; Lothian
and Borders at Edinburgh.
Lothian Region
City of Edinburgh District.

Gollanfield, Inverness; Grampian,
Highland and Islands at Inverness.
Highland Region
Inverness District.

Golspie, Sutherland; Grampian, Highland and Islands at Dornoch.
Highland Region
Sutherland District.

Gometra, Ulva Ferry, Isle of Mull; North Strathclyde at Oban.
Strathclyde Region
Argyll and Bute District.

Gonfirth, Voe, Shetland; Grampian, Highland and Islands at Lerwick.
Shetland Islands Council.

Gordon Arms, Melrose, Roxburghshire; Lothian and Borders at Selkirk.
Borders Region
Ettrick and Lauderdale District.

Gordon, Berwickshire; Lothian and Borders at Duns.
Borders Region
Berwickshire District.

Gordonstown, Duffus, Morayshire; Grampian, Highland and Islands at Elgin.
Grampian Region
Moray District.

Gorebridge, Midlothian; Lothian and Borders at Edinburgh.
Lothian Region
Midlothian District.

Gorgie, Edinburgh; Lothian and Borders at Edinburgh.
Lothian Region
City of Edinburgh District.

Gorthleck, Inverness; Grampian, Highland and Islands at Inverness.
Highland Region
Inverness District.

Gott, Shetland; Grampian, Highland and Islands at Lerwick.
Shetland Islands Council.

Goular, Lochmaddy, Isle of North Uist; Grampian, Highland and Islands at Lochmaddy.
Western Isles Islands Council.

Gourdon, Laurencekirk, Kincardineshire; Grampian, Highland and Islands at Stonehaven.
Grampian Region
Kincardine and Deeside District.

Gourock, Renfrewshire; North Strathclyde at Greenock.
Strathclyde Region
Inverclyde District.

Govan, Glasgow; Glasgow and Strathkelvin at Glasgow.
Strathclyde Region
City of Glasgow District.

Govig, Isle of Harris; Grampian, Highland and Islands at Stornoway.
Western Isles Islands Council.

Gowanbank, Forfar, Angus; Tayside, Central and Fife at Forfar.
Tayside Region
Angus District.

Gowkhill, Dunfermline, Fife; Tayside, Central and Fife at Dunfermline.
Fife Region
Dunfermline District.

Gowkshill, Gorebridge, Midlothian;
Lothian and Borders at Edinburgh.
Lothian Region
Midlothian District.

Graemsay, Stromness, Orkney;
Grampian, Highland and Islands at
Kirkwall.
Orkney Islands Council.

Grahamston, Falkirk, Stirlingshire;
Tayside, Central and Fife at
Falkirk.
Central Region
Falkirk District.

Gramsdale, Isle of Benbecula;
Grampian, Highland and Islands at
Lochmaddy.
Western Isles Islands Council.

Grandhom, Aberdeen; Grampian,
Highland and Islands at Aberdeen.
Grampian Region
City of Aberdeen District.

Grandtully, Aberfeldy, Perthshire;
Tayside, Central and Fife at Perth.
Tayside Region
Perth and Kinross District.

Grange, Keith, Morayshire;
Grampian, Highland and Islands at
Elgin.
Grampian Region
Moray District.

Grange of Lindores, Newburgh,
Fife; Tayside, Central and Fife at
Cupar.
Fife Region
North East Fife District.

Grangemouth, Stirlingshire;
Tayside, Central and Fife at
Falkirk.
Central Region
Falkirk District.

Granton, Edinburgh; Lothian and
Borders at Edinburgh.
Lothian Region
City of Edinburgh District.

Grantown-on-Spey, Inverness-
shire; Grampian, Highland and
Islands at Inverness.
Highland Region
Badenoch and Strathspey District.

Grantshouse, Duns, Berwickshire;
Lothian and Borders at Duns.
Borders Region
Berwickshire District.

Gravir, Isle of Lewis; Grampian,
Highland and Islands at
Stornoway.
Western Isles Islands Council.

Grean, Castlebay, Isle of Barra;
Grampian, Highland and Islands at
Lochmaddy.
Western Isles Islands Council.

Great Bernera, Isle of Lewis;
Grampian, Highland and Islands at
Stornoway.
Western Isles Islands Council.

Greeness, Turriff, Banffshire;
Grampian, Highland and Islands at
Banff.
Grampian Region
Banff and Buchan District.

Greengairs, Airdrie, Lanarkshire; South Strathclyde, Dumfries and Galloway at Airdrie.
Strathclyde Region
Monklands District.

Greenhill, Scarinish, Isle of Tiree; North Strathclyde at Oban.
Strathclyde Region
Argyll and Bute District.

Greenhillstair, Moffat, Dumfriesshire; South Strathclyde, Dumfries and Galloway at Dumfries.
Dumfries and Galloway Region
Annandale and Eskdale District.

Greenlaw, Duns, Berwickshire; Lothian and Borders at Duns.
Borders Region
Berwickshire District.

Greenloaning, Dunblane, Stirlingshire; Tayside, Central and Fife at Perth.
Tayside Region
Perth and Kinross District.

Greenock, Renfrewshire; North Strathclyde at Greenock.
Strathclyde Region
Inverclyde District.

Greens, Turriff, Banffshire; Grampian, Highland and Islands at Banff.
Grampian Region
Banff and Buchan District.

Grenitote, Lochmaddy, Isle of North Uist; Grampian, Highland and Islands at Lochmaddy.
Western Isles Islands Council.

Gress, Isle of Lewis; Grampian, Highland and Islands at Stornoway.
Western Isles Islands Council.

Gretna, Annan, Dumfriesshire; South Strathclyde, Dumfries and Galloway at Dumfries.
Dumfries and Galloway Region
Annandale and Eskdale District.

Greystone, Arbroath, Angus; Tayside, Central and Fife at Arbroath.
Tayside Region
Angus District.

Gribun, Isle of Mull; North Strathclyde at Oban.
Strathclyde Region
Argyll and Bute District.

Grimersta, Isle of Lewis; Grampian, Highland and Islands at Stornoway.
Western Isles Islands Council.

Griminish, Isle of Benbecula; Grampian, Highland and Islands at Lochmaddy.
Western Isles Islands Council.

Griminish, Lochmaddy, Isle of North Uist; Grampian, Highland and Islands at Lochmaddy.
Western Isles Islands Council.

Grimsay Island, Isle of Benbecula; Grampian, Highland and Islands at Lochmaddy.
Western Isles Islands Council.

Grimshader, Isle of Lewis; Grampian, Highland and Islands at Stornoway.
Western Isles Islands Council.

Grobsness, Voe, Shetland;
Grampian, Highland and Islands at
Lerwick.
Shetland Islands Council.

Grogary, Lochboisdale, Isle of
South Uist; Grampian, Highland
and Islands at Lochmaddy.
Western Isles Islands Council.

Grogport, Campbeltown, Argyll;
North Strathclyde at
Campbeltown.
Strathclyde Region
Argyll and Bute District.

Grose-Clete, Isle of Harris;
Grampian, Highland and Islands at
Stornoway.
Western Isles Islands Council.

Grossbay, Isle of Harris; Grampian,
Highland and Islands at
Stornoway.
Western Isles Islands Council.

Gruinard, Dundonnell, Ross-shire;
Grampian, Highland and Islands at
Dingwall.
Highland Region
Ross and Cromarty District.

Gruinart, Bridgend, Isle of Islay;
North Strathclyde at
Campbeltown.
Strathclyde Region
Argyll and Bute District.

Gruline, Isle of Mull; North
Strathclyde at Oban.
Strathclyde Region
Argyll and Bute District.

Gruting, Bridge of Walls, Shetland;
Grampian, Highland and Islands at
Lerwick.
Shetland Islands Council.

Guardbridge, St Andrews, Fife;
Tayside, Central and Fife at
Cupar.
Fife Region
North East Fife District.

Guay, Ballinluig, Perthshire;
Tayside, Central and Fife at Perth.
Tayside Region
Perth and Kinross District.

Guershader, Isle of Lewis;
Grampian, Highland and Islands at
Stornoway.
Western Isles Islands Council.

Guildtown, Perth; Tayside, Central
and Fife at Perth.
Tayside Region
Perth and Kinross District.

Gulberwick, Shetland; Grampian,
Highland and Islands at Lerwick.
Shetland Islands Council.

Gullane, East Lothian; Lothian and
Borders at Haddington.
Lothian Region
East Lothian District.

Gunnister, Ham, Shetland;
Grampian, Highland and Islands at
Lerwick.
Shetland Islands Council.

Gutcher, Yell, Shetland; Grampian,
Highland and Islands at Lerwick.
Shetland Islands Council.

Guthrie, Forfar, Angus; Tayside,
Central and Fife at Forfar.
Tayside Region
Angus District.

Habost, Lochs, Isle of Lewis;
Grampian, Highland and Islands at
Stornoway.
Western Isles Islands Council.

Habost, Port of Ness, Isle of Lewis;
Grampian, Highland and Islands at
Stornoway.
Western Isles Islands Council.

Hacklett, Isle of Benbecula;
Grampian, Highland and Islands at
Lochmaddy.
Western Isles Islands Council.

Haclete, Isle of Lewis; Grampian,
Highland and Islands at
Stornoway.
Western Isles Islands Council.

Haddington, East Lothian; Lothian
and Borders at Haddington.
Lothian Region
East Lothian District.

Haddo House, Ellon,
Aberdeenshire; Grampian,
Highland and Islands at Aberdeen.
Grampian Region
Gordon District.

Haggs, Bonnybridge, Stirlingshire;
Tayside, Central and Fife at
Falkirk.
Central Region
Falkirk District.

Halbeath, Dunfermline, Fife;
Tayside, Central and Fife at
Dunfermline.
Fife Region
Dunfermline District.

Haldane, Alexandria,
Dunbartonshire; North Strathclyde
at Dumbarton.
Strathclyde Region
Dumbarton District.

Halfway, Cambuslang, Glasgow;
Glasgow and Strathkelvin at
Glasgow.
Strathclyde Region
City of Glasgow District.

Halkirk, Caithness; Grampian,
Highland and Islands at Wick.
Highland Region
Caithness District.

Hallin, Portree, Isle of Skye;
Grampian, Highland and Islands at
Portree.
Highland Region
Skye and Lochalsh District.

Hallside, Cambuslang, Glasgow;
Glasgow and Strathkelvin at
Glasgow.
Strathclyde Region
City of Glasgow District.

Ham, Foula, Shetland; Grampian,
Highland and Islands at Lerwick.
Shetland Islands Council.

Hamar, Shetland; Grampian,
Highland and Islands at Lerwick.
Shetland Islands Council.

Hamilton, Lanarkshire; South Strathclyde, Dumfries and Galloway at Hamilton.
Strathclyde Region
Hamilton District.

Hamnavoe, Shetland; Grampian, Highland and Islands at Lerwick.
Shetland Islands Council.

Hardgate, Castle Douglas, Kirkcudbrightshire; South Strathclyde, Dumfries and Galloway at Kirkcudbright.
Dumfries and Galloway Region
Stewartry District.

Hardgate, Clydebank, Dunbartonshire; North Strathclyde at Dumbarton.
Strathclyde Region
Dumbarton District.

Harlosh, Portree, Isle of Skye; Grampian, Highland and Islands at Portree.
Highland Region
Skye and Lochalsh District.

Haroldswick, Unst, Shetland; Grampian, Highland and Islands at Lerwick.
Shetland Islands Council.

Harpsdale, Halkirk, Caithness; Grampian, Highland and Islands at Wick.
Highland Region
Caithness District.

Harris, Isle of Harris; Grampian, Highland and Islands at Stornoway.
Western Isles Islands Council.

Harthill, Shotts, Lanarkshire; South Strathclyde, Dumfries and Galloway at Hamilton.
Strathclyde Region
Motherwell District.

Haster, Wick, Caithness; Grampian, Highland and Islands at Wick.
Highland Region
Caithness District.

Hatton, Peterhead, Aberdeenshire; Grampian, Highland and Islands at Peterhead.
Grampian Region
Banff and Buchan District.

Hatton of Fintray, Dyce, Aberdeenshire; Grampian, Highland and Islands at Aberdeen.
Grampian Region
City of Aberdeen District.

Haugh of Urr, Castle Douglas, Kirkcudbrightshire; South Strathclyde, Dumfries and Galloway at Kirkcudbright.
Dumfries and Galloway Region
Stewartry District.

Haun, Eriskay, Lochboisdale, Isle of South Uist; Grampian, Highland and Islands at Lochmaddy.
Western Isles Islands Council.

Hawick, Roxburghshire; Lothian and Borders at Jedburgh.
Borders Region
Roxburgh District.

Hawksland, Lesmahagow, Lanarkshire; South Strathclyde, Dumfries and Galloway at Lanark.
Strathclyde Region
Clydesdale District.

Haywood, Forth, Lanarkshire;
South Strathclyde, Dumfries and
Galloway at Lanark.
Strathclyde Region
Clydesdale District.

Hazelbank, Lanark; South
Strathclyde, Dumfries and
Galloway at Lanark.
Strathclyde Region
Clydesdale District.

Hazelhead, Aberdeen; Grampian,
Highland and Islands at Aberdeen.
Grampian Region
City of Aberdeen District.

Heanish, Scarinish, Isle of Tiree;
North Strathclyde at Oban.
Strathclyde Region
Argyll and Bute District.

Heaste, Broadford, Isle of Skye;
Grampian, Highland and Islands at
Portree.
Highland Region
Skye and Lochalsh District.

Heathhall, Dumfries; South
Strathclyde, Dumfries and
Galloway at Dumfries.
Dumfries and Galloway Region
Nithsdale District.

Heiton, Kelso, Roxburghshire;
Lothian and Borders at Jedburgh.
Borders Region
Roxburgh District.

Helensburgh, Dunbartonshire;
North Strathclyde at Dumbarton.
Strathclyde Region
Dumbarton District.

Helensfield, Alloa,
Clackmannanshire; Tayside,
Central and Fife at Alloa.
Central Region
Clackmannan District.

Helmsdale, Sutherland; Grampian,
Highland and Islands at Dornoch.
Highland Region
Sutherland District.

Heriot, Midlothian; Lothian and
Borders at Edinburgh.
Lothian Region
Midlothian District.

Hermiston, Currie, Midlothian;
Lothian and Borders at Edinburgh.
Lothian Region
Midlothian District.

Heylipool, Scarinish, Isle of Tiree;
North Strathclyde at Oban.
Strathclyde Region
Argyll and Bute District.

Heylor, Shetland; Grampian,
Highland and Islands at Lerwick.
Shetland Islands Council.

Heynish, Scarinish, Isle of Tiree;
North Strathclyde at Oban.
Strathclyde Region
Argyll and Bute District.

High Blantyre, Glasgow; South
Strathclyde, Dumfries and
Galloway at Hamilton.
Strathclyde Region
Hamilton District.

High Bonnybridge, Bonnybridge,
Stirlingshire; Tayside, Central and
Fife at Falkirk.
Central Region
Falkirk District.

High Borve, Isle of Lewis;
Grampian, Highland and Islands at
Stornoway.
Western Isles Islands Council.

High Valleyfield, Newmills,
Dunfermline, Fife; Tayside, Central
and Fife at Dunfermline.
Fife Region
Dunfermline District.

Hightae, Lockerbie, Dumfriesshire;
South Strathclyde, Dumfries and
Galloway at Dumfries.
Dumfries and Galloway Region
Annandale and Eskdale District.

Hill of Beath, Cowdenbeath, Fife;
Tayside, Central and Fife at
Dunfermline.
Fife Region
Dunfermline District.

Hill of Fearn, Tain, Ross-shire;
Grampian, Highland and Islands at
Tain.
Highland Region
Ross and Cromarty District.

Hill View, Alexandria,
Dunbartonshire; North Strathclyde
at Dumbarton.
Strathclyde Region
Dumbarton District.

Hillend, Dunfermline, Fife; Tayside,
Central and Fife at Dunfermline.
Fife Region
Dunfermline District.

Hillend, Edinburgh; Lothian and
Borders at Edinburgh.
Strathclyde Region
City of Edinburgh District.

Hillington, Glasgow; Glasgow and
Strathkelvin at Glasgow.
Strathclyde Region
City of Glasgow District.

Hillington Industrial Estate,
Glasgow; North Strathclyde at
Paisley.
Strathclyde Region
Renfrew District.

Hillside, Montrose, Angus; Tayside,
Central and Fife at Arbroath.
Tayside Region
Angus District.

Hillside, Portlethen, Aberdeenshire;
Grampian, Highland and Islands at
Stonehaven.
Grampian Region
Kincardine and Deeside District.

Hillswick, Shetland; Grampian,
Highland and Islands at Lerwick.
Shetland Islands Council.

Hilton, Fearn, Tain, Ross-shire;
Grampian, Highland and Islands at
Tain.
Highland Region
Ross and Cromarty District.

Hilton, Inverness; Grampian,
Highland and Islands at Inverness.
Highland Region
Inverness District.

Hindhousefield, Jedburgh,
Roxburghshire; Lothian and
Borders at Jedburgh.
Borders Region
Roxburgh District.

Hoddam, Lockerbie, Dumfriesshire;
South Strathclyde, Dumfries and
Galloway at Dumfries.
Dumfries and Galloway Region
Annandale and Eskdale District.

Hoebeg, Lochmaddy, Isle of North
Uist; Grampian, Highland and
Islands at Lochmaddy.
Western Isles Islands Council.

Hollybush, Ayr; South Strathclyde,
Dumfries and Galloway at Ayr.
Strathclyde Region
Kyle and Carrick District.

Holm, Isle of Lewis; Grampian,
Highland and Islands at
Stornoway.
Western Isles Islands Council.

Holm, Orkney; Grampian, Highland
and Islands at Kirkwall.
Orkney Islands Council.

Holmar, Lochboisdale, Isle of South
Uist; Grampian, Highland and
Islands at Lochmaddy.
Western Isles Islands Council.

Holmend, Moffat, Dumfriesshire;
South Strathclyde, Dumfries and
Galloway at Dumfries.
Dumfries and Galloway Region
Annandale and Eskdale District.

Holytown, Lanarkshire; South
Strathclyde, Dumfries and
Galloway at Hamilton.
Strathclyde Region
Hamilton District.

Holywood, Dumfries; South
Strathclyde, Dumfries and
Galloway at Dumfries.
Dumfries and Galloway Region
Nithsdale District.

Hopeman, Lossiemouth,
Morayshire; Grampian, Highland
and Islands at Elgin.
Grampian Region
Moray District.

Horgabost, Isle of Harris;
Grampian, Highland and Islands at
Stornoway.
Western Isles Islands Council.

Horsaclete, Isle of Harris;
Grampian, Highland and Islands at
Stornoway.
Western Isles Islands Council.

Horve, Castlebay, Isle of Barra;
Grampian, Highland and Islands at
Lochmaddy.
Western Isles Islands Council.

Hosta, Lochmaddy, Isle of North
Uist; Grampian, Highland and
Islands at Lochmaddy.
Western Isles Islands Council.

Hoswick, Sandwick, Shetland;
Grampian, Highland and Islands at
Lerwick.
Shetland Islands Council.

Hough, Scarinish, Isle of Tiree;
North Strathclyde at Oban.
Strathclyde Region
Argyll and Bute District.

Hougharry, Lochmaddy, Isle of
North Uist; Grampian, Highland
and Islands at Lochmaddy.
Western Isles Islands Council.

Houston, Johnstone, Renfrewshire;
North Strathclyde at Paisley.
Strathclyde Region
Renfrew District.

Howbeg, Lochboisdale, Isle of
South Uist; Grampian, Highland
and Islands at Lochmaddy.
Western Isles Islands Council.

Howgate, Penicuik, Midlothian;
Lothian and Borders at Edinburgh.
Lothian Region
Midlothian District.

Howmore, Lochboisdale, Isle of
South Uist; Grampian, Highland
and Islands at Lochmaddy.
Western Isles Islands Council.

Hownam, Kelso, Roxburghshire;
Lothian and Borders at Jedburgh.
Borders Region
Roxburgh District.

Howwood, Johnstone,
Renfrewshire; North Strathclyde at
Paisley.
Strathclyde Region
Renfrew District.

Hoy, Stromness, Orkney;
Grampian, Highland and Islands at
Kirkwall.
Shetland Islands Council.

Hughton, Kiltarlity, Inverness-shire;
Grampian, Highland and Islands at
Inverness.
Highland Region
Inverness District.

Humbie, East Lothian; Lothian and
Borders at Haddington.
Lothian Region
East Lothian District.

Huna, John o' Groats, Caithness;
Grampian, Highland and Islands at
Wick.
Highland Region
Caithness District.

Hunter's Quay, Dunoon, Argyll;
North Strathclyde at Dunoon.
Strathclyde Region
Argyll and Bute District.

Hunterston, West Kilbride,
Ayrshire; North Strathclyde at
Kilmarnock.
Strathclyde Region
Cunninghame District.

Huntingtower, Perth; Tayside,
Central and Fife at Perth.
Tayside Region
Perth and Kinross District.

Huntly, Aberdeenshire; Grampian,
Highland and Islands at Aberdeen.
Grampian Region
Gordon District.

Hurlet, Glasgow; North Strathclyde
at Paisley.
Strathclyde Region
Renfrew District.

Hurlford, Kilmarnock, Ayrshire;
North Strathclyde at Kilmarnock.
Strathclyde Region
Kilmarnock and Louden District.

Hurliness, Hoy, Orkney; Grampian,
Highland and Islands at Kirkwall.
Orkney Islands Council.

Hushinish, Isle of Harris;
Grampian, Highland and Islands at
Stornoway.
Western Isles Islands Council.

Hyndford Bridge, Lanarkshire;
South Strathclyde, Dumfries and
Galloway at Lanark.
Strathclyde Region
Clydesdale District.

Hyndland, Glasgow; Glasgow and
Strathkelvin at Glasgow.
Strathclyde Region
City of Glasgow District.

Hynish, Isle of Tiree; North
Strathclyde at Oban.
Strathclyde Region
Argyll and Bute District.

Ianstown, Buckie, Morayshire;
Grampian, Highland and Islands at
Elgin.
Grampian Region
Moray District.

Idvies, Forfar, Angus; Tayside,
Central and Fife at Forfar.
Tayside Region
Angus District.

Illery, Locheport, Isle of North Uist;
Grampian, Highland and Islands at
Lochmaddy.
Western Isles Islands Council.

Inchbare, Brechin, Angus; Tayside,
Central and Fife at Forfar.
Tayside Region
Angus District.

Inchberry, Fochabers, Morayshire;
Grampian, Highland and Islands at
Elgin.
Grampian Region
Moray District.

Inchinnan, Renfrew; North
Strathclyde at Paisley.
Strathclyde Region
Renfrew District.

Inchnadamph, Ledmore,
Sutherland; Grampian, Highland
and Islands at Dornoch.
Highland Region
Sutherland District.

Inchture, Perthshire; Tayside,
Central and Fife at Perth.
Tayside Region
Perth and Kinross District.

Ineray, Baleshare, Isle of North
Uist; Grampian, Highland and
Islands at Lochmaddy.
Western Isles Islands Council.

Inglesmaldie, Laurencekirk,
Kincardineshire; Grampian,
Highland and Islands at
Stonehaven.
Grampian Region
Kincardine and Deeside District.

Inglewood, Alloa,
Clackmannanshire; Tayside,
Central and Fife at Alloa.
Central Region
Clackmannan District.

Ingliston, Newbridge, Midlothian;
Lothian and Borders at Edinburgh.
Lothian Region
Midlothian District.

Innellan, Dunoon, Argyll; North
Strathclyde at Dunoon.
Strathclyde Region
Argyll and Bute District.

Innerleithen, Peeblesshire; Lothian
and Borders at Peebles.
Borders Region
Tweeddale District.

Innerwick, Dunbar, East Lothian;
Lothian and Borders at
Haddington.
Lothian Region
East Lothian District.

Insch, Aberdeenshire; Grampian,
Highland and Islands at Aberdeen.
Grampian Region
Gordon District.

Insch, Kingussie, Inverness-shire;
Grampian, Highland and Islands at
Inverness.
Highland Region
Badenoch and Strathspey District.

Inshes, Inverness; Grampian,
Highland and Islands at Inverness.
Highland Region
Inverness District.

Inver, Ballater, Kincardineshire;
Grampian, Highland and Islands at
Stonehaven.
Grampian Region
Kincardine and Deeside District.

Inver, Dunkeld, Perthshire;
Tayside, Central and Fife at Perth.
Tayside Region
Perth and Kinross District.

Inver, Fearn, Tain, Ross-shire;
Grampian, Highland and Islands at
Tain.
Highland Region
Ross and Cromarty District.

Inveraldie, Dundee; Tayside,
Central and Fife at Dundee.
Tayside Region
City of Dundee District.

Inverallochy, Fraserburgh,
Aberdeenshire; Grampian,
Highland and Islands at
Peterhead.
Grampian Region
Banff and Buchan District.

Inveraray, Argyll; North Strathclyde
at Dunoon.
Strathclyde Region
Argyll and Bute District.

Inverarity, Forfar, Angus; Tayside,
Central and Fife at Forfar.
Tayside Region
Angus District.

Inverasdale, Achnasheen, Ross-
shire; Grampian, Highland and
Islands at Dingwall.
Highland Region
Ross and Cromarty District.

Inveravon, Ballindalloch,
Morayshire; Grampian, Highland
and Islands at Elgin.
Grampian Region
Moray District.

Inverawe, Taynuilt, Argyll; North
Strathclyde at Oban.
Strathclyde Region
Argyll and Bute District.

Inverbeg, Alexandria,
Dunbartonshire; North Strathclyde
at Dumbarton.
Strathclyde Region
Dumbarton District.

Inverbervie, Stonehaven,
Kincardineshire; Grampian,
Highland and Islands at
Stonehaven.
Grampian Region
Kincardine and Deeside District.

Invercauld, Braemar,
Kincardineshire; Grampian,
Highland and Islands at
Stonehaven.
Grampian Region
Kincardine and Deeside District.

Inveresk, Musselburgh, East
Lothian; Lothian and Borders at
Haddington.
Lothian Region
East Lothian District.

Inverey, Braemar, Kincardineshire;
Grampian, Highland and Islands at
Stonehaven.
Grampian Region
Kincardine and Deeside District.

Inverfarigaig, Dores, Inverness;
Grampian, Highland and Islands at
Inverness.
Highland Region
Inverness District.

Invergarry, Inverness-shire;
Grampian, Highland and Islands at
Fort William.
Highland Region
Lochaber District.

Invergloy, Spean Bridge,
Inverness-shire; Grampian,
Highland and Islands at Fort
William.
Highland Region
Lochaber District.

Invergordon, Ross-shire;
Grampian, Highland and Islands at
Tain.
Highland Region
Ross and Cromarty District.

Invergowrie, Dundee; Tayside,
Central and Fife at Dundee.
Tayside Region
City of Dundee District.

Inverinan, Taynuilt, Argyll; North
Strathclyde at Oban.
Strathclyde Region
Argyll and Bute District.

Inverinate, Kyle of Lochalsh, Ross-
shire; Grampian, Highland and
Islands at Dingwall.
Highland Region
Skye and Lochalsh District.

Inverkeilor, Arbroath, Angus;
Tayside, Central and Fife at
Arbroath.
Tayside Region
Angus District.

Inverkeithing, Fife; Tayside,
Central and Fife at Dunfermline.
Fife Region
Dunfermline District.

Inverkeithny, Huntly,
Aberdeenshire; Grampian,
Highland and Islands at Aberdeen.
Grampian Region
Gordon District.

Inverkip, Greenock; North
Strathclyde at Greenock.
Strathclyde Region
Inverclyde District.

Inverkirkaig, Sutherland;
Grampian, Highland and Islands at
Dornoch.
Highland Region
Sutherland District.

Inverlochlarig, Lochearnhead,
Stirlingshire; Tayside, Central and
Fife at Stirling.
Central Region
Stirling District.

Inverlochy, Fort William,
Inverness-shire; Grampian,
Highland and Islands at Fort
William.
Highland Region
Lochaber District.

Inverlussa, Craighouse, Isle of
Jura; North Strathclyde at
Campbeltown.
Strathclyde Region
Argyll and Bute District.

Invermoriston, Inverness-shire;
Grampian, Highland and Islands at
Inverness.
Highland Region
Inverness District.

Inverneil, Ardrishaig, Argyll; North
Strathclyde at Dunoon.
Strathclyde Region
Argyll and Bute District.

Inverness; Grampian, Highland
and Islands at Inverness.
Highland Region
Inverness District.

Inversanda, Kingairloch, Morvern,
Inverness-shire; Grampian,
Highland and Islands at Fort
William.
Highland Region
Lochaber District.

Invershin, Lairg, Sutherland;
Grampian, Highland and Islands at
Dornoch.
Highland Region
Sutherland District.

Inversnaid, Stirling; Tayside,
Central and Fife at Stirling.
Central Region
Stirling District.

Invertrossachs, Callander,
Stirlingshire; Tayside, Central and
Fife at Stirling.
Central Region
Stirling District.

Inverugie, Peterhead,
Aberdeenshire; Grampian,
Highland and Islands at
Peterhead.
Grampian Region
Banff and Buchan District.

Inverurie, Aberdeenshire;
Grampian, Highland and Islands at
Aberdeen.
Grampian Region
Gordon District.

Irongray, Dumfries; South
Strathclyde, Dumfries and
Galloway at Dumfries.
Dumfries and Galloway Region
Nithsdale District.

Irvine, Ayrshire; North Strathclyde
at Kilmarnock.
Strathclyde Region
Cunninghame District.

Isbister, Shetland; Grampian,
Highland and Islands at Lerwick.
Shetland Islands Council.

Island Flodda, Isle of Benbecula;
Grampian, Highland and Islands at
Lochmaddy.
Western Isles Islands Council.

Isle of Arran; North Strathclyde at
Kilmarnock.
Strathclyde Region
Cunninghame District.

Isle of Benbecula; Grampian,
Highland and Islands at
Lochmaddy.
Western Isles Islands Council

Isle of Bute; North Strathclyde at
Rothesay.
Strathclyde Region
Argyll and Bute District.

Isle of Canna; Grampian, Highland
and Islands at Fort William.
Highland Region
Lochaber District.

Isle of Coll; North Strathclyde at
Oban.
Strathclyde Region
Argyll and Bute District.

Isle of Colonsay; North Strathclyde
at Oban.
Strathclyde Region
Argyll and Bute District.

Isle of Eigg; Grampian, Highland
and Islands at Fort William.
Highland Region
Lochaber District.

Isle of Gigha; North Strathclyde at
Campbeltown.
Strathclyde Region
Argyll and Bute District.

Isle of Iona; North Strathclyde at
Oban.
Strathclyde Region
Argyll and Bute District.

Isle of Islay; North Strathclyde at
Campbeltown.
Strathclyde Region
Argyll and Bute District.

Isle of Jura; North Strathclyde at
Campbeltown.
Strathclyde Region
Argyll and Bute District.

Isle of Muck; Grampian, Highland
and Islands at Fort William.
Highland Region
Lochaber District.

Isle of Raasay; Grampian,
Highland and Islands at Portree.
Highland Region
Skye and Lochalsh District.

Isle of Rhum; Grampian, Highland
and Islands at Fort William.
Highland Region
Lochaber District.

Isle of Rona; Grampian, Highland and Islands at Portree.
Highland Region
Skye and Lochalsh District.

Isle of Ronay; Grampian, Highland and Islands at Lochmaddy.
Western Isles Islands Council.

Isle of Scalpay, Isle of Harris; Grampian, Highland and Islands at Stornoway.
Western Isles Islands Council.

Isle of Scalpay, Isle of Skye; Grampian, Highland and Islands at Portree.
Highland Region
Skye and Lochalsh District.

Isle of Whithorn, Newton Stewart, Wigtownshire; South Strathclyde, Dumfries and Galloway at Stranraer.
Dumfries and Galloway Region
Wigtown District.

Isle Oronsay, Isle of Skye:
Grampian, Highland and Islands at Portree.
Highland Region
Skye and Lochalsh District.

Islesteps, Dumfries; South Strathclyde, Dumfries and Galloway at Dumfries.
Dumfries and Galloway Region
Nithsdale District.

Islivig, Isle of Lewis; Grampian, Highland and Islands at Stornoway.
Western Isles Islands Council.

Jair, Perthshire; Tayside, Central and Fife at Perth.
Tayside Region
Perth and Kinross District.

Jamestown, Alexandria, Dunbartonshire; North Strathclyde at Dumbarton.
Strathclyde Region
Dumbarton District.

Jamestown, Strathpeffer, Ross-shire; Grampian, Highland and Islands at Dingwall.
Highland Region
Ross and Cromarty District.

Janetstown, Thurso, Caithness; Grampian, Highland and Islands at Wick.
Highland Region
Caithness District.

Jedburgh, Roxburghshire; Lothian and Borders at Jedburgh.
Borders Region
Roxburgh District.

Jemimaville, Cromarty, Ross-shire; Grampian, Highland and Islands at Dingwall.
Highland Region
Ross and Cromarty District.

John o' Groats, Wick, Caithness; Grampian, Highland and Islands at Wick.
Highland Region
Caithness District.

Johnshaven, Laurencekirk, Kincardineshire; Grampian, Highland and Islands at Stonehaven.
Grampian Region
Kincardine and Deeside District.

Johnstone, Renfrewshire; North Strathclyde at Paisley.
Strathclyde Region
Renfrew District.

Johnstonebridge, Lockerbie, Dumfriesshire; South Strathclyde, Dumfries and Galloway at Dumfries.
Dumfries and Galloway Region
Annandale and Eskdale District.

Joppa, Edinburgh; Lothian and Borders at Edinburgh.
Lothian Region
City of Edinburgh District.

Jordanhill, Glasgow; Glasgow and Strathkelvin at Glasgow.
Strathclyde Region
City of Glasgow District.

Juniper Green, Edinburgh; Lothian and Borders at Edinburgh.
Lothian Region
City of Edinburgh District.

Kaimes, Edinburgh; Lothian and Borders at Edinburgh.
Lothian Region
City of Edinburgh District.

Kallin, Lochmaddy, Isle of North Uist; Grampian, Highland and Islands at Lochmaddy.
Western Isles Islands Council.

Kames, Tighnabruaich, Argyll; North Strathclyde at Dunoon.
Strathclyde Region
Argyll and Bute District.

Keig, Alford, Aberdeenshire; Grampian, Highland and Islands at Aberdeen.
Grampian Region
Gordon District.

Keilbeg, Tarbert, Argyll; North Strathclyde at Dunoon.
Strathclyde Region
Argyll and Bute District.

Keilis, Port Askaig, Isle of Islay; North Strathclyde at Campbeltown.
Strathclyde Region
Argyll and Bute District.

Keir, Dunblane, Stirlingshire; Tayside, Central and Fife at Stirling.
Central Region
Stirling District.

Keir, Thornhill, Dumfriesshire; South Strathclyde, Dumfries and Galloway at Dumfries.
Dumfries and Galloway Region
Nithsdale District.

Keiss, Wick, Caithness; Grampian, Highland and Islands at Wick.
Highland Region
Caithness District.

Keith, Morayshire; Grampian, Highland and Islands at Elgin.
Grampian Region
Moray District.

Keith Hall, Inverurie, Aberdeenshire; Grampian, Highland and Islands at Aberdeen.
Grampian Region
Gordon District.

Kelhead, Annan, Dumfriesshire; South Strathclyde, Dumfries and Galloway at Dumfries.
Dumfries and Galloway Region
Annandale and Eskdale District.

Kellas, Broughty Ferry, Dundee;
Tayside, Central and Fife at
Dundee.
Tayside Region
City of Dundee District.

Kelloholm, Sanquhar,
Dumfriesshire; South Strath-
clyde, Dumfries and Galloway at
Dumfries.
Dumfries and Galloway Region
Nithsdale District.

Kelso, Roxburghshire; Lothian and
Borders at Jedburgh.
Borders Region
Roxburgh District.

Keltie Bridge, Callander,
Stirlingshire; Tayside, Central and
Fife at Stirling.
Central Region
Stirling District.

Keltneyburn, Aberfeldy, Perthshire;
Tayside, Central and Fife at Perth.
Tayside Region
Perth and Kinross District.

Kelton, Castle Douglas,
Kirkcudbrightshire; South
Strathclyde, Dumfries and
Galloway at Kirkcudbright.
Dumfries and Galloway Region
Stewartry District.

Kelton, Dumfries; South
Strathclyde, Dumfries and
Galloway at Dumfries.
Dumfries and Galloway Region
Nithsdale District.

Kelty, Fife; Tayside, Central and
Fife at Dunfermline.
Fife Region
Dunfermline District.

Kemback, Cupar, Fife; Tayside,
Central and Fife at Cupar.
Fife Region
North East Fife District.

Kemnay, Inverurie, Aberdeenshire;
Grampian, Highland and Islands at
Aberdeen.
Grampian Region
Gordon District.

Ken Bridge, New Galloway,
Kirkcudbrightshire; South
Strathclyde, Dumfries and
Galloway at Kirkcudbright.
Dumfries and Galloway Region
Stewartry District.

Kendebig, Isle of Harris; Grampian,
Highland and Islands at
Stornoway.
Western Isles Islands Council.

Kendram, Portree, Isle of Skye;
Grampian, Highland and Islands at
Portree.
Highland Region
Skye and Lochalsh District.

Kenmore, Aberfeldy, Perthshire;
Tayside, Central and Fife at Perth.
Tayside Region
Perth and Kinross District.

Kennacraig, Tarbert, Argyll; North
Strathclyde at Campbeltown.
Strathclyde Region
Argyll and Bute District.

Kennet, Clackmannanshire;
Tayside, Central and Fife at Alloa.
Central Region
Clackmannan District.

Kennethmont, Huntly, Aberdeenshire; Grampian, Highland and Islands at Aberdeen.
Grampian Region
Gordon District.

Kennishead, Thornliebank, Glasgow; Glasgow and Strathkelvin at Glasgow.
Strathclyde Region
City of Glasgow District.

Kennoway, Leven, Fife; Tayside, Central and Fife at Kirkcaldy.
Fife Region
Kirkcaldy District.

Kenovay, Scarinish, Isle of Tiree; North Strathclyde at Oban.
Strathclyde Region
Argyll and Bute District.

Kentallen, Oban, Argyll; North Strathclyde at Oban.
Strathclyde Region
Argyll and Bute District.

Kentangavel, Castlebay, Isle of Barra; Grampian, Highland and Islands at Lochmaddy.
Western Isles Islands Council.

Kentra, Acharacle, Morvern, Inverness-shire; Grampian, Highland and Islands at Fort William.
Highland Region
Lochaber District.

Keose, Isle of Lewis; Grampian, Highland and Islands at Stornoway.
Western Isles Islands Council.

Kerrera, Oban, Argyll; North Strathclyde at Oban.
Strathclyde Region
Argyll and Bute District.

Kerrycroy, Rothesay, Isle of Bute; North Strathclyde at Rothesay.
Strathclyde Region
Argyll and Bute District.

Kersavagh, Lochmaddy, Isle of North Uist; Grampian, Highland and Islands at Lochmaddy.
Western Isles Islands Council.

Kersemill, Stirling; Tayside, Central and Fife at Stirling.
Central Region
Stirling District.

Kershader, Isle of Lewis; Grampian, Highland and Islands at Stornoway.
Western Isles Islands Council.

Kettins, Coupar Angus, Blairgowrie, Perthshire; Tayside, Central and Fife at Perth.
Tayside Region
Perth and Kinross District.

Kettlebridge, Cupar, Fife; Tayside, Central and Fife at Cupar.
Fife Region
North East Fife District.

Kettleholm, Lockerbie, Dumfriesshire; South Strathclyde, Dumfries and Galloway at Dumfries.
Dumfries and Galloway Region
Annandale and Eskdale District.

Kilaulay, Lochboisdale, Isle of South Uist; Grampian, Highland and Islands at Lochmaddy. Western Isles Islands Council.

Kilbagie, Alloa, Clackmannanshire; Tayside, Central and Fife at Alloa.
Central Region
Clackmannan District.

Kilbarchan, Johnstone, Renfrewshire; North Strathclyde at Paisley.
Strathclyde Region
Renfrew District.

Kilberry, Tarbert, Argyll; North Strathclyde at Campbeltown.
Strathclyde Region
Argyll and Bute District.

Kilbirnie, Ayrshire; North Strathclyde at Kilmarnock.
Strathclyde Region
Cunninghame District.

Kilbowie, Clydebank, Dunbartonshire; North Strathclyde at Dumbarton.
Strathclyde Region
Dumbarton District.

Kilbride, Oban, Argyll; North Strathclyde at Oban.
Strathclyde Region
Argyll and Bute District.

Kilbryde, Dunblane, Stirlingshire; Tayside, Central and Fife at Stirling.
Central Region
Stirling District.

Kilbucho, Biggar, Lanarkshire; South Strathclyde, Dumfries and Galloway at Lanark.
Strathclyde Region
Clydesdale District.

Kilchattan, Isle of Colonsay; North Strathclyde at Oban.
Strathclyde Region
Argyll and Bute District.

Kilchattan, Rothesay, Isle of Bute; North Strathclyde at Rothesay.
Strathclyde Region
Argyll and Bute District.

Kilchiaran, Isle of Islay; North Strathclyde at Campbeltown.
Strathclyde Region
Argyll and Bute District.

Kilchoan, Acharacle, Ardnamurchan, Inverness-shire; Grampian, Highland and Islands at Fort William.
Highland Region
Lochaber District.

Kilchoman, Bruichladdich, Isle of Islay; North Strathclyde at Campbeltown.
Strathclyde Region
Argyll and Bute District

Kilchrenan, Taynuilt, Argyll; North Strathclyde at Oban.
Strathclyde Region
Argyll and Bute District.

Kilconquhar, Leven, Fife; Tayside, Central and Fife at Cupar.
Fife Region
North East Fife District.

Kilcreggan, Helensburgh, Dunbartonshire; North Strathclyde at Dumbarton.
Strathclyde Region
Dumbarton District.

Kildalton, Port Ellen, Isle of Islay; North Strathclyde at Campbeltown.
Strathclyde Region
Argyll and Bute District.

Kildean, Stirling; Tayside, Central and Fife at Stirling.
Central Region
Stirling District.

Kildonan, Brodick, Isle of Arran; North Strathclyde at Kilmarnock.
Strathclyde Region
Cunninghame District.

Kildonan, Helmsdale, Sutherland; Grampian, Highland and Islands at Dornoch.
Highland Region
Sutherland District.

Kildonan, Lochboisdale, Isle of South Uist; Grampian, Highland and Islands at Lochmaddy.
Western Isles Islands Council.

Kildrummy, Alford, Aberdeenshire; Grampian, Highland and Islands at Aberdeen.
Grampian Region
Gordon District.

Kilerivagh, Isle of Benbecula; Grampian, Highland and Islands at Lochmaddy.
Western Isles Islands Council.

Kilfinan, Tighnabruiach, Argyll; North Strathclyde at Dunoon.
Strathclyde Region
Argyll and Bute District.

Kilkenneth, Scarinish, Isle of Tiree; North Strathclyde at Oban.
Strathclyde Region
Argyll and Bute District.

Kilkenzie, Campbeltown, Argyll; North Strathclyde at Campbeltown.
Strathclyde Region
Argyll and Bute District.

Kilkerran, Maybole, Ayrshire; South Strathclyde, Dumfries and Galloway at Ayr.
Strathclyde Region
Kyle and Carrick District.

Killearn, Glasgow; Tayside, Central and Fife at Stirling.
Central Region
Stirling District.

Killiechonan, Rannoch Station, Perthshire; Tayside, Central and Fife at Perth.
Tayside Region
Perth and Kinross District.

Killiechronan, Aros, Isle of Mull; North Strathclyde at Oban.
Strathclyde Region
Argyll and Bute District.

Killiecrankie, Pitlochry, Perthshire; Tayside, Central and Fife at Perth.
Tayside Region
Perth and Kinross District.

Killilan, Kyle of Lochalsh, Ross-shire; Grampian, Highland and Islands at Dingwall.
Highland Region
Skye and Lochalsh District.

Killin, Stirlingshire; Tayside, Central and Fife at Stirling.
Central Region
Stirling District.

Killochan, Girvan, Ayrshire; South Strathclyde, Dumfries and Galloway at Ayr.
Strathclyde Region
Kyle and Carrick District.

Kilmacolm, Renfrewshire; North Strathclyde at Greenock.
Strathclyde Region
Renfrew District.

Kilmahoe, Dumfries; South Strathclyde, Dumfries and Galloway at Dumfries.
Strathclyde Region
Nithsdale District.

Kilmahog, Callander, Stirlingshire; Tayside, Central and Fife at Stirling.
Central Region
Stirling District.

Kilmaluaig, Scarinish, Isle of Tiree; North Strathclyde at Oban.
Strathclyde Region
Argyll and Bute District.

Kilmany, Cupar, Fife; Tayside, Central and Fife at Cupar.
Fife Region
North East Fife District.

Kilmarnock, Ayrshire; North Strathclyde at Kilmarnock.
Strathclyde Region
Kilmarnock and Loudoun District.

Kilmartin, Lochgilphead, Argyll; North Strathclyde at Oban.
Strathclyde Region
Argyll and Bute District.

Kilmaurs, Kilmarnock, Ayrshire; North Strathclyde at Kilmarnock.
Strathclyde Region
Kilmarnock and Loudoun District.

Kilmelfort, Oban, Argyll; North Strathclyde at Oban.
Strathclyde Region
Argyll and Bute District.

Kilmichael, Lochgilphead, Argyll; North Strathclyde at Dunoon.
Strathclyde Region
Argyll and Bute District.

Kilmore, Oban, Argyll; North Strathclyde at Oban.
Strathclyde Region
Argyll and Bute District.

Kilmore, Teangue, Sleat, Isle of Skye; Grampian, Highland and Islands at Portree.
Highland Region
Skye and Lochalsh District.

Kilmory, Brodick, Isle of Arran; North Strathclyde at Kilmarnock.
Strathclyde Region
Cunninghame District.

Kilmory, Lochgilphead, Argyll; North Strathclyde at Dunoon.
Strathclyde Region
Argyll and Bute District.

Kilmuir, Portree, Isle of Skye;
Grampian, Highland and Islands at
Portree.
Highland Region
Skye and Lochalsh District.

Kilmun, Dunoon, Argyll; North
Strathclyde at Dunoon.
Strathclyde Region
Argyll and Bute District.

Kilninian, Tobermory, Isle of Mull;
North Strathclyde at Oban.
Strathclyde Region
Argyll and Bute District.

Kilninver, Oban, Argyll; North
Strathclyde at Oban.
Strathclyde Region
Argyll and Bute District.

Kilpheder, Lochboisdale, Isle of
South Uist; Grampian, Highland
and Islands at Lochmaddy.
Western Isles Islands Council.

Kilrenny, Anstruther, Fife; Tayside,
Central and Fife at Cupar.
Fife Region
North East Fife District.

Kilry, Alyth, Perthshire; Tayside,
Central and Fife at Perth.
Tayside Region
Perth and Kinross District.

Kilspindie, Errol, Perthshire;
Tayside, Central and Fife at Perth.
Tayside Region
Perth and Kinross District.

Kilsyth, Glasgow; South
Strathclyde, Dumfries and
Galloway at Airdrie.
Strathclyde Region
Monklands District.

Kiltarlity, Beauly, Inverness-shire;
Grampian, Highland and Islands at
Inverness.
Highland Region
Inverness District.

Kilwhipnach, Campbeltown, Argyll;
North Strathclyde at
Campbeltown.
Strathclyde Region
Argyll and Bute District.

Kilwinning, Ayrshire; North
Strathclyde at Kilmarnock.
Strathclyde Region
Cunninghame District.

Kin, Dunoon, Argyll; North
Strathclyde at Dunoon.
Strathclyde Region
Argyll and Bute District.

Kinaldie, Aberdeen; Grampian,
Highland and Islands at Aberdeen.
Grampian Region
City of Aberdeen District.

Kinbrace, Sutherland; Grampian,
Highland and Islands at Dornoch.
Highland Region
Sutherland District.

Kinbuck, Dunblane, Stirlingshire;
Tayside, Central and Fife at
Stirling.
Central Region
Stirling District.

Kincaldrum, Forfar, Angus;
Tayside, Central and Fife at
Forfar.
Tayside Region
Angus District.

Kincaple, St Andrews, Fife;
Tayside, Central and Fife at
Cupar.
Fife Region
North East Fife District.

Kincardine, Alloa,
Clackmannanshire; Tayside,
Central and Fife at Dunfermline.
Fife Region
Dunfermline District.

Kincardine, Ardgay, Sutherland;
Grampian, Highland and Islands at
Dornoch.
Highland Region
Sutherland District.

Kincardine O'Neil, Aboyne,
Kincardineshire; Grampian,
Highland and Islands at
Stonehaven.
Grampian Region
Kincardine and Deeside District.

Kinclaven, Blairgowrie, Perthshire;
Tayside, Central and Fife at Perth.
Tayside Region
Perth and Kinross District.

Kincraig, Kingussie, Inverness-
shire; Grampian, Highland and
Islands at Inverness.
Highland Region
Badenoch and Strathspey District.

Kindallachan, Ballinluig,
Perthshire; Tayside, Central and
Fife at Perth.
Tayside Region
Perth and Kinross District.

Kinellar, Aberdeen; Grampian,
Highland and Islands at Aberdeen.
Grampian Region
City of Aberdeen District.

Kinfauns, Perth; Tayside, Central
and Fife at Perth.
Tayside Region
Perth and Kinross District.

King Edward, Banff; Grampian,
Highland and Islands at Banff.
Grampian Region
Banff and Buchan District.

Kingairloch, Argour, Inverness-
shire; Grampian, Highland and
Islands at Fort William.
Highland Region
Lochaber District.

Kingarth, Rothesay, Isle of Bute;
North Strathclyde at Rothesay.
Strathclyde Region
Argyll and Bute District.

Kingeff, Montrose, Angus; Tayside,
Central and Fife at Arbroath.
Tayside Region
Angus District.

Kingennie, Broughty Ferry,
Dundee; Tayside, Central and Fife
at Dundee.
Tayside Region
City of Dundee District.

Kingholm Quay, Dumfries; South
Strathclyde, Dumfries and
Galloway at Dumfries.
Dumfries and Galloway Region
Nithsdale District.

Kinghorn, Burntisland, Fife;
Tayside, Central and Fife at
Kirkcaldy.
Fife Region
Kirkcaldy District.

Kinglassie, Lochgelly, Fife;
Tayside, Central and Fife at
Kirkcaldy.
Fife Region
Kirkcaldy District.

Kingoldrum, Kirriemuir, Angus;
Tayside, Central and Fife at
Forfar.
Tayside Region
Angus District.

Kingsbarns, St Andrews, Fife;
Tayside, Central and Fife at
Cupar.
Fife Region
North East Fife District.

Kingseat, Dunfermline, Fife;
Tayside, Central and Fife at
Dunfermline.
Fife Region
Dunfermline District.

Kingshouse, Ballachulish,
Glencoe, Inverness-shire;
Grampian, Highland and Islands at
Fort William.
Highland Region
Lochaber District.

Kingskettle, Cupar, Fife; Tayside,
Central and Fife at Cupar.
Fife Region
North East Fife District.

Kingsmuir, Forfar, Angus; Tayside,
Central and Fife at Forfar.
Tayside Region
Angus District.

Kingston, Garmouth, Fochabers,
Morayshire; Grampian, Highland
and Islands at Elgin.
Grampian Region
Moray District.

Kingston, North Berwick, East
Lothian; Lothian and Borders at
Haddington.
Lothian Region
East Lothian District.

Kingswells, Aberdeen; Grampian,
Highland and Islands at Aberdeen.
Grampian Region
City of Aberdeen District.

Kingussie, Inverness-shire;
Grampian, Highland and Islands at
Inverness.
Highland Region
Badenoch and Strathspey
District.

Kininmonth, Peterhead,
Aberdeenshire; Grampian,
Highland and Islands at
Peterhead.
Grampian Region
Banff and Buchan District.

Kinkell, Conon Bridge, Ross-shire;
Grampian, Highland and Islands at
Dingwall.
Highland Region
Ross and Cromarty District.

Kinloch, Blairgowrie, Perthshire;
Tayside, Central and Fife
at Perth.
Tayside Region
Perth and Kinross District.

Kinloch, Isle of Lewis; Grampian,
Highland and Islands at
Stornoway.
Western Isles Islands Council.

Kinloch Hourn, Knoydart,
Inverness-shire; Grampian,
Highland and Islands at Fort
William.
Highland Region
Lochaber District.

Kinloch Laggan, Newtonmore,
Inverness-shire; Grampian,
Highland and Islands at Inverness.
Highland Region
Badenoch and Strathspey District.

Kinloch Rannoch, Pitlochry,
Perthshire; Tayside, Central and
Fife at Perth.
Tayside Region
Perth and Kinross District.

Kinlochard, Stirling; Tayside,
Central and Fife at Stirling.
Central Region
Stirling District.

Kinlochbervie, Rhiconich, Lairg,
Sutherland; Grampian, Highland
and Islands at Dornoch.
Highland Region
Sutherland District.

Kinlocheil, Fort William, Inverness-
shire; Grampian, Highland and
Islands at Fort William.
Highland Region
Lochaber District.

Kinlochewe, Achnasheen, Ross-
shire; Grampian, Highland and
Islands at Dingwall.
Highland Region
Ross and Cromarty District.

Kinlochleven, Ballachulish,
Inverness-shire; Grampian,
Highland and Islands at Fort
William.
Highland Region
Lochaber District.

Kinlochmoidart, Lochailort,
Inverness-shire; Grampian,
Highland and Islands at Fort
William.
Highland Region
Lochaber District.

Kinlochroag, Isle of Lewis;
Grampian, Highland and Islands at
Stornoway.
Western Isles Islands Council.

Kinloss, Forres, Morayshire;
Grampian, Highland and Islands at
Elgin.
Grampian Region
Moray District.

Kinmuck, Inverurie, Aberdeenshire;
Grampian, Highland and Islands at
Aberdeen.
Grampian Region
Gordon District.

Kinnaird, Inchture, Perthshire;
Tayside, Central and Fife at Perth.
Tayside Region
Perth and Kinross District.

Kinneft, Inverbervie,
Kincardineshire; Grampian,
Highland and Islands at
Stonehaven.
Highland Region
Kincardine and Deeside District.

Kinnell, Arbroath, Angus; Tayside,
Central and Fife at Arbroath.
Tayside Region
Angus District.

Kinnell, Killin, Stirlingshire;
Tayside, Central and Fife at
Stirling.
Central Region
Stirling District.

Kinnesswood, Kinross; Tayside, Central and Fife at Perth.
Tayside Region
Perth and Kinross District.

Kinnettles, Forfar, Angus; Tayside, Central and Fife at Forfar.
Tayside Region
Angus District.

Kinnoir, Huntly, Aberdeenshire; Grampian, Highland and Islands at Aberdeen.
Grampian Region
Gordon District.

Kinross; Tayside, Central and Fife at Perth.
Tayside Region
Perth and Kinross District.

Kinrossie, Perth; Tayside, Central and Fife at Perth.
Tayside Region
Perth and Kinross District.

Kintessack, Forres, Morayshire; Grampian, Highland and Islands at Elgin.
Grampian Region
Moray District.

Kintore, Inverurie, Aberdeenshire; Grampian, Highland and Islands at Aberdeen.
Grampian Region
Gordon District.

Kintulavig, Isle of Lewis; Grampian, Highland and Islands at Stornoway.
Western Isles Islands Council.

Kippen, Stirling; Tayside, Central and Fife at Stirling.
Central Region
Stirling District.

Kippencross, Dunblane, Stirlingshire; Tayside, Central and Fife at Stirling.
Central Region
Stirling District.

Kippford, Dalbeattie, Kirkcudbrightshire; South Strathclyde, Dumfries and Galloway at Kirkcudbright.
Dumfries and Galloway Region
Stewartry District.

Kirk Yetholm, Kelso, Roxburghshire; Lothian and Borders at Jedburgh.
Borders Region
Roxburgh District.

Kirkapol, Scarinish, Isle of Tiree; North Strathclyde at Oban.
Strathclyde Region
Argyll and Bute District.

Kirkbean, Dumfries; South Strathclyde, Dumfries and Galloway at Dumfries.
Dumfries and Galloway Region
Nithsdale District.

Kirkbuddo, Forfar, Angus; Tayside, Central and Fife at Forfar.
Tayside Region
Angus District.

Kirkcaldy, Fife; Tayside, Central and Fife at Kirkcaldy.
Fife Region
Kirkcaldy District.

Kirkcolm, Stranraer, Wigtownshire; South Strathclyde, Dumfries and Galloway at Stranraer.
Dumfries and Galloway Region
Wigtown District.

Kirkconnel, Sanquhar, Dumfriesshire; South Strathclyde, Dumfries and Galloway at Dumfries.
Dumfries and Galloway Region
Nithsdale District.

Kirkcowan, Newton Stewart, Wigtownshire; South Strathclyde, Dumfries and Galloway at Stranraer.
Dumfries and Galloway Region
Wigtown District.

Kirkcudbright; South Strathclyde, Dumfries and Galloway at Kirkcudbright.
Dumfries and Galloway Region
Stewartry District.

Kirkfieldbank, Lanark; South Strathclyde, Dumfries and Galloway at Lanark.
Strathclyde Region
Clydesdale District.

Kirkgunzeon, Dumfries; South Strathclyde, Dumfries and Galloway at Dumfries.
Dumfries and Galloway Region
Nithsdale District.

Kirkhill, Inverness; Grampian, Highland and Islands at Inverness.
Highland Region
Inverness District.

Kirkibost, Isle of Lewis; Grampian, Highland and Islands at Stornoway.
Western Isles Islands Council.

Kirkinch, Blairgowrie, Perthshire; Tayside, Central and Fife at Perth.
Tayside Region
Perth and Kinross District.

Kirkinner, Newton Stewart, Wigtownshire; South Strathclyde, Dumfries and Galloway at Stranraer.
Dumfries and Galloway Region
Wigtown District.

Kirkintilloch, Glasgow; Glasgow and Strathkelvin at Glasgow.
Strathclyde Region
City of Glasgow District.

Kirkland, Thornhill, Dumfriesshire; South Strathclyde, Dumfries and Galloway at Dumfries.
Dumfries and Galloway Region
Nithsdale District.

Kirkliston, Edinburgh; Lothian and Borders at Edinburgh.
Lothian Region
City of Edinburgh District.

Kirkmabreck, Creetown, Wigtownshire; South Strathclyde, Dumfries and Galloway at Stranraer.
Dumfries and Galloway Region
Wigtown District.

Kirkmichael, Ballindalloch, Morayshire; Grampian, Highland and Islands at Elgin.
Grampian Region
Moray District.

Kirkmichael, Blairgowrie,
Perthshire; Tayside, Central and
Fife at Perth.
Tayside Region
Perth and Kinross District.

Kirkmichael, Maybole, Ayrshire;
South Strathclyde, Dumfries and
Galloway at Ayr.
Strathclyde Region
Kyle and Carrick District.

Kirkmuirhill, Lanark; South
Strathclyde, Dumfries and
Galloway at Lanark.
Strathclyde Region
Clydesdale District.

Kirknewton, Midlothian; Lothian
and Borders at Edinburgh.
Lothian Region
Midlothian District.

Kirkoswald, Maybole, Ayrshire;
South Strathclyde, Dumfries and
Galloway at Ayr.
Strathclyde Region
Kyle and Carrick District.

Kirkpatrick, Thornhill,
Dumfriesshire; South Strathclyde,
Dumfries and Galloway at
Dumfries.
Dumfries and Galloway Region
Nithsdale District.

Kirkpatrick Durham,
Kirkcudbrightshire; South
Strathclyde, Dumfries and
Galloway at Kirkcudbright.
Dumfries and Galloway Region
Stewartry District.

Kirkpatrick Fleming,
Kirkcudbrightshire; South
Strathclyde, Dumfries and
Galloway at Kirkcudbright.
Dumfries and Galloway Region
Stewartry District.

Kirkton, Dumfries; South
Strathclyde, Dumfries and
Galloway at Dumfries.
Dumfries and Galloway Region
Nithsdale District.

Kirkton, Lochearnhead,
Stirlingshire; Tayside, Central and
Fife at Stirling.
Central Region
Stirling District.

Kirkton of Rayne, Inverurie,
Aberdeenshire; Grampian,
Highland and Islands at Aberdeen.
Grampian Region
Gordon District.

Kirkton of Skene, Skene,
Aberdeenshire; Grampian,
Highland and Islands at Aberdeen.
Grampian Region
City of Aberdeen District.

Kirktown of Auchterless, Turriff,
Banffshire; Grampian, Highland
and Islands at Banff.
Grampian Region
Banff and Buchan District.

Kirktown of Clatt, Rhynie,
Aberdeenshire; Grampian,
Highland and Islands at Aberdeen.
Grampian Region
Gordon District.

Kirkwall, Orkney; Grampian,
Highland and Islands at Kirkwall.
Orkney Islands Council.

Kirn, Dunoon, Argyll; North
Strathclyde at Dunoon.
Strathclyde Region
Argyll and Bute District.

Kirriemuir, Angus; Tayside, Central
and Fife at Forfar.
Tayside Region
Angus District.

Kirtlebridge, Lockerbie,
Dumfriesshire; South Strath-
clyde, Dumfries and Galloway at
Dumfries.
Dumfries and Galloway Region
Annandale and Eskdale District.

Kirvick, Isle of Lewis; Grampian,
Highland and Islands at
Stornoway.
Western Isles Islands Council.

Kishorn, Lochcarron, Ross-shire;
Grampian, Highland and Islands at
Dingwall.
Highland Region
Ross and Cromarty District.

Kneep, Isle of Lewis; Grampian,
Highland and Islands at
Stornoway.
Western Isles Islands Council.

Knipoch, Oban, Argyll; North
Strathclyde at Oban.
Strathclyde Region
Argyll and Bute District.

Knock, Carloway, Isle of Lewis;
Grampian, Highland and Islands at
Stornoway.
Western Isles Islands Council.

Knock, Huntly, Aberdeenshire;
Grampian, Highland and Islands at
Aberdeen.
Grampian Region
Gordon District.

Knockaird, Isle of Lewis;
Grampian, Highland and Islands at
Stornoway.
Western Isles Islands Council.

Knockando, Forres, Morayshire;
Grampian, Highland and Islands at
Elgin.
Grampian Region
Moray District.

Knockcuien, Lochmaddy, Isle of
North Uist; Grampian, Highland
and Islands at Lochmaddy.
Western Isles Islands Council.

Knockentiber, Kilmarnock,
Ayrshire; North Strathclyde at
Kilmarnock.
Strathclyde Region
Kilmarnock and Louden District.

Knockintorran, Lochmaddy, Isle of
North Uist; Grampian, Highland
and Islands at Lochmaddy.
Western Isles Islands Council.

Knockline, Lochmaddy, Isle of
North Uist; Grampian, Highland
and Islands at Lochmaddy.
Western Isles Islands Council.

Knockvennie, Castle Douglas,
Kirkcudbrightshire; South
Strathclyde, Dumfries and
Galloway at Kirkcudbright.
Dumfries and Galloway Region
Stewartry District.

Knowe, Newton Stewart,
Wigtownshire; South Strathclyde,
Dumfries and Galloway at
Stranraer.
Dumfries and Galloway Region
Wigtown District.

Knoydart, Mallaig, Inverness-shire;
Grampian, Highland and Islands at
Fort William.
Highland Region
Lochaber.

Kyle of Lochalsh, Ross-shire;
Grampian, Highland and Islands at
Dingwall.
Highland Region
Skye and Lochalsh District.

Kyleakin, Isle of Skye; Grampian,
Highland and Islands at Portree.
Highland Region
Skye and Lochalsh District.

Kylerhea, Isle of Skye; Grampian,
Highland and Islands at Portree.
Highland Region
Skye and Lochalsh District.

Kyles Flodda, Isle of Benbecula;
Grampian, Highland and Islands at
Lochmaddy.
Western Isles Islands Council.

Kyles Harris, Isle of Harris;
Grampian, Highland and Islands at
Stornoway.
Western Isles Islands Council.

Kyles Morar, Mallaig, Inverness-
shire; Grampian, Highland and
Islands at Fort William.
Highland Region
Lochaber District.

Kyles Paible, Lochmaddy, Isle of
North Uist; Grampian, Highland
and Islands at Lochmaddy.
Western Isles Islands Council.

Kylesku, Lairg, Sutherland;
Grampian, Highland and Islands at
Dornoch.
Highland Region
Sutherland District.

Kylestrome, Kylesku, Lairg,
Sutherland; Grampian, Highland
and Islands at Dornoch.
Highland Region
Sutherland District.

Lacklea, Harris; Grampian,
Highland and Islands at
Stornoway.
Western Isles Islands Council.

Ladybank, Cupar, Fife; Tayside,
Central and Fife at Cupar.
Fife Region
North East Fife District.

Ladykirk, Berwick-upon-Tweed;
Lothian and Borders at Duns.
Borders Region
Berwickshire District.

Ladysbridge, Banff; Grampian,
Highland and Islands at Banff.
Grampian Region
Banff and Buchan District.

Laga, Acharacle, Ardnamurchan,
Inverness-shire; Grampian,
Highland and Islands at Fort
William.
Highland Region
Lochaber District.

Lagavullin, Port Ellen, Isle of Islay;
North Strathclyde at
Campbeltown.
Strathclyde Region
Argyll and Bute District.

Lagg, Craighouse, Isle of Jura;
North Strathclyde at
Campbeltown.
Strathclyde Region
Argyll and Bute District.

Laggan, Newtonmore, Inverness-
shire; Grampian, Highland and
Islands at Inverness.
Highland Region
Badenoch and Strathspey District.

Laggandoin, Isle of Scalpay,
Harris; Grampian, Highland and
Islands at Stornoway.
Western Isles Islands Council.

Laide, Aultbea, Gairloch, Ross-
shire; Grampian, Highland and
Islands at Dingwall.
Highland Region
Ross and Cromarty District.

Lair, Blairgowrie, Perthshire;
Tayside, Central and Fife at Perth.
Tayside Region
Perth and Kinross District.

Lairg, Sutherland; Grampian,
Highland and Islands at Dornoch.
Highland Region
Sutherland District.

Lamancha, West Linton,
Peeblesshire; Lothian and Borders
at Peebles.
Borders Region
Tweeddale District.

Lamington, Biggar, Lanarkshire;
South Strathclyde, Dumfries and
Galloway at Lanark.
Strathclyde Region
Clydesdale District.

Lamington, Kildary, Ross-shire;
Grampian, Highland and Islands at
Tain.
Highland Region
Ross and Cromarty District.

Lamlash, Brodick, Isle of Arran;
North Strathclyde at Kilmarnock.
Strathclyde Region
Cunninghame District.

Lanark; South Strathclyde,
Dumfries and Galloway at Lanark.
Strathclyde Region
Clydesdale District.

Langass, Lochmaddy, Isle of North
Uist; Grampian, Highland and
Islands at Lochmaddy.
Western Isles Islands Council.

Langbank, Port Glasgow,
Renfrewshire; North Strathclyde at
Paisley.
Strathclyde Region
Renfrew District.

Langholm, Dumfriesshire; South
Strathclyde, Dumfries and
Galloway at Dumfries.
Dumfries and Galloway Region
Annandale and Eskdale District.

Lanton, Jedburgh, Roxburghshire;
Lothian and Borders at Jedburgh.
Borders Region
Roxburgh District.

Laphroaig, Port Ellen, Isle of Islay; North Strathclyde at Campbeltown.
Strathclyde Region
Argyll and Bute District.

Larbert, Stirlingshire; Tayside, Central and Fife at Stirling.
Central Region
Stirling District.

Largo, Anstruther, Fife; Tayside, Central and Fife at Cupar.
Fife Region
North East Fife District.

Largoward, Anstruther, Fife; Tayside, Central and Fife at Cupar.
Fife Region
North East Fife District.

Largs, Ayrshire; North Strathclyde at Kilmarnock.
Strathclyde Region
Cunninghame District.

Larkhall, Lanarkshire; South Strathclyde, Dumfries and Galloway at Hamilton.
Strathclyde Region
Hamilton District.

Lassodie, Dunfermline, Fife; Tayside, Central and Fife at Dunfermline.
Fife Region
Dunfermline District.

Lasswade, Midlothian; Lothian and Borders at Edinburgh.
Lothian Region
Midlothian District.

Latheron, Caithness; Grampian, Highland and Islands at Wick.
Highland Region
Caithness District.

Latheronwheel, Caithness; Grampian, Highland and Islands at Wick.
Highland Region
Caithness District.

Lauder, Berwickshire; Lothian and Borders at Selkirk.
Borders Region
Ettrick and Lauderdale District.

Laurencekirk, Kincardineshire; Grampian, Highland and Islands at Stonehaven.
Grampian Region
Kincardine and Deeside District.

Laurieston, Castle Douglas, Kirkcudbrightshire; South Strathclyde, Dumfries and Galloway at Kirkcudbright.
Dumfries and Galloway Region
Stewartry District.

Laurieston, Falkirk, Stirlingshire; Tayside, Central and Fife at Falkirk.
Central Region
Falkirk District.

Law, Carluke, Lanarkshire; South Strathclyde, Dumfries and Galloway at Lanark.
Strathclyde Region
Clydesdale District.

Lawers, Aberfeldy, Perthshire; Tayside, Central and Fife at Perth.
Tayside Region
Perth and Kinross District.

Laxay, Isle of Lewis; Grampian, Highland and Islands at Stornoway.
Western Isles Islands Council.

Laxford Bridge, Sutherland; Grampian, Highland and Islands at Dornoch.
Highland Region
Sutherland District.

Laxo, Shetland; Grampian, Highland and Islands at Lerwick.
Shetland Islands Council.

Leachkin, Isle of Harris; Grampian, Highland and Islands at Stornoway.
Western Isles Islands Council.

Leadburn, West Linton, Peeblesshire; Lothian and Borders at Peebles.
Borders Region
Tweeddale District.

Leadhills, Biggar, Lanarkshire; South Strathclyde, Dumfries and Galloway at Lanark.
Strathclyde Region
Clydesdale District.

Leanish, Castlebay, Isle of Barra; Grampian, Highland and Islands at Lochmaddy.
Western Isles Islands Council.

Ledaig, Castlebay, Isle of Barra; Grampian, Highland and Islands at Lochmaddy.
Western Isles Islands Council.

Ledaig, Connel, Argyll; North Strathclyde at Oban.
Strathclyde Region
Argyll and Bute District.

Ledaig, Tobermory, Isle of Mull; North Strathclyde at Oban.
Strathclyde Region
Argyll and Bute District.

Ledmore Junction, Sutherland; Grampian, Highland and Islands at Dornoch.
Highland Region
Sutherland District.

Leith, Edinburgh; Lothian and Borders at Edinburgh.
Lothian Region
City of Edinburgh District.

Leitholm, Coldstream, Berwickshire; Lothian and Borders at Duns.
Borders Region
Berwickshire District.

Lempitlaw, Kelso, Roxburghshire; Lothian and Borders at Jedburgh.
Borders Region
Roxburgh District.

Lemreway, Isle of Lewis; Grampian, Highland and Islands at Stornoway.
Western Isles Islands Council.

Lennel, Coldstream, Berwickshire; Lothian and Borders at Duns.
Borders Region
Roxburgh District.

Lennoxtown, Glasgow; Glasgow and Strathkelvin at Glasgow.
Strathclyde Region
City of Glasgow District.

Lentran, Inverness; Grampian, Highland and Islands at Inverness.
Highland Region
Inverness District.

Lenzie, Kirkintilloch, Glasgow;
Glasgow and Strathkelvin at
Glasgow.
Strathclyde Region
City of Glasgow District.

Lerags, Oban, Argyll; North
Strathclyde at Oban.
Strathclyde Region
Argyll and Bute District.

Lerwick, Shetland; Grampian,
Highland and Islands at Lerwick.
Shetland Islands Council.

Leslie, Glenrothes, Fife; Tayside,
Central and Fife at Kirkcaldy.
Fife Region
Kirkcaldy District.

Leslie, Insch, Aberdeenshire;
Grampian, Highland and Islands at
Aberdeen.
Grampian Region
Gordon District.

Lesmahagow, Lanarkshire; South
Strathclyde, Dumfries and
Galloway at Lanark.
Strathclyde Region
Clydesdale District.

Leswalt, Stranraer, Wigtownshire;
South Strathclyde, Dumfries and
Galloway at Stranraer.
Dumfries and Galloway Region
Wigtown District.

Letham, Cupar, Fife; Tayside,
Central and Fife at Cupar.
Fife Region
North East Fife District.

Letham, Falkirk, Stirlingshire;
Tayside, Central and Fife at
Falkirk.
Central Region
Falkirk District.

Letham, Forfar, Angus; Tayside,
Central and Fife at Forfar.
Tayside Region
Angus District.

Letham Grange, Arbroath, Angus;
Tayside, Central and Fife at
Arbroath.
Tayside Region
Angus District.

Lethenty, Turriff, Banffshire;
Grampian, Highland and Islands at
Banff.
Grampian Region
Banff and Buchan District.

Lethnot, Brechin, Angus; Tayside,
Central and Fife at Forfar.
Tayside Region
Angus District.

Letterfearn, Kyle of Lochalsh,
Ross-shire; Grampian, Highland
and Islands at Dingwall.
Highland Region
Skye and Lochalsh District.

Letterfinlay, Spean Bridge,
Inverness-shire; Grampian,
Highland and Islands at Fort
William.
Highland Region
Lochaber District.

Leuchars, St Andrews, Fife;
Tayside, Central and Fife at
Cupar.
Fife Region
North East Fife District.

Leurbost, Isle of Lewis; Grampian, Highland and Islands at Stornoway.
Western Isles Islands Council.

Leven, Fife; Tayside, Central and Fife at Kirkcaldy.
Fife Region
Kirkcaldy District.

Levenhall, East Lothian; Lothian and Borders at Haddington.
Lothian Region
East Lothian District.

Levenwick, Shetland; Grampian, Highland and Islands at Lerwick.
Shetland Islands Council.

Leverburgh, Isle of Harris; Grampian, Highland and Islands at Stornoway.
Western Isles Islands Council.

Leysmill, Arbroath, Angus; Tayside, Central and Fife at Arbroath.
Tayside Region
Angus District.

Lhanbryde, Elgin, Morayshire; Grampian, Highland and Islands at Elgin.
Grampian Region
Moray District.

Libberton, Carnwath, Lanarkshire; South Strathclyde, Dumfries and Galloway at Lanark.
Strathclyde Region
Clydesdale District.

Liberton, Edinburgh; Lothian and Borders at Edinburgh.
Lothian Region
City of Edinburgh District.

Lickisto, Isle of Harris; Grampian, Highland and Islands at Stornoway.
Western Isles Islands Council

Liff, Dundee; Tayside, Central and Fife at Dundee.
Tayside Region
City of Dundee District.

Lighthill, Back, Isle of Lewis; Grampian, Highland and Islands at Stornoway.
Western Isles Islands Council.

Lilliesleaf, Melrose, Roxburghshire; Lothian and Borders at Selkirk.
Borders Region
Ettrick and Lauderdale District.

Limekilns, Dunfermline, Fife; Tayside, Central and Fife at Dunfermline.
Fife Region
Dunfermline District.

Lindores, Newburgh, Fife; Tayside, Central and Fife at Cupar.
Fife Region
Argyll and Bute District.

Lingerbay, Isle of Harris; Grampian, Highland and Islands at Stornoway.
Western Isles Islands Council.

Liniclate, Isle of Benbecula; Grampian, Highland and Islands at Lochmaddy.
Western Isles Islands Council.

Linicro, Portree, Isle of Skye; Grampian, Highland and Islands at Portree.
Highland Region
Skye and Lochalsh District.

Linique, Lochboisdale, Isle of South Uist; Grampian, Highland and Islands at Lochmaddy. Western Isles Islands Council.

Linktown, Kirkcaldy, Fife; Tayside, Central and Fife at Kirkcaldy. Fife Region Kirkcaldy District.

Linlithgow, West Lothian; Lothian and Borders at Linlithgow. Lothian Region West Lothian District.

Linn of Dee, Braemar, Kincardineshire; Grampian, Highland and Islands at Stonehaven. Grampian Region Kincardine and Deeside District.

Linshader, Isle of Lewis; Grampian, Highland and Islands at Stornoway. Western Isles Islands Council.

Lintmill, Cullen, Buckie, Morayshire; Grampian, Highland and Islands at Elgin. Grampian Region Moray District.

Lintrathen, Kirriemuir, Angus; Tayside, Central and Fife at Forfar. Tayside Region Angus District.

Linwood, Paisley, Renfrewshire; North Strathclyde at Paisley. Strathclyde Region Renfrew District.

Lionel, Isle of Lewis; Grampian, Highland and Islands at Stornoway. Western Isles Islands Council.

Lismore, Oban, Argyll; North Strathclyde at Oban. Strathclyde Region Argyll and Bute District.

Little Vantage, Midlothian; Lothian and Borders at Edinburgh. Lothian Region Midlothian District.

Livingston, West Lothian; Lothian and Borders at Linlithgow. Lothian Region West Lothian District.

Loanhead, Midlothian; Lothian and Borders at Edinburgh. Lothian Region Midlothian District.

Loans, Troon, Ayrshire; South Strathclyde, Dumfries and Galloway at Ayr. Strathclyde Region Kyle and Carrick District.

Loch Eck, Dunoon, Argyll; North Strathclyde at Dunoon. Strathclyde Region Argyll and Bute District.

Loch Katrine, Callander, Stirlingshire; Tayside, Central and Fife at Stirling. Central Region Stirling District.

Lochailort, Fort William, Inverness-shire; Grampian, Highland and Islands at Fort William.
Highland Region
Lochaber District.

Lochaline, Morvern, Inverness-shire; Grampian, Highland and Islands at Fort William.
Highland Region
Lochaber District.

Lochans, Stranraer, Wigtownshire; South Strathclyde, Dumfries and Galloway at Stranraer.
Dumfries and Galloway Region
Wigtown District.

Locharbriggs, Dumfries; South Strathclyde, Dumfries and Galloway at Dumfries.
Dumfries and Galloway Region
Nithsdale District.

Lochavich, Taynuilt, Argyll; North Strathclyde at Oban.
Strathclyde Region
Argyll and Bute District.

Lochawe, Dalmally, Argyll; North Strathclyde at Oban.
Strathclyde Region
Argyll and Bute District.

Lochboisdale, Isle of South Uist; Grampian, Highland and Islands at Lochmaddy.
Western Isles Islands Council.

Lochbroom, Garve, Ross-shire; Grampian, Highland and Islands at Dingwall.
Highland Region
Ross and Cromarty District.

Lochbuie, Isle of Mull; North Strathclyde at Oban.
Strathclyde Region
Argyll and Bute District.

Lochcarnan, Lochboisdale, Isle of South Uist; Grampian; Highland and Islands at Lochmaddy.
Western Isles Islands Council.

Lochcarron, Strathcarron, Ross-shire; Grampian, Highland and Islands at Dingwall.
Highland Region
Ross and Cromarty District.

Lochcroistean, Isle of Lewis; Grampian, Highland and Islands at Stornoway.
Western Isles Islands Council.

Lochdonhead, Isle of Mull; North Strathclyde at Oban.
Strathclyde Region
Argyll and Bute District.

Lochearnhead, Stirlingshire; Tayside, Central and Fife at Stirling.
Central Region
Stirling District.

Lochee, Dundee; Tayside, Central and Fife at Dundee.
Tayside Region
City of Dundee District.

Lochend, Inverness; Grampian, Highland and Islands at Inverness.
Highland Region
Inverness District.

Lochend, Shetland; Grampian, Highland and Islands at Lerwick.
Shetland Islands Council.

150

Locheport, Lochmaddy, Isle of
North Uist; Grampian, Highland
and Islands at Lochmaddy.
Western Isles Islands Council.

Lochetive, Taynuilt, Oban, Argyll;
North Strathclyde at Oban.
Strathclyde Region
Argyll and Bute District.

Locheynort, Lochboisdale, Isle of
South Uist; Grampian, Highland
and Islands at Lochmaddy.
Western Isles Islands Council.

Lochfoot, Dumfries; South
Strathclyde, Dumfries and
Galloway at Dumfries.
Dumfries and Galloway Region
Nithsdale District.

Lochgair, Lochgilphead, Argyll;
North Strathclyde at Dunoon.
Strathclyde Region
Argyll and Bute District.

Lochganvich, Isle of Lewis;
Grampian, Highland and Islands at
Stornoway.
Western Isles Islands Council.

Lochgelly, Fife; Tayside, Central
and Fife at Dunfermline.
Fife Region
Dunfermline District.

Lochgilphead, Argyll; North
Strathclyde at Dunoon.
Strathclyde Region
Argyll and Bute District.

Lochgoilhead, Argyll; North
Strathclyde at Dunoon.
Strathclyde Region
Argyll and Bute District.

Lochinver, Sutherland; Grampian,
Highland and Islands at Dornoch.
Highland Region
Sutherland District.

Lochlee, Angus; Tayside, Central
and Fife at Forfar.
Tayside Region
Angus District.

Lochluichart, Garve, Ross-shire;
Grampian, Highland and Islands at
Dingwall.
Highland Region
Ross and Cromarty District.

Lochmaben, Lockerbie,
Dumfriesshire; South Strath-
clyde, Dumfries and Galloway at
Dumfries.
Dumfries and Galloway Region
Annandale and Eskdale District.

Lochmaddy, Isle of North Uist;
Grampian, Highland and Islands at
Lochmaddy.
Western Isles Islands Council.

Lochmaree, Kinlochewe, Ross-
shire; Grampian, Highland and
Islands at Dingwall.
Highland Region
Ross and Cromarty District.

Lochore, Lochgelly, Fife; Tayside,
Central and Fife at Dunfermline.
Fife Region
Dunfermline District.

Lochportan, Lochmaddy, Isle of
North Uist; Grampian, Highland
and Islands at Lochmaddy.
Western Isles Islands Council.

Lochranza, Isle of Arran; North
Strathclyde at Kilmarnock.
Strathclyde Region
Cunninghame District.

Lochrutton, Dumfries; South
Strathclyde, Dumfries and
Galloway at Dumfries.
Dumfries and Galloway Region
Nithsdale District.

Lochskipport, Lochboisdale, Isle of
South Uist; Grampian, Highland
and Islands at Lochmaddy.
Western Isles Islands Council.

Lochussie, Conon Bridge, Ross-
shire; Grampian, Highland and
Islands at Dingwall.
Highland Region
Ross and Cromarty District.

Lochwinnoch, Renfrewshire; North
Strathclyde at Paisley.
Strathclyde Region
Renfrew District.

Lockerbie, Dumfriesshire; South
Strathclyde, Dumfries and
Galloway at Dumfries.
Dumfries and Galloway Region
Annandale and Eskdale District.

Logan, Cumnock, Ayrshire; South
Strathclyde, Dumfries and
Galloway at Ayr.
Strathclyde Region
Cumnock and Doon Valley District.

Loganswell, Newton Mearns,
Glasgow; North Strathclyde at
Paisley.
Strathclyde Region
Renfrew District.

Logie, Cupar, Fife; Tayside, Central
and Fife at Cupar.
Fife Region
North East Fife District.

Logie, Kirriemuir, Angus; Tayside,
Central and Fife at Forfar.
Tayside Region
Angus District.

Logie, Stirling; Tayside, Central
and Fife at Stirling.
Central Region
Stirling District.

Logie Coldstone, Kincardineshire;
Grampian, Highland and Islands at
Stonehaven.
Grampian Region
Kincardine and Deeside District.

Logiealmond, Perth; Tayside,
Central and Fife at Perth.
Tayside Region
Perth and Kinross District.

Logierait, Ballinluig, Pitlochry,
Perthshire; Tayside, Central and
Fife at Perth.
Tayside Region
Perth and Kinross District.

Logierieve, Ellon, Aberdeenshire;
Grampian, Highland and Islands at
Aberdeen.
Grampian Region
Gordon District.

Long Hermiston, Midlothian;
Lothian and Borders at Edinburgh.
Lothian Region
Midlothian District.

Longannet, Alloa,
Clackmannanshire; Tayside,
Central and Fife at Alloa.
Central Region
Clackmannan District.

Longbar, Glengarnock, Beith,
Ayrshire; North Strathclyde at
Kilmarnock.
Strathclyde Region
Cunninghame District.

Longcroft, Bonnybridge,
Stirlingshire; Tayside, Central and
Fife at Falkirk.
Central Region
Falkirk District.

Longforgan, Dundee; Tayside,
Central and Fife at Dundee.
Tayside Region
City of Dundee District.

Longformacus, Duns,
Berwickshire; Lothian and Borders
at Duns.
Borders Region
Berwickshire District.

Longhaven, Peterhead,
Aberdeenshire; Grampian,
Highland and Islands at
Peterhead.
Grampian Region
Banff and Buchan District.

Longhill, Huntly, Aberdeenshire;
Grampian, Highland and Islands at
Aberdeen.
Grampian Region
Gordon District.

Longhope, Stromness, Orkney;
Grampian, Highland and Islands at
Kirkwall.
Orkney Islands Council.

Longmanhill, Banffshire;
Grampian, Highland and Islands at
Banff.
Grampian Region
Banff and Buchan District.

Longmorn, Elgin, Morayshire;
Grampian, Highland and Islands at
Elgin.
Grampian Region
Moray District.

Longniddry, East Lothian; Lothian
and Borders at Haddington.
Lothian Region
East Lothian District.

Longridge, Bathgate, West
Lothian; Lothian and Borders at
Linlithgow.
Lothian Region
West Lothian District.

Longriggend, Airdrie, Lanarkshire;
South Strathclyde, Dumfries and
Galloway at Airdrie.
Strathclyde Region
Monklands District.

Longside, Peterhead,
Aberdeenshire; Grampian,
Highland and Islands at Banff.
Grampian Region
Banff and Buchan District.

Lonmay, Fraserburgh,
Aberdeenshire; Grampian,
Highland and Islands at
Peterhead.
Grampian Region
Banff and Buchan District.

Lossiemouth, Morayshire;
Grampian, Highland and Islands at
Elgin.
Grampian Region
Moray District.

Loth, Helmsdale, Sutherland;
Grampian, Highland and Islands at
Dornoch.
Highland Region
Sutherland District.

Lotts, Port Ellen, Isle of Islay; North
Strathclyde at Campbeltown.
Strathclyde Region
Argyll and Bute District.

Loudounhill, Darvel, Ayrshire;
North Strathclyde at Kilmarnock.
Strathclyde Region
Kilmarnock and Loudoun District.

Low Valleyfield, Dunfermline, Fife;
Tayside, Central and Fife at
Dunfermline.
Fife Region
North East Fife District.

Lower Barvas, Isle of Lewis;
Grampian, Highland and Islands at
Stornoway.
Western Isles Islands Council.

Lower Bayble, Isle of Lewis;
Grampian, Highland and Islands at
Stornoway.
Western Isles Islands Council.

Lower Cabrach, Huntly,
Aberdeenshire; Grampian,
Highland and Islands at Aberdeen.
Grampian Region
Gordon District.

Lower Largo, Leven, Fife; Tayside,
Central and Fife at Cupar.
Fife Region
North East Fife District.

Lower Mains, Dollar,
Clackmannanshire; Tayside,
Central and Fife at Alloa.
Central Region
Clackmannan District.

Lower Shader, Isle of Lewis;
Grampian, Highland and Islands at
Stornoway.
Western Isles Islands Council.

Lowthertown, Annan,
Dumfriesshire; South Strathclyde,
Dumfries and Galloway at
Dumfries.
Dumfries and Galloway Region
Annandale and Eskdale District.

Ludag, Lochboisdale, Isle of South
Uist; Grampian, Highland and
Islands at Lochmaddy.
Western Isles Islands Council.

Lugar, Cumnock, Ayrshire; South
Strathclyde, Dumfries and
Galloway at Ayr.
Strathclyde Region
Cumnock and Doon Valley District.

Luggiebank, Cumbernauld,
Glasgow; South Strathclyde,
Dumfries and Galloway at Airdrie.
Strathclyde Region
Monklands District.

Lugton, Kilmarnock, Ayrshire;
North Strathclyde at Kilmarnock.
Strathclyde Region
Kilmarnock and Loudoun District.

Luib, Broadford, Isle of Skye;
Grampian, Highland and Islands at
Portree.
Highland Region
Skye and Lochalsh District.

Luib, Crianlarich, Stirlingshire;
Tayside, Central and Fife at
Stirling.
Central Region
Stirling District.

Lumphanan, Banchory,
Kincardineshire; Grampian,
Highland and Islands at
Stonehaven.
Grampian Region
Kincardine and Deeside District.

Lumphinnans, Cowdenbeath, Fife;
Tayside, Central and Fife at
Dunfermline.
Fife Region
Dunfermline District.

Lumsden, Huntly, Aberdeenshire;
Grampian, Highland and Islands at
Aberdeen.
Grampian Region
Gordon District.

Lunanhead, Forfar, Angus;
Tayside, Central and Fife at
Forfar.
Tayside Region
Angus District.

Luncarty, Perth; Tayside, Central
and Fife at Perth.
Tayside Region
Perth and Kinross District.

Lundale, Isle of Lewis; Grampian,
Highland and Islands at
Stornoway.
Western Isles Islands Council.

Lundie, Dundee; Tayside, Central
and Fife at Dundee.
Tayside Region
City of Dundee District.

Lundin Links, Leven, Fife;
Tayside, Central and Fife at
Cupar.
Fife Region
North East Fife District.

Lunna, Shetland; Grampian,
Highland and Islands at Lerwick.
Shetland Islands Council.

Luskentyre, Isle of Harris;
Grampian, Highland and Islands at
Stornoway.
Western Isles Islands Council.

Luss, Alexandria, Dunbartonshire;
North Strathclyde at Dumbarton.
Strathclyde Region
Dumbarton District.

Lussagiven, Craighouse, Isle of
Jura; North Strathclyde at
Campbeltown.
Strathclyde Region
Argyll and Bute District.

Luthermuir, Laurencekirk,
Kincardineshire; Grampian,
Highland and Islands at
Stonehaven.
Grampian Region
Kincardine and Deeside District.

Luthrie, Cupar, Fife; Tayside,
Central and Fife at Cupar.
Fife Region
North East Fife District.

Lybster, Caithness; Grampian, Highland and Islands at Wick.
Highland Region
Caithness District.

Lynchat, Kingussie, Inverness-shire; Grampian, Highland and Islands at Inverness.
Highland Region
Badenoch and Strathspey District.

Lyne of Skene, Skene, Aberdeenshire; Grampian, Highland and Islands at Aberdeen.
Grampian Region
City of Aberdeen District.

Lyness, Stromness, Orkney; Grampian, Highland and Islands at Kirkwall.
Orkney Islands Council.

Mabie, Dumfries; South Strathclyde, Dumfries and Galloway at Dumfries.
Dumfries and Galloway Region
Nithsdale District.

Macduff, Banffshire; Grampian, Highland and Islands at Banff.
Grampian Region
Banff and Buchan District.

Machrie, Brodick, Isle of Arran; North Strathclyde at Kilmarnock.
Strathclyde Region
Cunninghame District.

Machrihanish, Campbeltown, Argyll; North Strathclyde at Campbeltown.
Strathclyde Region
Argyll and Bute District.

Macmerry, Tranent, East Lothian; Lothian and Borders at Haddington.
Lothian Region
East Lothian District.

Madderty, Crieff, Perthshire; Tayside, Central and Fife at Perth.
Tayside Region
Perth and Kinross District.

Maddiston, Falkirk, Stirlingshire; Tayside, Central and Fife at Falkirk.
Central Region
Falkirk District.

Maggieknockater, Craigellachie, Morayshire; Grampian, Highland and Islands at Elgin.
Grampian Region
Moray District.

Maidens, Girvan, Ayrshire; South Strathclyde, Dumfries and Galloway at Ayr.
Strathclyde Region
Kyle and Carrick District.

Mainholm, Ayr; South Strathclyde, Dumfries and Galloway at Ayr.
Strathclyde Region
Kyle and Carrick District.

Mainsriddle, Dumfries; South Strathclyde, Dumfries and Galloway at Dumfries.
Dumfries and Galloway Region
Nithsdale District.

Makerston, Kelso, Roxburghshire; Lothian and Borders at Jedburgh.
Borders Region
Roxburgh District.

Malaclate, Lochmaddy, Isle of
North Uist; Grampian, Highland
and Islands at Lochmaddy.
Western Isles Islands Council.

Mallaig, Fort William, Inverness-
shire; Grampian, Highland and
Islands at Fort William.
Highland Region
Lochaber District.

Mamus, Forfar, Angus; Tayside,
Central and Fife at Forfar.
Tayside Region
Angus District.

Mangersta, Isle of Lewis;
Grampian, Highland and Islands at
Stornoway.
Western Isles Islands Council.

Manish, Isle of Harris; Grampian,
Highland and Islands at
Stornoway.
Western Isles Islands Council.

Marchmont, Greenlaw,
Berwickshire; Lothian and Borders
at Duns.
Borders Region
Berwickshire District.

Marig, Isle of Harris; Grampian,
Highland and Islands at
Stornoway.
Western Isles Islands Council.

Markinch, Glenrothes, Fife;
Tayside, Central and Fife at
Kirkcaldy.
Fife Region
Kirkcaldy District.

Marrburn, Thornhill, Dumfriesshire;
South Strathclyde, Dumfries and
Galloway at Dumfries.
Dumfries and Galloway Region
Nithsdale District.

Marrel, Helmsdale, Sutherland;
Grampian, Highland and Islands at
Dornoch.
Highland Region
Sutherland District.

Marvig, Isle of Lewis; Grampian,
Highland and Islands at
Stornoway.
Western Isles Islands Council.

Marybank, Isle of Lewis; Grampian,
Highland and Islands at
Stornoway.
Western Isles Islands Council.

Marybank, Muir of Ord, Ross-shire;
Grampian, Highland and Islands at
Dingwall.
Highland Region
Ross and Cromarty District.

Maryculter, Aberdeenshire;
Grampian, Highland and Islands at
Stonehaven.
Grampian Region
Kincardine and Deeside District.

Maryhill, Glasgow; Glasgow and
Strathkelvin at Glasgow.
Strathclyde Region
City of Glasgow District.

Maryhill, Isle of Lewis; Grampian,
Highland and Islands at
Stornoway.
Western Isles Islands Council.

Marykirk, Laurencekirk,
Kincardineshire; Grampian,
Highland and Islands at
Stonehaven.
Grampian Region
Kincardine and Deeside District.

Marypark, Ballindalloch,
Morayshire; Grampian, Highland
and Islands at Elgin.
Grampian Region
Moray District.

Maryton, Kirriemuir, Angus;
Tayside, Central and Fife at
Forfar.
Tayside Region
Angus District.

Marywell, Aberdeenshire;
Grampian, Highland and Islands at
Stonehaven.
Grampian Region
Kincardine and Deeside District.

Masterton, Dunfermline, Fife;
Tayside, Central and Fife at
Dunfermline.
Fife Region
Dunfermline District.

Mauchline, Ayrshire; South
Strathclyde, Dumfries and
Galloway at Ayr.
Strathclyde Region
Kyle and Carrick District.

Maud, Peterhead, Aberdeenshire;
Grampian, Highland and Islands at
Peterhead.
Grampian Region
Banff and Buchan District.

Maxton, Melrose, Roxburghshire;
Lothian and Borders at Selkirk.
Borders Region
Ettrick and Lauderdale District.

Maxwelltown, Dumfries; South
Strathclyde, Dumfries and
Galloway at Dumfries.
Dumfries and Galloway Region
Nithsdale District.

Maybole, Ayrshire; South
Strathclyde, Dumfries and
Galloway at Ayr.
Strathclyde Region
Kyle and Carrick District.

Maybury, Edinburgh; Lothian and
Borders at Edinburgh.
Lothian Region
City of Edinburgh District.

Mayfield, Edinburgh; Lothian and
Borders at Edinburgh.
Lothian Region
City of Edinburgh District.

Meavaig, Isle of Harris; Grampian,
Highland and Islands at
Stornoway.
Western Isles Islands Council.

Meigle, Perthshire; Tayside,
Central and Fife at Perth.
Tayside Region
Perth and Kinross District.

Meigle, Skelmorlie, Ayrshire; North
Strathclyde at Kilmarnock.
Strathclyde Region
Kyle and Carrick District.

Meikle Wartle, Inverurie, Aberdeenshire; Grampian, Highland and Islands at Aberdeen.
Grampian Region
Gordon District.

Meikleour, Perth; Tayside, Central and Fife at Perth.
Tayside Region
Perth and Kinross District.

Melbost, Isle of Lewis; Grampian, Highland and Islands at Stornoway.
Western Isles Islands Council.

Melrose, Roxburghshire; Lothian and Borders at Selkirk.
Borders Region
Ettrick and Lauderdale District.

Melvaig, Gairloch, Ross-shire; Grampian, Highland and Islands at Dingwall.
Highland Region
Ross and Cromarty District.

Melvich, Thurso, Caithness; Grampian, Highland and Islands at Dornoch.
Highland Region
Sutherland District.

Memsie, Fraserburgh, Aberdeenshire; Grampian, Highland and Islands at Peterhead.
Grampian Region
Banff and Buchan District.

Menmuir, Brechin, Angus; Tayside, Central and Fife at Forfar.
Tayside Region
Angus District.

Mennock, Sanquhar, Dumfriesshire; South Strath-clyde, Dumfries and Galloway at Dumfries.
Dumfries and Galloway Region
Nithsdale District.

Menstrie, Clackmannanshire; Tayside, Central and Fife at Alloa.
Central Region
Clackmannan District.

Merchiston, Edinburgh; Lothian and Borders at Edinburgh.
Lothian Region
City of Edinburgh District.

Methil, Leven, Fife; Tayside, Central and Fife at Kirkcaldy.
Fife Region
Kirkcaldy District.

Methilhill, Leven, Fife; Tayside, Central and Fife at Kirkcaldy.
Fife Region
Kirkcaldy District.

Methlick, Ellon, Aberdeenshire; Grampian, Highland and Islands at Aberdeen.
Grampian Region
Gordon District.

Methven, Perth; Tayside, Central and Fife at Perth.
Tayside Region
Perth and Kinross District.

Mey, Thurso, Caithness; Grampian, Highland and Islands at Wick.
Highland Region
Caithness District.

Miavaig, Isle of Lewis; Grampian, Highland and Islands at Stornoway.
Western Isles Islands Council.

Mid Calder, Livingston, West Lothian; Lothian and Borders at Linlithgow.
Lothian Region
West Lothian District.

Mid Clyth, Lybster, Caithness; Grampian, Highland and Islands at Wick.
Highland Region
Caithness District.

Mid Yell, Shetland; Grampian, Highland and Islands at Lerwick.
Shetland Islands Council.

Middlebie, Lockerbie, Dumfriesshire; South Strathclyde, Dumfries and Galloway at Dumfries.
Dumfries and Galloway Region
Annandale and Eskdale District.

Middlequarter, Lochmaddy, Isle of North Uist; Grampian, Highland and Islands at Lochmaddy.
Western Isles Islands Council.

Middleton, Scarinish, Isle of Tiree; North Strathclyde at Oban.
Strathclyde Region
Argyll and Bute District.

Midlem, Selkirk; Lothian and Borders at Selkirk.
Borders Region
Ettrick and Lauderdale District.

Milarochy, Balmaha, Glasgow; Tayside, Central and Fife at Stirling.
Central Region
Stirling District.

Millbrex, Turriff, Banffshire; Grampian, Highland and Islands at Banff.
Grampian Region
Banff and Buchan District.

Millerhill, Midlothian; Lothian and Borders at Edinburgh.
Lothian Region
Midlothian District.

Millerston, Glasgow; Glasgow and Strathkelvin at Glasgow.
Strathclyde Region
City of Glasgow District.

Millhall, Stirling; Tayside, Central and Fife at Stirling.
Central Region
Stirling District.

Millhouse, Tighnabruaich, Argyll; North Strathclyde at Dunoon.
Strathclyde Region
Argyll and Bute District.

Millhousebridge, Lockerbie, Dumfriesshire; South Strathclyde, Dumfries and Galloway at Dumfries.
Dumfries and Galloway Region
Annandale and Eskdale District.

Milliken Park, Johnstone, Renfrewshire; North Strathclyde at Paisley.
Strathclyde Region
Renfrew District.

Millisle, Garlieston, Wigtownshire;
South Strathclyde, Dumfries and
Galloway at Stranraer.
Dumfries and Galloway Region
Wigtown District.

Millport, Isle of Cumbrae; North
Strathclyde at Kilmarnock.
Strathclyde Region
Cunninghame District.

Milltimber, Aberdeen; Grampian,
Highland and Islands at Aberdeen.
Grampian Region
City of Aberdeen District.

Milnathort, Kinross; Tayside,
Central and Fife at Perth.
Tayside Region
Perth and Kinross District.

Milngavie, Glasgow; North
Strathclyde at Dumbarton.
Strathclyde Region
Bearsden and Milngavie District.

Milovaig, Isle of Skye; Grampian,
Highland and Islands at Portree.
Highland Region
Skye and Lochalsh District.

Milton, Drumnadrochit, Inverness-
shire; Grampian, Highland and
Islands at Inverness.
Highland Region
Inverness District.

Milton, Dumbarton; North
Strathclyde at Dumbarton.
Strathclyde Region
Dumbarton District.

Milton, Dumfries; South
Strathclyde, Dumfries and
Galloway at Dumfries.
Dumfries and Galloway Region
Nithsdale District.

Milton, Glasgow; Glasgow and
Strathkelvin at Glasgow.
Strathclyde Region
City of Glasgow District.

Milton, Kildary, Ross-shire;
Grampian, Highland and Islands at
Tain.
Highland Region
Ross and Cromarty District.

Milton, Lochboisdale, Isle of South
Uist; Grampian, Highland and
Islands at Lochmaddy.
Western Isles Islands Council.

Milton, Wick, Caithness; Grampian,
Highland and Islands at Wick.
Highland Region
Caithness District.

Milton Bridge, Penicuik,
Midlothian; Lothian and Borders at
Edinburgh.
Lothian Region
Midlothian District.

Milton of Balgonie, Glenrothes,
Fife; Tayside, Central and Fife at
Kirkcaldy.
Fife Region
Kirkcaldy District.

Milton of Culloden, Inverness;
Grampian, Highland and Islands at
Inverness.
Highland Region
Inverness District.

Miltonduff, Elgin, Morayshire; Grampian, Highland and Islands at Elgin.
Grampian Region
Moray District.

Minigaff, Newton Stewart, Wigtownshire; South Strathclyde, Dumfries and Galloway at Stranraer.
Dumfries and Galloway Region
Wigtown District.

Minish, Lochmaddy, Isle of North Uist; Grampian, Highland and Islands at Lochmaddy.
Western Isles Islands Council.

Minishant, Maybole, Ayrshire; South Strathclyde, Dumfries and Galloway at Ayr.
Strathclyde Region
Kyle and Carrick District.

Mintlaw, Peterhead, Aberdeenshire; Grampian, Highland and Islands at Peterhead.
Grampian Region
Banff and Buchan District.

Minto, Hawick, Roxburghshire; Lothian and Borders at Jedburgh.
Borders Region
Roxburgh District.

Mochrum, Newton Stewart, Wigtownshire.
South Strathclyde, Dumfries and Galloway at Stranraer.
Dumfries and Galloway Region
Wigtown District.

Moffat, Dumfriesshire; South Strathclyde, Dumfries and Galloway at Dumfries.
Dumfries and Galloway Region
Annandale and Eskdale District.

Mollinsburn, Stepps, Glasgow; Glasgow and Strathkelvin at Glasgow.
Strathclyde Region
City of Glasgow District.

Moniaive, Thornhill, Dumfries; South Strathclyde, Dumfries and Galloway at Dumfries.
Dumfries and Galloway Region
Nithsdale District.

Monifieth, Dundee; Tayside, Central and Fife at Dundee.
Tayside Region
City of Dundee District.

Monikie, Broughty Ferry, Dundee; Tayside, Central and Fife at Dundee.
Tayside Region
City of Dundee District.

Monkton, Prestwick, Ayrshire; South Strathclyde, Dumfries and Galloway at Ayr.
Strathclyde Region
Kyle and Carrick District.

Monktonhall, Musselburgh, Midlothian; Lothian and Borders at Edinburgh.
Lothian Region
Midlothian District.

Monreith, Newton Stewart, Wigtownshire; South Strathclyde, Dumfries and Galloway at Stranraer.
Dumfries and Galloway Region
Wigtown District.

Montgarrie, Alford, Aberdeenshire; Grampian, Highland and Islands at Aberdeen.
Grampian Region
Gordon District.

Montgreenan, Kilwinning, Ayrshire; North Strathclyde at Kilmarnock.
Strathclyde Region
Cunninghame District.

Montrave, Cupar, Fife; Tayside, Central and Fife at Cupar.
Fife Region
North East Fife District.

Montrose, Angus; Tayside, Central and Fife at Arbroath.
Tayside Region
Angus District.

Monymusk, Inverurie, Aberdeenshire; Grampian, Highland and Islands at Aberdeen.
Grampian Region
Gordon District.

Moodiesburn, Chryston, Glasgow; Glasgow and Strathkelvin at Glasgow.
Strathclyde Region
City of Glasgow District.

Moorpark, Renfrew; North Strathclyde at Paisley.
Strathclyde Region
Renfrew District.

Morar, Mallaig, Inverness-shire; Grampian, Highland and Islands at Fort William.
Highland Region
Lochaber District.

Morebattle, Kelso, Roxburghshire; Lothian and Borders at Jedburgh.
Borders Region
Roxburgh District.

Morningside, Edinburgh; Lothian and Borders at Edinburgh.
Lothian Region
City of Edinburgh District.

Mornish, Tobermory, Isle of Mull; North Strathclyde at Oban.
Strathclyde Region
Argyll and Bute District.

Morrington, Dumfries; South Strathclyde, Dumfries and Galloway at Dumfries.
Dumfries and Galloway Region
Nithsdale District.

Morsgail, Isle of Lewis; Grampian, Highland and Islands at Stornoway.
Western Isles Islands Council.

Moscow, Galston, Ayrshire; South Strathclyde, Dumfries and Galloway at Ayr.
Strathclyde Region
Kyle and Carrick District.

Moss, Scarinish, Isle of Tiree; North Strathclyde at Oban.
Strathclyde Region
Argyll and Bute District.

Mossat, Alford, Aberdeenshire;
Grampian, Highland and Islands at
Aberdeen.
Grampian Region
Gordon District.

Mossbank, Shetland; Grampian,
Highland and Islands at Lerwick.
Shetland Islands Council.

Mossdale, Castle Douglas,
Kirkcudbrightshire; South
Strathclyde, Dumfries and
Galloway at Kirkcudbright.
Dumfries and Galloway Region
Stewartry District.

Mosspaul Inn, Langholm,
Dumfriesshire; South Strath-
clyde, Dumfries and Galloway at
Dumfries.
Dumfries and Galloway Region
Annandale and Eskdale District.

Mosstodloch, Fochabers,
Morayshire; Grampian, Highland
and Islands at Elgin.
Grampian Region
Moray District.

Mosstowie, Elgin, Morayshire;
Grampian, Highland and Islands at
Elgin.
Grampian Region
Moray District.

Mossyard, Castle Douglas,
Kirkcudbrightshire; South
Strathclyde, Dumfries and
Galloway at Kirkcudbright.
Dumfries and Galloway Region
Stewartry District.

Motherwell, Lanarkshire; South
Strathclyde, Dumfries and
Galloway at Hamilton.
Strathclyde Region
Motherwell District.

Moulin, Pitlochry, Perthshire;
Tayside, Central and Fife at Perth.
Tayside Region
Perth and Kinross District.

Mound, Sutherland; Grampian,
Highland and Islands at Dornoch.
Highland Region
Sutherland District.

Mount Stuart, Rothesay, Isle of
Bute; North Strathclyde at
Rothesay.
Strathclyde Region
Argyll and Bute District.

Mount Vernon, Glasgow; Glasgow
and Strathkelvin at Glasgow.
Strathclyde Region
City of Glasgow District.

Mountblairy, Banff; Grampian,
Highland and Islands at Banff.
Grampian Region
Banff and Buchan District.

Mounteagle, Fortrose, Ross-shire;
Grampian, Highland and Islands at
Dingwall.
Highland Region
Ross and Cromarty District.

Mouswald, Dumfries; South
Strathclyde, Dumfries and
Galloway at Dumfries.
Dumfries and Galloway Region
Nithsdale District.

Moy, Tomatin, Inverness;
Grampian, Highland and Islands at
Inverness.
Highland Region
Inverness District.

Muasdale, Tarbert, Argyll; North
Strathclyde at Campbeltown.
Strathclyde Region
Argyll and Bute District.

Muchalls, Stonehaven,
Kincardineshire; Grampian,
Highland and Islands at
Stonehaven.
Grampian Region
Kincardine and Deeside District.

Muckart, Dollar,
Clackmannanshire; Tayside,
Central and Fife at Alloa.
Central Region
Clackmannan District.

Muckle Roe, Shetland; Grampian,
Highland and Islands at Lerwick.
Shetland Islands Council.

Mugdock, Milngavie, Glasgow;
North Strathclyde at Dumbarton.
Strathclyde Region
Dumbarton District.

Muir of Fowlis, Alford,
Aberdeenshire; Grampian,
Highland and Islands at Aberdeen.
Grampian Region
Gordon District.

Muir of Ord, Ross-shire; Grampian,
Highland and Islands at Dingwall.
Highland Region
Ross and Cromarty District.

Muiravonside, Linlithgow, West
Lothian; Lothian and Borders at
Linlithgow.
Lothian Region
West Lothian District.

Muirdrum, Carnoustie, Angus;
Tayside, Central and Fife at
Arbroath.
Tayside Region
Angus District.

Muirhead, Dundee; Tayside,
Central and Fife at Dundee.
Tayside Region
City of Dundee District.

Muirhead, Falkland, Fife; Tayside,
Central and Fife at Cupar.
Fife Region
North East Fife District.

Muirhead, Glasgow; Glasgow and
Strathkelvin at Glasgow.
Strathclyde Region
City of Glasgow District.

Muirhouse, Edinburgh; Lothian and
Borders at Edinburgh.
Lothian Region
City of Edinburgh District.

Muirkirk, Cumnock, Ayrshire;
South Strathclyde, Dumfries and
Galloway at Ayr.
Strathclyde Region
Cumnock and Doon Valley District.

Muirton, Auchterarder, Perthshire;
Tayside, Central and Fife at Perth.
Tayside Region
Perth and Kinross District.

Mulben, Keith, Morayshire; Grampian, Highland and Islands at Elgin.
Grampian Region
Moray District.

Munlochy, Ross-shire; Grampian, Highland and Islands at Dingwall.
Highland Region
Ross and Cromarty District.

Murkle, Thurso, Caithness; Grampian, Highland and Islands at Wick.
Highland Region
Caithness District.

Murroes, Broughty Ferry, Dundee; Tayside, Central and Fife at Dundee.
Tayside Region
City of Dundee District.

Murthly, Perth; Tayside, Central and Fife at Perth.
Tayside Region
Perth and Kinross District.

Musselburgh, Midlothian; Lothian and Borders at Edinburgh.
Lothian Region
Midlothian District.

Muthill, Crieff, Perthshire; Tayside, Central and Fife at Perth.
Tayside Region
Perth and Kinross District.

Nairn; Grampian, Highland and Islands at Inverness.
Highland Region
Nairn District.

Nairnside, Inverness; Grampian, Highland and Islands at Inverness.
Highland Region
Inverness District.

Navidale, Helmsdale, Sutherland; Grampian, Highland and Islands at Dornoch.
Highland Region
Sutherland District.

Neap, Lerwick, Shetland; Grampian, Highland and Islands at Lerwick.
Shetland Islands Council.

Neilston, Glasgow; North Strathclyde at Paisley.
Strathclyde Region
Renfrew District.

Nemphlar, Lanark; South Strathclyde, Dumfries and Galloway at Lanark.
Strathclyde Region
Clydesdale District.

Nenthorn, Kelso, Roxburghshire; Lothian and Borders at Jedburgh.
Borders Region
Roxburgh District.

Ness, Isle of Lewis; Grampian, Highland and Islands at Stornoway.
Western Isles Islands Council.

Nether Kinmundy, Peterhead, Aberdeenshire; Grampian, Highland and Islands at Peterhead.
Grampian Region
Banff and Buchan District.

Netherburn, Larkhall, Lanarkshire; South Strathclyde, Dumfries and Galloway at Hamilton.
Strathclyde Region
Hamilton District.

Nethercleugh, Lockerbie, Dumfriesshire; South Strathclyde, Dumfries and Galloway at Dumfries.
Dumfries and Galloway Region
Annandale and Eskdale District.

Netherley, Stonehaven, Kincardineshire; Grampian, Highland and Islands at Stonehaven.
Grampian Region
Kincardine and Deeside District.

Netherthird, Cumnock, Ayrshire; South Strathclyde, Dumfries and Galloway at Ayr.
Strathclyde Region
Cumnock and Doon Valley District.

Netherton, Brechin, Angus; Tayside, Central and Fife at Forfar.
Tayside Region
Angus District.

Nethybridge, Inverness-shire; Grampian, Highland and Islands at Inverness.
Highland Region
Badenoch and Strathspey District.

New Abbey, Dumfries; South Strathclyde, Dumfries and Galloway at Dumfries.
Dumfries and Galloway Region
Nithsdale District.

New Aberdour, Fraserburgh, Aberdeenshire; Grampian, Highland and Islands at Peterhead.
Grampian Region
Banff and Buchan District.

New Alyth, Blairgowrie, Perthshire; Tayside, Central and Fife at Perth.
Tayside Region
Perth and Kinross District.

New Byth, Turriff, Banffshire; Grampian, Highland and Islands at Banff.
Grampian Region
Banff and Buchan District.

New Clunie, Murthly, Perth; Tayside, Central and Fife at Perth.
Tayside Region
Perth and Kinross District.

New Craighall, Midlothian; Lothian and Borders at Edinburgh.
Lothian Region
Midlothian District.

New Cumnock, Cumnock, Ayrshire; South Strathclyde, Dumfries and Galloway at Ayr.
Strathclyde Region
Cumnock and Doon Valley District.

New Deer, Peterhead, Aberdeenshire; Grampian, Highland and Islands at Peterhead.
Grampian Region
Banff and Buchan District.

New Elgin, Elgin, Morayshire; Grampian, Highland and Islands at Elgin.
Grampian Region
Moray District.

New Galloway, Castle Douglas, Kirkcudbrightshire; South Strathclyde, Dumfries and Galloway at Kirkcudbright.
Dumfries and Galloway Region
Stewartry District.

New Garrabost, Isle of Lewis; Grampian, Highland and Islands at Stornoway.
Western Isles Islands Council.

New Gilston, Leven, Fife; Tayside, Central and Fife at Cupar.
Fife Region
North East Fife District.

New Leeds, Peterhead, Aberdeenshire; Grampian, Highland and Islands at Peterhead.
Grampian Region
Banff and Buchan District.

New Luce, Newton Stewart, Wigtownshire; South Strathclyde, Dumfries and Galloway at Stranraer.
Dumfries and Galloway Region
Wigtown District.

New Machar, Inverurie, Aberdeenshire; Grampian, Highland and Islands at Aberdeen.
Grampian Region
Gordon District.

New Monkland, Airdrie, Lanarkshire; South Strathclyde, Dumfries and Galloway at Airdrie.
Strathclyde Region
Monklands District.

New Pitsligo, Fraserburgh, Aberdeenshire; Grampian, Highland and Islands at Banff.
Grampian Region
Banff and Buchan District.

New Scone, Perth; Tayside, Central and Fife at Perth.
Tayside Region
Perth and Kinross District.

New Selma, Argyll; North Strathclyde at Oban.
Strathclyde Region
Argyll and Bute District.

New Shawbost, Isle of Lewis; Grampian, Highland and Islands at Stornoway.
Western Isles Islands Council.

New Tolsta, Isle of Lewis; Grampian, Highland and Islands at Stornoway.
Western Isles Islands Council.

New Winton, Tranent, East Lothian; Lothian and Borders at Haddington.
Lothian Region
East Lothian District.

Newarthill, Motherwell, Lanarkshire; South Strathclyde, Dumfries and Galloway at Hamilton.
Strathclyde Region
Motherwell District.

Newbattle, Dalkeith, Midlothian; Lothian and Borders at Edinburgh.
Lothian Region
Midlothian District.

Newbie, Annan, Dumfriesshire;
South Strathclyde, Dumfries and
Galloway at Dumfries.
Dumfries and Galloway Region
Annandale and Eskdale District.

Newbigging, Broughty Ferry,
Dundee; Tayside, Central and Fife
at Dundee.
Tayside Region
City of Dundee District.

Newbigging, Carnwath,
Lanarkshire; South Strathclyde,
Dumfries and Galloway at Lanark.
Strathclyde Region
Clydesdale District.

Newbridge, Dumfries; South
Strathclyde, Dumfries and
Galloway at Dumfries.
Dumfries and Galloway Region
Nithsdale District.

Newbridge, Midlothian; Lothian and
Borders at Edinburgh.
Lothian Region
Midlothian District.

Newburgh, Cupar, Fife; Tayside,
Central and Fife at Cupar.
Fife Region
North East Fife District.

Newburgh, Ellon, Aberdeenshire;
Grampian, Highland and Islands at
Aberdeen.
Grampian Region
Gordon District.

Newcastleton, Roxburghshire;
Lothian and Borders at Jedburgh.
Borders Region
Roxburgh District.

Newhouse, Motherwell,
Lanarkshire; South Strathclyde,
Dumfries and Galloway at
Hamilton.
Strathclyde Region
Motherwell District.

Newington, Edinburgh; Lothian and
Borders at Edinburgh.
Lothian Region
City of Edinburgh District.

Newlands, Glasgow; Glasgow and
Strathkelvin at Glasgow.
Strathclyde Region
City of Glasgow District.

Newmains, Lanarkshire; South
Strathclyde, Dumfries and
Galloway at Hamilton.
Strathclyde Region
Motherwell District.

Newmarket, Stornoway, Isle of
Lewis; Grampian, Highland and
Islands at Stornoway.
Western Isles Islands Council.

Newmill, Keith, Morayshire;
Grampian, Highland and Islands at
Elgin.
Grampian Region
Moray District.

Newmill on Teviot, Hawick,
Roxburghshire; Lothian and
Borders at Jedburgh.
Borders Region
Roxburgh District.

Newmills, Dunfermline, Fife;
Tayside, Central and Fife at
Dunfermline.
Fife Region
Dunfermline District.

Newmilns, Ayrshire; North
Strathclyde at Kilmarnock.
Strathclyde Region
Kilmarnock and Louden District.

Newpark, Callanish, Isle of Lewis;
Grampian, Highland and Islands at
Stornoway.
Western Isles Island Council.

Newport, Fionnphort, Isle of Mull;
North Strathclyde at Oban.
Strathclyde Region
Argyll and Bute District.

Newport-on-Tay, Fife; Tayside,
Central and Fife at Cupar.
Tayside Region
North East Fife District.

Newstead, Melrose,
Roxburghshire; Lothian and
Borders at Selkirk.
Borders Region
Ettrick and Lauderdale District.

Newton, Broxburn, West Lothian;
Lothian and Borders at Linlithgow.
Lothian Region
West Lothian District.

Newton, Dumbarton; North
Strathclyde at Dumbarton.
Strathclyde Region
Dumbarton District.

Newton, Lochmaddy, Isle of North
Uist; Grampian, Highland and
Islands at Lochmaddy.
Western Isles Islands Council.

Newton, Winchburgh, West
Lothian; Lothian and Borders at
Linlithgow.
Lothian Region
West Lothian District.

Newton Bridge, Amulree,
Perthshire; Tayside, Central and
Fife at Perth.
Tayside Region
Perth and Kinrose District.

Newton Mearns, Glasgow; North
Strathclyde at Paisley.
Strathclyde Region
Renfrew District.

Newton of Belltrees, Lochwinnoch,
Renfrewshire; North Strathclyde at
Paisley.
Strathclyde Region
Renfrew District.

Newton of Falkland, Cupar, Fife;
Tayside, Central and Fife at
Cupar.
Fife Region
North East Fife District.

Newton of Ferintosh, Muir of Ord,
Ross-shire; Grampian, Highland
and Islands at Dingwall.
Highland Region
Ross and Cromarty District.

Newton Stewart, Wigtownshire;
South Strathclyde, Dumfries and
Galloway at Stranraer.
Dumfries and Galloway Region
Wigtown District.

Newtonairds, Dumfries; South
Strathclyde, Dumfries and
Galloway at Dumfries.
Dumfries and Galloway Region
Nithsdale District.

Newtongrange, Dalkeith,
Midlothian; Lothian and Borders at
Edinburgh.
Lothian Region
Midlothian District.

Newtonhill, Lentran, Inverness;
Grampian, Highland and Islands at
Inverness.
Highland Region
Inverness District.

Newtonhill, Stonehaven,
Kincardineshire; Grampian,
Highland and Islands at
Stonehaven.
Grampian Region
Kincardine and Deeside District.

Newtonmore, Inverness-shire;
Grampian, Highland and Islands at
Inverness.
Highland Region
Badenoch and Strathspey District.

Newtown, Inverarary, Argyll; North
Strathclyde at Dunoon.
Strathclyde Region
Argyll and Bute District.

Newtown St Boswells,
Roxburghshire; Lothian and
Borders at Selkirk.
Borders Region
Ettrick and Lauderdale District.

Newtyle, Angus, Tayside; Tayside,
Central and Fife at Forfar.
Tayside Region
Angus District.

Newvalley, Isle of Lewis;
Grampian, Highland and Islands at
Stornoway.
Western Isles Islands Council.

Nigg, Aberdeen; Grampian,
Highland and Islands at Aberdeen.
Grampian Region
City of Aberdeen District.

Nigg, Fearn, Ross-shire; Grampian,
Highland and Islands at Tain.
Highland Region
Ross and Cromarty District.

Ninemileburn, Penicuik,
Midlothian; Lothian and Borders at
Edinburgh.
Lothian Region
Midlothian District.

Nisbet, Jedburgh, Roxburghshire;
Lothian and Borders at Jedburgh.
Borders Region
Roxburgh District.

Nitshill, Glasgow; Glasgow and
Strathkelvin at Glasgow.
Strathclyde Region
City of Glasgow District.

Norham, Berwick-Upon-Tweed,
Berwickshire; Lothian and Borders
at Duns.
Borders Region
Berwickshire District.

North Berwick, East Lothian;
Lothian and Borders at
Haddington.
Lothian Region
East Lothian District.

North Boisdale, Lochboisdale,
South Uist; Grampian, Highland
and Islands at Lochmaddy.
Western Isles Islands Council.

North Bragar, Isle of Lewis;
Grampian, Highland and Islands at
Stornoway.
Western Isles Islands Council.

North Collafirth, Shetland;
Grampian, Highland and Islands at
Lerwick.
Shetland Islands Council.

North Dell, Isle of Lewis;
Grampian, Highland and Islands at
Stornoway.
Western Isles Islands Council.

North Duntulm, Portree, Isle of
Skye; Grampian, Highland and
Islands at Portree.
Highland Region
Skye and Lochalsh District.

North Galson, Isle of Lewis;
Grampian, Highland and Islands at
Stornoway.
Western Isles Islands Council.

North Glendale, Lochboisdale,
South Uist; Grampian, Highland
and Islands at Lochmaddy.
Western Isles Islands Council.

North Kessock, Ross-shire;
Grampian, Highland and Islands at
Dingwall.
Highland Region
Ross and Cromarty District.

North Locheynort, Lochboisdale,
South Uist; Grampian, Highland
and Islands at Lochmaddy.
Western Isles Islands Council.

North Middleton, Gorebridge,
Midlothian; Lothian and Borders at
Edinburgh.
Lothian Region
Midlothian District.

North Queensferry, Dunfermline,
Fife; Tayside, Central and Fife at
Dunfermline.
Fife Region
Dunfermline District.

North Roe, Shetland; Grampian,
Highland and Islands at Lerwick.
Shetland Islands Council.

North Ronaldsay, Orkney;
Grampian, Highland and Islands at
Kirkwall.
Orkney Islands Council.

North Shawbost, Isle of Lewis;
Grampian, Highland and Islands at
Stornoway.
Western Isles Islands Council.

North Tolsta, Isle of Lewis;
Grampian, Highland and Islands at
Stornoway.
Western Isles Islands Council.

Northbay, Castlebay, Isle of Barra;
Grampian, Highland and Islands at
Lochmaddy.
Western Isles Islands Council.

Northmuir, Kirriemuir, Angus;
Tayside, Central and Fife at
Forfar.
Tayside Region
Angus District.

Northton, Isle of Harris; Grampian,
Highland and Islands at
Stornoway.
Western Isles Islands Council.

Northwaa, Sanday, Orkney; Grampian, Highland and Islands at Kirkwall.
Orkney Islands Council.

Northwaterbridge, Laurencekirk, Kincardineshire; Grampian, Highland and Islands at Stonehaven.
Grampian Region
Kincardine and Deeside District.

Nostie, Kyle, Ross-shire; Grampian, Highland and Islands at Dingwall.
Highland Region
Skye and Lochalsh District.

Nunraw, East Lothian; Lothian and Borders at Haddington.
Lothian Region
East Lothian District.

Nunton, Isle of Benbecula; Grampian, Highland and Islands at Lochmaddy.
Western Isles Islands Council.

Oakley, Dunfermline, Fife; Tayside, Central and Fife at Dunfermline.
Fife Region
Dunfermline District.

Oathlaw, Forfar, Angus; Tayside, Central and Fife at Forfar.
Tayside Region
Angus District.

Oban, Argyll; North Strathclyde at Oban.
Strathclyde Region
Argyll and Bute District.

Ochiltree, Cumnock, Ayrshire; South Strathclyde, Dumfries and Galloway at Ayr.
Strathclyde Region
Cumnock and Doon Valley District.

Old Craighall, Musselburgh, Midlothian; Lothian and Borders at Edinburgh.
Lothian Region
Midlothian District.

Old Dailly, Girvan, Ayrshire; South Strathclyde, Dumfries and Galloway at Ayr.
Strathclyde Region
Kyle and Carrick District.

Old Deer, Peterhead, Aberdeenshire; Grampian, Highland and Islands at Peterhead.
Grampian Region
Banff and Buchan District.

Old Kilmadock, Doune, Stirlingshire; Tayside, Central and Fife at Stirling.
Central Region
Stirling District.

Old Kilpatrick, Glasgow; North Strathclyde at Dumbarton.
Strathclyde Region
Dumbarton District.

Old Meldrum, Inverurie, Aberdeenshire; Grampian, Highland and Islands at Aberdeen.
Grampian Region
Gordon District.

Old Plean, Stirling; Tayside, Central and Fife at Stirling.
Central Region
Stirling District.

Old Rayne, Insch, Aberdeenshire; Grampian, Highland and Islands at Aberdeen.
Grampian Region
Gordon District.

Old Sauchie, Stirling; Tayside, Central and Fife at Stirling.
Central Region
Stirling District.

Oldhall, Paisley; North Strathclyde at Paisley.
Strathclyde Region
Renfrew District.

Oldhamstocks, Cockburnspath, Berwickshire; Lothian and Borders at Haddington.
Lothian Region
East Lothian District.

Ollaberry, Shetland; Grampian, Highland and Islands at Lerwick.
Shetland Islands Council.

Onich, Fort William, Inverness-shire; Grampian, Highland and Islands at Fort William.
Grampian Region
Lochaber District.

Opinan, Gairloch, Ross-shire; Grampian, Highland and Islands at Dingwall.
Grampian Region
Ross and Cromarty District.

Ordhead, Inverurie, Aberdeenshire; Grampian, Highland and Islands at Aberdeen.
Grampian Region
Gordon District.

Ordie, Aboyne, Kincardineshire; Grampian, Highland and Islands at Stonehaven.
Grampian Region
Kincardine and Deeside District.

Orinsay, Isle of Lewis; Grampian, Highland and Islands at Stornoway.
Western Isles Islands Council.

Ormiclate, Lochboisdale, Isle of South Uist; Grampian, Highland and Islands at Lochmaddy.
Western Isles Islands Council.

Ormiston, East Lothian; Lothian and Borders at Haddington.
Lothian Region
East Lothian District.

Ormsary, Lochgilphead, Argyll; North Strathclyde at Dunoon.
Strathclyde Region
Argyll and Bute District.

Orphir, Stromness, Orkney; Grampian, Highland and Islands at Kirkwall.
Shetland Islands Council.

Orton, Fochabers, Morayshire; Grampian, Highland and Islands at Elgin.
Grampian Region
Moray District.

Otter Ferry, Tighnabruaich, Argyll; North Strathclyde at Dunoon.
Strathclyde Region
Argyll and Bute District.

Otterswick, Yell, Shetland; Grampian, Highland and Islands at Lerwick.
Shetland Islands Council.

Outend, Isle of Scalpay, Harris; Grampian, Highland and Islands at Stornoway.
Western Isles Islands Council.

Overtown, Wishaw, Lanarkshire; South Strathclyde, Dumfries and Galloway at Hamilton.
Strathclyde Region
Hamilton District.

Oxnam, Jedburgh, Roxburghshire; Lothian and Borders at Jedburgh.
Borders Region
Roxburgh District.

Oxton, Lauder, Berwickshire; Lothian and Borders at Selkirk.
Borders Region
Ettrick and Lauderdale District.

Oykel Bridge, Bonar Bridge, Sutherland; Grampian, Highland and Islands at Dornoch.
Highland Region
Sutherland District.

Oyne, Insch, Aberdeenshire; Grampian, Highland and Islands at Aberdeen.
Grampian Region
Gordon District.

Padanaram, Forfar, Angus; Tayside, Central and Fife at Forfar.
Tayside Region
Angus District.

Paiblesgarry, Lochmaddy, Isle of North Uist; Grampian, Highland and Islands at Lochmaddy.
Western Isles Islands Council.

Paisley, Renfrewshire; North Strathclyde at Paisley.
Strathclyde Region
Renfrew District.

Palnackie, Castle Douglas, Kirkcudbrightshire; South Strathclyde, Dumfries and Galloway at Kirkcudbright.
Dumfries and Galloway Region
Stewartry District.

Palnure, Newton Stewart, Wigtownshire; South Strathclyde, Dumfries and Galloway at Stranraer.
Dumfries and Galloway Region
Wigtown District.

Panbridge, Carnoustie, Angus; Tayside, Central and Fife at Arbroath.
Tayside Region
Angus District.

Papa Stour, Shetland; Grampian, Highland and Islands at Lerwick.
Shetland Islands Council.

Papa Westray, Orkney; Grampian, Highland and Islands at Kirkwall.
Orkney Islands Council.

Papdale, Kirkwall, Orkney; Grampian, Highland and Islands at Kirkwall.
Orkney Islands Council.

Papigoe, Wick, Caithness; Grampian, Highland and Islands at Wick.
Highland Region
Caithness District.

Park, Banchory, Kincardineshire; Grampian, Highland and Islands at Stonehaven.
Grampian Region
Kincardine and Deeside District.

Park, Barvas, Isle of Lewis; Grampian, Highland and Islands at Stornoway.
Western Isles Islands Council.

Park, Carloway, Isle of Lewis; Grampian, Highland and Islands at Stornoway.
Western Isles Islands Council.

Park, Thornhill, Dumfriesshire; South Strathclyde, Dumfries and Galloway at Dumfries.
Dumfries and Galloway Region
Nithsdale District.

Parkgate, Dumfries; South Strathclyde, Dumfries and Galloway at Dumfries.
Dumfries and Galloway Region
Nithsdale District.

Parks, Eriskay, Isle of South Uist; Grampian, Highland and Islands at Lochmaddy.
Western Isles Council.

Partick, Glasgow; Glasgow and Strathkelvin at Glasgow.
Strathclyde Region
City of Glasgow District.

Parton, Castle Douglas, Kirkcudbrightshire; South Strathclyde, Dumfries and Galloway at Kirkcudbright.
Dumfries and Galloway Region
Stewartry District.

Pathhead, Midlothian; Lothian and Borders at Edinburgh.
Lothian Region
Midlothian District.

Pathstruie, Perth; Tayside, Central and Fife at Perth.
Tayside Region
Perth and Kinross District.

Patna, Ayr; South Strathclyde, Dumfries and Galloway at Ayr.
Strathclyde Region
Kyle and Carrick District.

Patterton, Newton Mearns, Glasgow; North Strathclyde at Paisley.
Strathclyde Region
Renfrew District.

Paxton, Berwickshire; Lothian and Borders at Duns.
Borders Region
Berwickshire District.

Peebles; Lothian and Borders at Peebles.
Borders Region
Tweeddale District.

Peiness, Portree, Isle of Skye; Grampian, Highland and Islands at Portree.
Highland Region
Skye and Lochalsh District.

Penan, Fraserburgh, Aberdeenshire; Grampian, Highland and Islands at Banff.
Grampian Region
Banff and Buchan District.

Pencaitland, East Lothian; Lothian and Borders at Haddington.
Lothian Region
East Lothian District.

Penicuik, Midlothian; Lothian and Borders at Edinburgh.
Lothian Region
Midlothian District.

Penifiler, Portree, Isle of Skye; Grampian, Highland and Islands at Portree.
Highland Region
Skye and Lochalsh District.

Peninerine, Lochboisdale, Isle of South Uist; Grampian, Highland and Islands at Lochmaddy.
Western Isles Islands Council.

Peninver, Campbeltown, Argyll; North Strathclyde at Campbeltown.
Strathclyde Region
Argyll and Bute District.

Penmore, Dervaig, Tobermory, Isle of Mull; North Strathclyde at Oban.
Strathclyde Region
Argyll and Bute District.

Penninghame, Newton Stewart, Wigtownshire; South Strathclyde, Dumfries and Galloway at Stranraer.
Strathclyde Region
Wigtown District.

Pennyghael, Isle of Mull; North Strathclyde at Oban.
Strathclyde Region
Argyll and Bute District.

Penpoint, Thornhill, Dumfriesshire; South Strathclyde, Dumfries and Galloway at Dumfries.
Dumfries and Galloway Region
Nithsdale District.

Persley, Aberdeen; Grampian, Highland and Islands at Aberdeen.
Grampian Region
City of Aberdeen District.

Perth; Tayside, Central and Fife at Perth.
Tayside Region
Perth and Kinross District.

Peterculter, Aberdeen; Grampian, Highland and Islands at Aberdeen.
Grampian Region
City of Aberdeen District.

Peterhead, Aberdeenshire; Grampian, Highland and Islands at Peterhead.
Grampian Region
Banff and Buchan District.

Peters Port, Isle of Benbecula; Grampian, Highland and Islands at Lochmaddy.
Western Isles Islands Council.

Pettinain, Lanark; South Strathclyde, Dumfries and Galloway at Lanark.
Strathclyde Region
Clydesdale District.

Pettycur, Kinghorn, Fife; Tayside, Central and Fife at Kirkcaldy.
Fife Region
Kirkcaldy District.

Philpstoun, Linlithgow, West Lothian; Lothian and Borders at Linlithgow.
Lothian Region
West Lothian District.

Pierowall, Westray, Orkney; Grampian, Highland and Islands at Kirkwall.
Orkney Islands Council.

Pilton, Edinburgh; Lothian and Borders at Edinburgh.
Lothian Region
City of Edinburgh District.

Pinmore, Girvan, Ayrshire; South Strathclyde, Dumfries and Galloway at Ayr.
Strathclyde Region
Kyle and Carrick District.

Pinwherry, Girvan, Ayrshire; South Strathclyde, Dumfries and Galloway at Ayr.
Strathclyde Region
Kyle and Carrick District.

Pirnmill, Brodick, Isle of Arran; North Strathclyde at Kilmarnock.
Strathclyde Region
Cunninghame District.

Pitcairngreen, Perth; Tayside, Central and Fife at Perth.
Tayside Region
Perth and Kinross District.

Pitcaple, Inverurie, Aberdeenshire; Grampian, Highland and Islands at Aberdeen.
Grampian Region
Gordon District.

Pitfodels, Cults, Aberdeen; Grampian, Highland and Islands at Aberdeen.
Grampian Region
City of Aberdeen District.

Pitlessie, Cupar, Fife; Tayside, Central and Fife at Cupar.
Fife Region
North East Fife District.

Pitlochry, Perthshire; Tayside, Central and Fife at Perth.
Tayside Region
Perth and Kinross District.

Pitmeddon, Ellon, Aberdeenshire; Grampian, Highland and Islands at Aberdeen.
Grampian Region
Gordon District.

Pitroddie, Perth; Tayside, Central and Fife at Perth.
Tayside Region
Perth and Kinross District.

Pitscottie, Cupar, Fife; Tayside, Central and Fife at Cupar.
Fife Region
North East Fife District.

Pittenweem, Anstruther, Fife; Tayside, Central and Fife at Cupar.
Fife Region
North East Fife District.

Pladda Isle, Brodick, Isle of Arran; North Strathclyde at Kilmarnock.
Strathclyde Region
Cunninghame District.

Plains, Airdrie, Lanarkshire; South
Strathclyde, Dumfries and
Galloway at Airdrie.
Strathclyde Region
Monklands District.

Plasterfield, Stornoway, Isle of
Lewis; Grampian, Highland and
Islands at Stornoway.
Western Isles Islands Council.

Plean, Stirling; Tayside, Central
and Fife at Stirling.
Central Region
Stirling District.

Plockropool, Isle of Harris;
Grampian, Highland and Islands at
Stornoway.
Western Isles Islands Council.

Plockton, Kyle of Lochalsh, Ross-
shire; Grampian, Highland and
Islands at Dingwall.
Highland Region
Skye and Lochalsh District.

Pluscarden, Elgin, Morayshire;
Grampian, Highland and Islands at
Elgin.
Grampian Region
Moray District.

Polbeth, West Calder, West
Lothian; Lothian and Borders at
Linlithgow.
Lothian Region
West Lothian District.

Pollock, Glasgow; Glasgow and
Strathkelvin at Glasgow.
Strathclyde Region
City of Glasgow District.

Pollokshaws, Glasgow; Glasgow
and Strathkelvin at Glasgow.
Strathclyde Region
City of Glasgow District.

Pollokshields, Glasgow; Glasgow
and Strathkelvin at Glasgow.
Strathclyde Region
City of Glasgow District.

Polmadie, Glasgow; Glasgow and
Strathkelvin at Glasgow.
Strathclyde Region
City of Glasgow District.

Polmont, Falkirk, Stirlingshire;
Tayside, Central and Fife at
Falkirk.
Central Region
Falkirk District.

Polwarth, Greenlaw, Berwickshire;
Lothian and Borders at Duns.
Borders Region
Berwickshire District.

Poolewe, Gairloch, Ross-shire;
Grampian, Highland and Islands at
Dingwall.
Highland Region
Ross and Cromarty District.

Port Ann, Lochgilphead, Argyll;
North Strathclyde at Dunoon.
Strathclyde Region
Argyll and Bute District.

Port Appin, Appin, Argyll; North
Strathclyde at Oban.
Strathclyde Region
Argyll and Bute District.

Port Askaig, Isle of Islay; North
Strathclyde at Campbeltown.
Strathclyde Region
Argyll and Bute District.

Port Bannatyne, Rothesay, Isle of
Bute; North Strathclyde at
Rothesay.
Strathclyde Region
Argyll and Bute District.

Port Charlotte, Isle of Islay; North
Strathclyde at Campbeltown.
Strathclyde Region
Argyll and Bute District.

Port Ellen, Isle of Islay; North
Strathclyde at Campbeltown.
Strathclyde Region
Argyll and Bute District.

Port Elphinstone, Inverurie,
Aberdeenshire; Grampian,
Highland and Islands at Aberdeen.
Grampian Region
Gordon District.

Port Glasgow, Renfrewshire; North
Strathclyde at Greenock.
Strathclyde Region
Renfrew District.

Port Logan, Stranraer,
Wigtownshire; South Strathclyde,
Dumfries and Galloway at
Stranraer.
Dumfries and Galloway Region
Wigtown District.

Port of Menteith, Stirling; Tayside,
Central and Fife at Stirling.
Central Region
Stirling District.

Port of Ness, Isle of Lewis;
Grampian, Highland and Islands at
Stornoway.
Western Isles Islands Council.

Port Seton, Prestonpans, East
Lothian; Lothian and Borders at
Haddington.
Lothian Region
East Lothian District.

Port Sonachan, Dalmally, Argyll;
North Strathclyde at Oban.
Strathclyde Region
Argyll and Bute District.

Port Wemyss, Portnahaven, Isles
of Islay; North Strathclyde at
Campbeltown.
Strathclyde Region
Argyll and Bute District.

Port William, Newton Stewart,
Wigtownshire; South Strathclyde,
Dumfries and Galloway at
Stranraer.
Dumfries and Galloway Region
Wigtown District.

Portencross, West Kilbride,
Ayrshire; North Strathclyde at
Kilmarnock.
Strathclyde Region
Cunninghame District.

Portessie, Buckie, Morayshire;
Grampian, Highland and Islands at
Elgin.
Grampian Region
Moray District.

Portgordon, Buckie, Morayshire;
Grampian, Highland and Islands at
Elgin.
Grampian Region
Moray District.

Portgower, Helmsdale, Sutherland;
Grampian, Highland and Islands at
Dornoch.
Highland Region
Sutherland District.

Portinnisherrich, Dalmally, Argyll;
North Strathclyde at Oban.
Strathclyde Region
Argyll and Bute District.

Portlethen, Aberdeen; Grampian,
Highland and Islands at
Stonehaven.
Grampian Region
Kincardine and Deeside District.

Portling, Dalbeattie,
Kirkcudbrightshire; South
Strathclyde, Dumfries and
Galloway at Kirkcudbright.
Dumfries and Galloway Region
Stewartry District.

Portmahomack, Fearn, Ross-shire;
Grampian, Highland and Islands at
Tain.
Highland Region
Ross and Cromarty District.

Portnacroish, Argyll; North
Strathclyde at Oban.
Strathclyde Region
Argyll and Bute District.

Portnaguran, Isle of Lewis;
Grampian, Highland and Islands at
Stornoway.
Western Isles Islands Council.

Portnahaven, Isle of Islay; North
Strathclyde at Campbeltown.
Strathclyde Region
Argyll and Bute District.

Portnalong, Carbost, Isle of Skye;
Grampian, Highland and Islands at
Portree.
Highland Region
Skye and Lochalsh District.

Portnockie, Buckie, Morayshire;
Grampian, Highland and Islands at
Elgin.
Grampian Region
Moray District.

Portobello, Edinburgh; Lothian and
Borders at Edinburgh.
Lothian Region
City of Edinburgh District.

Portpatrick, Stranraer,
Wigtownshire; South Strathclyde,
Dumfries and Galloway at
Stranraer.
Dumfries and Galloway Region
Wigtown District.

Portree, Isle of Skye; Grampian,
Highland and Islands at Portree.
Highland Region
Skye and Lochalsh District.

Portsoy, Banff; Grampian,
Highland and Islands at Banff.
Grampian Region
Banff and Buchan.

Portvoller, Isle of Lewis; Grampian,
Highland and Islands at
Stornoway.
Western Isles Islands Council.

Possilpark, Glasgow; Glasgow and
Strathkelvin at Glasgow.
Strathclyde Region
City of Glasgow District.

Potarch, Banchory,
Kincardineshire; Grampian,
Highland and Islands at
Stonehaven.
Grampian Region
Kincardine and Deeside District.

Potterton, Aberdeen; Grampian,
Highland and Islands at Aberdeen.
Grampian Region
City of Aberdeen District.

Powfoot, Annan, Dumfrieshire;
South Strathclyde, Dumfries and
Galloway at Dumfries.
Dumfries and Galloway Region
Annandale and Eskdale District.

Powmill, Dollar,
Clackmannanshire; Tayside,
Central and Fife at Alloa.
Central Region
Clackmannan District.

Poyntzfield, Cromarty, Conon
Bridge, Ross-shire; Grampian,
Highland and Islands at Dingwall.
Highland Region
Ross and Cromarty District.

Premnay, Insch, Aberdeenshire;
Grampian, Highland and Islands at
Aberdeen.
Grampian Region
Gordon District.

Preston, Dumfries; South
Strathclyde, Dumfries and
Galloway at Dumfries.
Dumfries and Galloway Region
Nithsdale District.

Preston, Duns, Berwickshire;
Lothian and Borders at Duns.
Borders Region
Berwickshire District.

Prestonhall, Pathhead, Midlothian;
Lothian and Borders at Edinburgh.
Lothian Region
Midlothian District.

Prestonpans, East Lothian; Lothian
and Borders at Haddington.
Lothian Region
East Lothian District.

Prestwick, Ayrshire; South
Strathclyde, Dumfries and
Galloway at Ayr.
Strathclyde Region
Kyle and Carrick District.

Pumpherston, Livingston, West
Lothian; Lothian and Borders at
Linlithgow.
Lothian Region
West Lothian District.

Quarff, Shetland; Grampian,
Highland and Islands at Lerwick.
Shetland Islands Council.

Quarter, Glassford, Lanarkshire;
South Strathclyde, Dumfries and
Galloway at Hamilton.
Strathclyde Region
Clydesdale District.

Quay, Berneray, Lochmaddy, Isle
of North Uist; Grampian, Highland
and Islands at Lochmaddy.
Western Isles Islands Council.

Queenzieburn, Kilsyth, Glasgow;
South Strathclyde, Dumfries and
Galloway at Airdrie.
Strathclyde Region
Cumbernauld and Kilsyth District.

Quidinish, Isle of Harris; Grampian, Highland and Islands at Stornoway.
Western Isles Islands Council.

Quothquan, Biggar, Lanarkshire; South Strathclyde, Dumfries and Galloway at Lanark.
Strathclyde Region
Clydesdale District.

Quoyloo, Stromness; Grampian, Highland and Islands at Kirkwall.
Shetland Islands Council.

Racks, Dumfries; South Strathclyde, Dumfries and Galloway at Dumfries.
Dumfries and Galloway Region
Nithsdale District.

Radernie, Cupar, Fife; Tayside, Central and Fife at Cupar.
Fife Region
North East Fife District.

Radnor Park, Clydebank, Dunbartonshire; North Strathclyde at Dumbarton.
Strathclyde Region
Dumbarton District.

Raemoir, Banchory, Kincardineshire; Grampian, Highland and Islands at Stonehaven.
Grampian Region
Kincardine and Deeside District.

Raewick, Shetland; Grampian, Highland and Islands at Lerwick.
Shetland Islands Council.

Rafford, Forres, Morayshire; Grampian, Highland and Islands at Elgin.
Grampian Region
Moray District.

Rait, Perth; Tayside, Central and Fife at Perth.
Tayside Region
Perth and Kinross District.

Ralston, Paisley, Renfrewshire; North Strathclyde at Paisley.
Strathclyde Region
Renfrew District.

Ramoyle, Dunblane, Stirlingshire; Tayside, Central and Fife at Stirling.
Central Region
Stirling District.

Ranish, Isle of Lewis; Grampian, Highland and Islands at Stornoway.
Western Isles Islands Council.

Rankinston, Ayr; South Strathclyde, Dumfries and Galloway at Ayr.
Strathclyde Region
Kyle and Carrick District.

Rannoch Station, Perthshire; Tayside, Central and Fife at Perth.
Tayside Region
Perth and Kinross District.

Rapness, Westray, Orkney; Grampian, Highland and Islands at Kirkwall.
Orkney Islands Council.

Rarnish, Isle of Benbecula;
Grampian, Highland and Islands at
Lochmaddy.
Western Isles Islands Council.

Rashfield, Dunoon, Argyll; North
Strathclyde at Dunoon.
Strathclyde Region
Argyll and Bute District.

Rathen, Fraserburgh,
Aberdeenshire; Grampian,
Highland and Islands at
Peterhead.
Grampian Region
Banff and Buchan District.

Rathillet, Cupar, Fife; Tayside,
Central and Fife at Cupar.
Fife Region
North East Fife District.

Ratho, Newbridge, Midlothian;
Lothian and Borders at Edinburgh.
Lothian Region
Midlothian District.

Rathven, Buckie, Morayshire;
Grampian, Highland and Islands at
Elgin.
Grampian Region
Moray District.

Rattray, Blairgowrie, Perthshire;
Tayside, Central and Fife at Perth.
Tayside Region
Perth and Kinross District.

Rattray, Peterhead, Aberdeenshire;
Grampian, Highland and Islands at
Peterhead.
Grampian Region
Banff and Buchan District.

Ravenstruther, Lanark; South
Strathclyde, Dumfries and
Galloway at Lanark.
Strathclyde Region
Clydesdale District.

Rawyards, Airdrie, Lanarkshire;
South Strathclyde, Dumfries and
Galloway at Airdrie.
Strathclyde Region
Monklands District.

Reading, Falkirk, Stirlingshire;
Tayside, Central and Fife at
Falkirk.
Central Region
Falkirk District.

Reay, Thurso, Caithness;
Grampian, Highland and Islands at
Wick.
Highland Region
Caithness District.

Reddingmuirhead, Falkirk
Stirlingshire; Tayside, Central and
Fife at Falkirk.
Central Region
Falkirk District.

Redgorton, Perth; Tayside, Central
and Fife at Perth.
Tayside Region
Perth and Kinross District.

Redland, Orkney; Grampian,
Highland and Islands at Kirkwall.
Orkney Islands Council.

Redpath, Earlston, Berwickshire;
Lothian and Borders at Selkirk.
Borders Region
Ettrick and Lauderdale District.

Reef, Isle of Lewis; Grampian, Highland and Islands at Stornoway.
Western Isles Islands Council.

Reiss, Wick, Caithness; Grampian, Highland and Islands at Wick.
Highland Region
Caithness District.

Rendall, Orkney; Grampian, Highland and Islands at Kirkwall.
Orkney Islands Council.

Renfrew, North Strathclyde at Paisley.
Strathclyde Region
Renfrew District.

Renton, Dumbarton; North Strathclyde at Dumbarton.
Strathclyde Region
Dumbarton District.

Resaurie, Smithton, Inverness; Grampian, Highland and Islands at Inverness.
Highland Region
Inverness District.

Rest-and-be-thankful, Arrochar, Dunbartonshire; North Strathclyde at Dumbarton.
Strathclyde Region
Dumbarton District.

Reston, Eyemouth, Berwickshire; Lothian and Borders at Duns.
Borders Region
Berwickshire District.

Rhenigidale, Isle of Harris; Grampian, Highland and Islands at Stornoway.
Western Isles Islands Council.

Rhiconich, Laxford Bridge, Sutherland; Grampian, Highland and Islands at Dornoch.
Highland Region
Sutherland District.

Ronehouse, Castle Douglas, Kirkcudbrightshire; South Strathclyde, Dumfries and Galloway at Kirkcudbright.
Dumfries and Galloway Region
Stewartry District.

Rhu, Helensburgh, Dunbartonshire; North Strathclyde at Dumbarton.
Strathclyde Region
Dumbarton District.

Rhu, Port Charlotte, Isle of Islay; North Strathclyde at Campbeltown.
Strathclyde Region
Argyll and Bute District.

Rhubadoch, Isle of Bute; North Strathclyde at Rothesay.
Strathclyde Region
Argyll and Bute District.

Rhuda Ban, Eriskay, Isle of South Uist; Grampian, Highland and Islands at Lochmaddy.
Western Isles Islands Council.

Rhugashinish, Lochboisdale, Isle of South Uist; Grampian, Highland and Islands at Lochmaddy.
Western Isles Islands Council.

Rhunahaorine, Tarbert, Argyll; North Strathclyde at Campbeltown.
Strathclyde Region
Argyll and Bute District.

Rhuvanish, Berneray, Isle of North
Uist; Grampian, Highland and
Islands at Lochmaddy.
Western Isles Islands Council.

Rhynd, Perth; Tayside, Central and
Fife at Perth.
Tayside Region
Perth and Kinross District.

Rhynie, Huntly, Aberdeenshire;
Grampian, Highland and Islands at
Aberdeen.
Grampian Region
Gordon District.

Riccarton, Hawick, Roxburghshire;
Lothian and Borders at Jedburgh.
Borders Region
Roxburgh District.

Riccarton, Kilmarnock, Ayrshire;
North Strathclyde at Kilmarnock.
Strathclyde Region
Kilmarnock and Loudoun District.

Rickarton, Stonehaven,
Kincardineshire; Grampian,
Highland and Islands at
Stonehaven.
Grampian Region
Kincardine and Deeside District.

Rigg, Gretna, Dumfriesshire; South
Strathclyde, Dumfries and
Galloway at Dumfries.
Dumfries and Galloway Region
Annandale and Eskdale District.

Riggend, Airdrie, Lanarkshire;
South Strathclyde, Dumfries and
Galloway at Airdrie.
Strathclyde Region
Monklands District.

Rigside, Lanark; South Strathclyde,
Dumfries and Galloway at Lanark.
Strathclyde Region
Clydesdale District.

Ringford, Castle Douglas,
Kirkcudbrightshire; South
Strathclyde, Dumfries and
Galloway at Kirkcudbright.
Dumfries and Galloway Region
Stewartry District.

Roadside, Inverbervie,
Kincardineshire; Grampian,
Highland and Islands at
Stonehaven.
Grampian Region
Kincardine and Deeside District.

Roberton, Biggar, Lanarkshire;
South Strathclyde, Dumfries and
Galloway at Lanark.
Strathclyde Region
Clydesdale District.

Roberton, Hawick, Roxburghshire;
Lothian and Borders at Jedburgh.
Borders Region
Roxburgh District.

Rockcliffe, Dalbeattie,
Kirkcudbrightshire; South
Strathclyde, Dumfries and
Galloway at Kirkcudbright.
Dumfries and Galloway Region
Stewartry District.

Rodel, Leverburgh, Isle of Harris;
Grampian, Highland and Islands at
Stornoway.
Western Isles Islands Council.

Rogart, Sutherland; Grampian,
Highland and Islands at Dornoch.
Highland Region
Sutherland District.

Romanno Bridge, West Linton, Peeblesshire; Lothian and Borders at Peebles.
Borders Region
Tweeddale District.

Ronay Islands, Lochmaddy, Isle of North Uist; Grampian, Highland and Islands at Lochmaddy.
Western Isles Islands Council.

Rora, Peterhead, Aberdeenshire; Grampian, Highland and Islands at Peterhead.
Grampian Region
Banff and Buchan District.

Roscobie, Forfar, Angus; Tayside, Central and Fife at Forfar.
Tayside Region
Angus District.

Rosebank, Stonehouse, Lanarkshire; South Strathclyde, Dumfries and Galloway at Hamilton.
Strathclyde Region
Hamilton District.

Rosehall, Lairg, Sutherland; Grampian, Highland and Islands at Dornoch.
Highland Region
Sutherland District.

Rosehearty, Fraserburgh, Aberdeenshire; Grampian, Highland and Islands at Banff.
Grampian Region
Banff and Buchan District.

Roseisle, Burghead, Morayshire; Grampian, Highland and Islands at Elgin.
Grampian Region
Moray District.

Rosemarkie, Fortrose, Ross-shire; Grampian, Highland and Islands at Dingwall.
Highland Region
Ross and Cromarty District.

Rosemount, Blairgowrie, Perthshire; Tayside, Central and Fife at Perth.
Tayside Region
Perth and Kinross District.

Roseneath, Helensburgh, Dunbartonshire; North Strathclyde at Dumbarton.
Strathclyde Region
Dumbarton District.

Rosewell, Midlothian; Lothian and Borders at Edinburgh.
Lothian Region
Midlothian District.

Rosinish, Eriskay, Isle of South Uist; Grampian, Highland and Islands at Lochmaddy.
Western Isles Islands Council.

Roslin, Midlothian; Lothian and Borders at Edinburgh.
Lothian Region
Midlothian District.

Rosslynlee, Roslin, Midlothian; Lothian and Borders at Edinburgh.
Lothian Region
Midlothian District.

Rosyth, Dunfermline, Fife; Tayside, Central and Fife at Dunfermline.
Fife Region
Dunfermline District.

Rothes, Elgin, Morayshire;
Grampian, Highland and Islands at
Elgin.
Grampian Region
Moray District.

Rothesay, Isle of Bute; North
Strathclyde at Rothesay.
Strathclyde Region
Argyll and Bute District.

Rothiemay, Keith, Morayshire;
Grampian, Highland and Islands at
Elgin.
Grampian Region
Moray District.

Rothienorman, Turriff, Banffshire;
Grampian, Highland and Islands at
Banff.
Grampian Region
Banff and Buchan District.

Roundyhill, Forfar, Angus;
Tayside, Central and Fife at
Forfar.
Tayside Region
Angus District.

Rousay, Orkney; Grampian,
Highland and Islands at Kirkwall.
Orkney Islands Council.

Rowanburn, Canonbie,
Dumfriesshire; South Strath-
clyde, Dumfries and Galloway at
Dumfries.
Dumfries and Galloway Region
Annandale and Eskdale District.

Rowardennan, Glasgow; Tayside,
Central and Fife at Stirling.
Central Region
Stirling District.

Roxburgh, Kelso, Roxburghshire;
Lothian and Borders at Jedburgh.
Borders Region
Roxburgh District.

Roy Bridge, Spean Bridge,
Inverness-shire; Grampian,
Highland and Islands at Fort
William.
Highland Region
Lochaber District.

Ruaig, Scarinish, Isle of Tiree;
North Strathclyde at Oban.
Strathclyde Region
Argyll and Bute District.

Rudhu, Lochmaddy, Isle of North
Uist; Grampian, Highland and
Islands at Lochmaddy.
Western Isles Islands Council.

Rumbling Bridge, Kinross;
Tayside, Central and Fife at Perth.
Tayside Region
Perth and Kinross District.

Rumford, Falkirk, Stirlingshire;
Tayside, Central and Fife at
Falkirk.
Central Region
Falkirk District.

Rushgarry, Berneray, Isle of North
Uist; Grampian, Highland and
Islands at Lochmaddy.
Western Isles Islands Council.

Ruskie, Stirling; Tayside, Central
and Fife at Stirling.
Central Region
Stirling District.

Rutherglen, Glasgow; Glasgow
and Strathkelvin at Glasgow.
Strathclyde Region
City of Glasgow District.

Ruthven, Blairgowrie, Perthshire;
Tayside, Central and Fife at Perth.
Tayside Region
Perth and Kinross District.

Ruthven, Huntly, Aberdeenshire;
Grampian, Highland and Islands at
Aberdeen.
Grampian Region
Gordon District.

Ruthven, Kingussie, Inverness-
shire; Grampian, Highland and
Islands at Inverness.
Highland Region
Badenoch and Strathspey District.

Ruthwell, Dumfries; South
Strathclyde, Dumfries and
Galloway at Dumfries.
Dumfries and Galloway Region
Nithsdale District.

Ryelands, Strathaven, Lanarkshire;
South Strathclyde, Dumfries and
Galloway at Hamilton.
Strathclyde Region
Hamilton District.

Saddell, Campbeltown, Argyll;
North Strathclyde at
Campbeltown.
Strathclyde Region
Argyll and Bute District.

Salen, Acharacle, Strontian, Argyll;
Grampian, Highland and Islands at
Fort William.
Highland Region
Lochaber District.

Salen, Isle of Mull; North
Strathclyde at Oban.
Strathclyde Region
Argyll and Bute District.

Saline, Dunfermline; Tayside,
Central and Fife at Dunfermline.
Tayside Region
Dunfermline District.

Salmondsmuir, Arbroath, Angus;
Tayside, Central and Fife at
Arbroath.
Tayside Region
Angus District.

Salsburgh, Shotts, Lanarkshire;
South Strathclyde, Dumfries and
Galloway at Airdrie.
Strathclyde Region
Motherwell District.

Saltburn, Invergordon, Ross-shire;
Grampian, Highland and Islands at
Tain.
Highland Region
Ross and Cromarty District.

Saltcoats, Ayrshire; North
Strathclyde at Kilmarnock.
Strathclyde Region
Cunninghame District.

Sanaigmore, Isle of Islay; North
Strathclyde at Campbeltown.
Strathclyde Region
Argyll and Bute District.

Sand Laide, Isle of Tiree; North
Strathclyde at Oban.
Strathclyde Region
Argyll and Bute District.

Sanday, Orkney; Grampian,
Highland and Islands at Kirkwall.
Orkney Islands Council.

Sandbank, Dunoon, Argyll; North
Strathclyde at Dunoon.
Strathclyde Region
Argyll and Bute District.

Sandend, Banff; Grampian,
Highland and Islands at Banff.
Grampian Region
Banff and Buchan District.

Sandford, Strathaven, Lanarkshire;
South Strathclyde, Dumfries and
Galloway at Hamilton.
Strathclyde Region
Hamilton District.

Sandgarth, Shapinsay, Orkney;
Grampian, Highland and Islands at
Kirkwall.
Orkney Islands Council.

Sandhaven, Fraserburgh,
Aberdeenshire; Grampian,
Highland and Islands at Banff.
Grampian Region
Banff and Buchan District.

Sandhead, Stranraer,
Wigtownshire; South Strathclyde,
Dumfries and Galloway at
Stranraer.
Dumfries and Galloway Region
Wigtown District.

Sandilands, Lanark; South
Strathclyde, Dumfries and
Galloway at Lanark.
Strathclyde Region
Clydesdale District.

Sandness, Lerwick, Shetland;
Grampian, Highland and Islands at
Lerwick.
Shetland Islands Council.

Sandveien, Lerwick, Shetland;
Grampian, Highland and Islands at
Lerwick.
Shetland Islands Council.

Sandvig, Lochcarnan, Isle of South
Uist; Grampian, Highland and
Islands at Lochmaddy.
Western Isles Islands Council.

Sandwick, Isle of Lewis; Grampian,
Highland and Islands at
Stornoway.
Western Isles Islands Council.

Sandwick, Shetland; Grampian,
Highland and Islands at Lerwick.
Shetland Islands Council.

Sandwick, Stromness, Orkney;
Grampian, Highland and Islands at
Kirkwall.
Orkney Islands Council.

Sandyhills, Dalbeattie,
Kirkcudbrightshire; South
Strathclyde, Dumfries and
Galloway at Kirkcudbright.
Dumfries and Galloway Region
Stewartry District.

Sandyhills, Glasgow; Glasgow and
Strathkelvin at Glasgow.
Strathclyde Region
City of Glasgow District.

Sangobeg, Durness, Lairg,
Sutherland; Grampian, Highland
and Islands at Dornoch.
Highland Region
Sutherland District.

Sangomore, Durness, Lairg,
Sutherland; Grampian, Highland
and Islands at Dornoch.
Highland Region
Sutherland District.

Sannox, Brodick, Isle of Arran;
North Strathclyde at Kilmarnock.
Strathclyde Region
Cunninghame District.

Sanquhar, Dumfriesshire; South
Strathclyde, Dumfries and
Galloway at Dumfries.
Dumfries and Galloway Region
Nithsdale District.

Sarclet, Thrumster, Wick,
Caithness; Grampian, Highland
and Islands at Wick.
Highland Region
Caithness District.

Sartle, Staffin, Portree, Isle of Skye;
Grampian, Highland and Islands at
Portree.
Highland Region
Skye and Lochalsh District.

Satran, Carbost, Sligachan, Isle of
Skye; Grampian, Highland and
Islands at Portree.
Highland Region
Skye and Lochalsh District.

Sauchen, Inverurie, Aberdeenshire;
Grampian, Highland and Islands at
Aberdeen.
Grampian Region
Gordon District.

Sauchie, Alloa, Clackmannanshire;
Tayside, Central and Fife at Alloa.
Central Region
Clackmannan District.

Sauchieburn, Stirling; Tayside,
Central and Fife at Stirling.
Central Region
Stirling District.

Saughton, Edinburgh; Lothian and
Borders at Edinburgh.
Lothian Region
City of Edinburgh District.

Saughtree, Hawick, Roxburghshire;
Lothian and Borders at Jedburgh.
Borders Region
Roxburgh District.

Scadabay, Isle of Harris;
Grampian, Highland and Islands at
Stornoway.
Western Isles Islands Council.

Scaladale, Isle of Harris; Grampian,
Highland and Islands at
Stornoway.
Western Isles Islands Council.

Scalasaig, Isle of Colonsay; North
Strathclyde at Oban.
Strathclyde Region
Argyll and Bute District.

Scaliscro, Isle of Lewis; Grampian,
Highland and Islands at
Stornoway.
Western Isles Islands Council.

Scalloway, Lerwick, Shetland;
Grampian, Highland and Islands at
Lerwick.
Shetland Islands Council.

Scardroy, Marybank, Strathconan,
Ross-shire; Grampian, Highland
and Islands at Dingwall.
Highland Region
Ross and Cromarty District.

Scarfskerry, Thurso, Caithness;
Grampian, Highland and Islands at
Wick.
Highland Region
Caithness District.

Scarinish, Isle of Tiree; North
Strathclyde at Oban.
Strathclyde Region
Argyll and Bute District.

Scarista, Isle of Harris; Grampian,
Highland and Islands at
Stornoway.
Western Isles Islands Council.

Scarp, Isle of Harris; Grampian,
Highland and Islands at
Stornoway.
Western Isles Islands Council.

Scolpaig, Lochmaddy, Isle of North
Uist; Grampian, Highland and
Islands at Lochmaddy.
Western Isles Islands Council.

Scone, Perth; Tayside, Central and
Fife at Perth.
Tayside Region
Perth and Kinross District.

Sconser, Broadford, Isle of Skye;
Grampian, Highland and Islands at
Portree.
Highland Region
Skye and Lochalsh District.

Scorguie, Inverness; Grampian,
Highland and Islands at Inverness.
Highland Region
Inverness District.

Scotlandwell, Kinross; Tayside,
Central and Fife at Perth.
Tayside Region
Perth and Kinross District.

Scotscalder, Halkirk, Caithness;
Grampian, Highland and Islands at
Wick.
Highland Region
Caithness District.

Scotvein, Lochmaddy, Isle of North
Uist; Grampian, Highland and
Islands at Lochmaddy.
Western Isles Islands Council.

Scourie, Lairg, Sutherland;
Grampian, Highland and Islands at
Dornoch.
Highland Region
Sutherland District.

Scousburgh, Shetland; Grampian,
Highland and Islands at Lerwick.
Shetland Islands Council.

Scrabster, Thurso, Caithness;
Grampian, Highland and Islands at
Wick.
Highland Region
Caithness District.

Seafield, Bathgate, West Lothian;
Lothian and Borders at Linlithgow.
Lothian Region
West Lothian District.

Seaforth Head, Isle of Lewis;
Grampian, Highland and Islands at
Stornoway.
Western Isles Islands Council.

Seamill, Ardrossan, Ayrshire; North
Strathclyde at Kilmarnock.
Strathclyde Region
Cunninghame District.

Seilebost, Isle of Harris; Grampian,
Highland and Islands at
Stornoway.
Western Isles Islands Council.

Selkirk; Lothian and Borders at
Selkirk.
Borders Region
Ettrick and Lauderdale District.

Sellafirth, Yell, Shetland;
Grampian, Highland and Islands at
Lerwick.
Shetland Islands Council.

Shandon, Helensburgh,
Dunbartonshire; North Strathclyde
at Dumbarton.
Strathclyde Region
Dumbarton District.

Shandwick, Fearn, Ross-shire;
Grampian, Highland and Islands at
Tain.
Highland Region
Ross and Cromarty District.

Shannochie, Brodick, Isle of Arran;
North Strathclyde at Kilmarnock.
Strathclyde Region
Cunninghame District.

Shawbost, Isle of Lewis; Grampian,
Highland and Islands at
Stornoway.
Western Isles Islands Council.

Shawhead, Dumfries; South
Strathclyde, Dumfries and
Galloway at Dumfries.
Dumfries and Galloway Region
Nithsdale District.

Sheardale, Dollar,
Clackmannanshire; Tayside,
Central and Fife at Alloa.
Central Region
Clackmannan District.

Shearington, Dumfries; South
Strathclyde, Dumfries and
Galloway at Dumfries.
Dumfries and Galloway Region
Nithsdale District.

Shebster, Thurso, Caithness;
Grampian, Highland and Islands at
Wick.
Highland Region
Caithness District.

Sheriffmuir, Dunblane, Perthshire;
Tayside, Central and Fife at Perth.
Tayside Region
Perth and Kinross District.

Sheshader, Isle of Lewis;
Grampian, Highland and Islands at
Stornoway.
Western Isles Islands Council.

Shielbridge, Kyle of Lochalsh,
Ross-shire; Grampian, Highland
and Islands at Dingwall.
Highland Region
Skye and Lochalsh District.

Shieldaig, Strathcarron, Ross-
shire; Grampian, Highland and
Islands at Dingwall.
Highland Region
Ross and Cromarty District.

Shieldhill, Falkirk, Stirlingshire;
Tayside, Central and Fife at
Falkirk.
Central Region
Falkirk District.

Shieldhill, Lochmaben,
Dumfriesshire; South Strath-
clyde, Dumfries and Galloway at
Dumfries.
Dumfries and Galloway Region
Annandale and Eskdale District.

Shieldnish, Isle of Lewis; Grampian, Highland and Islands at Stornoway.
Western Isles Islands Council.

Shillford, Barrhead, Renfrewshire; North Strathclyde at Paisley.
Strathclyde Region
Renfrew District.

Shiskine, Brodick, Isle of Arran; North Strathclyde at Kilmarnock.
Strathclyde Region
Cunninghame District.

Shotts, Lanarkshire; South Strathclyde, Dumfries and Galloway at Hamilton.
Strathclyde Region
Motherwell District.

Shulishader, Isle of Lewis; Grampian, Highland and Islands at Stornoway.
Western Isles Islands Council.

Shuna Island, Appin, Argyll; North Strathclyde at Oban.
Strathclyde Region
Argyll and Bute District.

Sibbaldie, Lockerbie, Dumfriesshire; South Strathclyde, Dumfries and Galloway at Dumfries.
Dumfries and Galloway Region
Annandale and Eskdale District.

Sidinish, Lochmaddy, Isle of North Uist; Grampian, Highland and Islands at Lochmaddy.
Western Isles Islands Council.

Sighthill, Edinburgh; Lothian and Borders at Edinburgh.
Lothian Region
City of Edinburgh District.

Silverburn, Penicuik, Midlothian; Lothian and Borders at Edinburgh.
Lothian Region
Midlothian District.

Sinclairshill, Duns, Berwickshire; Lothian and Borders at Duns.
Borders Region
Berwickshire District.

Sinclairston, Cumnock, Ayrshire; South Strathclyde, Dumfries and Galloway at Ayr.
Strathclyde Region
Cumnock and Doon Valley District.

Sinnahard, Glenkindie, Alford, Aberdeenshire; Grampian, Highland and Islands at Aberdeen.
Grampian Region
Gordon District.

Skail, Orkney; Grampian, Highland and Islands at Kirkwall.
Orkney Islands Council.

Skaill, Thurso, Caithness; Grampian, Highland and Islands at Wick.
Highland Region
Caithness District.

Skallary, Castlebay, Isle of Barra; Grampian, Highland and Islands at Lochmaddy.
Western Isles Islands Council.

Skares, Cumnock, Ayrshire; South Strathclyde, Dumfries and Galloway at Ayr.
Strathclyde Region
Cumnock and Doon Valley District.

Skeabost Bridge, Portree, Isle of Skye; Grampian, Highland and Islands at Portree.
Highland Region
Skye and Lochalsh District.

Skelbo, Dornoch, Sutherland; Grampian, Highland and Islands at Dornoch.
Highland Region
Sutherland District.

Skellister, Shetland; Grampian, Highland and Islands at Lerwick.
Shetland Islands Council.

Skelmorlie, Ayrshire; North Strathclyde at Kilmarnock.
Strathclyde Region
Cunninghame District.

Skene, Aberdeenshire; Grampian, Highland and Islands at Aberdeen.
Grampian Region
City of Aberdeen District.

Skerray, Tongue, Sutherland; Grampian, Highland and Islands at Dornoch.
Highland Region
Sutherland District.

Skigersta, Isle of Lewis; Grampian, Highland and Islands at Stornoway.
Western Isles Islands Council.

Skinflats, Falkirk; Tayside, Central and Fife at Falkirk.
Central Region
Falkirk District.

Skinidin, Dunvegan, Isle of Skye; Grampian, Highland and Islands at Portree.
Highland Region
Skye and Lochalsh District.

Skinnet, Talmine, Tongue, Sutherland; Grampian, Highland and Islands at Dornoch.
Highland Region
Sutherland District.

Skipness, Tarbert, Argyll; North Strathclyde at Campbeltown.
Strathclyde Region
Argyll and Bute District.

Skirling, Biggar, Lanarkshire; Lothian and Borders at Peebles.
Borders Region
Tweeddale District.

Skulamus, Broadford, Isle of Skye; Grampian, Highland and Islands at Portree.
Highland Region
Skye and Lochalsh District.

Slamannan, Falkirk, Stirlingshire; Tayside, Central and Fife at Falkirk.
Central Region
Falkirk District.

Slateford, Edinburgh; Lothian and Borders at Edinburgh.
Lothian Region
City of Edinburgh District.

Slattadale, Achnasheen, Ross-shire; Grampian, Highland and Islands at Dingwall.
Highland Region
Ross and Cromarty District.

Sliddery, Brodick, Isle of Arran; North Strathclyde at Kilmarnock.
Strathclyde Region
Cunninghame District.

Sligachan, Portree, Isle of Skye; Grampian, Highland and Islands at Portree.
Highland Region
Skye and Lochalsh District.

Sluggans, Portree, Isle of Skye; Grampian, Highland and Islands at Portree.
Highland Region
Skye and Lochalsh District.

Smailholm, Kelso, Roxburghshire; Lothian and Borders at Jedburgh.
Borders Region
Roxburgh District.

Smerclate, Lochboisdale, Isle of South Uist; Grampian, Highland and Islands at Lochmaddy.
Western Isles Islands Council.

Smithton, Inverness; Grampian, Highland and Islands at Inverness.
Highland Region
Inverness District.

Snishival, Lochboisdale, Isle of South Uist; Grampian, Highland and Islands at Lochmaddy.
Western Isles Islands Council.

Snizort, Portree, Isle of Skye; Grampian, Highland and Islands at Portree.
Highland Region
Skye and Lochalsh District.

Sollas, Lochmaddy, Isle of North Uist; Grampian, Highland and Islands at Lochmaddy.
Western Isles Islands Council.

Solsgirth, Dollar, Clackmannanshire; Tayside, Central and Fife at Dunfermline.
Fife Region
Dunfermline District.

Sorbie, Newton Stewart, Wigtownshire; South Strathclyde, Dumfries and Galloway at Stranraer.
Dumfries and Galloway Region
Wigtown District.

Sorisdale, Isle of Coll; North Strathclyde at Oban.
Strathclyde Region
Argyll and Bute District.

Sorn, Mauchline, Ayrshire; South Strathclyde, Dumfries and Galloway at Ayr.
Strathclyde Region
Kyle and Carrick District.

Soroba, Oban, Argyll; North Strathclyde at Oban.
Strathclyde Region
Argyll and Bute District.

South Bragar, Isle of Lewis; Grampian, Highland and Islands at Stornoway.
Western Isles Islands Council.

South Clunes, Kirkhill, Inverness; Grampian, Highland and Islands at Inverness.
Highland Region
Inverness District.

South Cuan, Oban, Argyll; North Strathclyde at Oban.
Strathclyde Region
Argyll and Bute District.

South Dell, Isle of Lewis; Grampian, Highland and Islands at Stornoway.
Western Isles Islands Council.

South Duntulm, Portree, Isle of Skye; Grampian, Highland and Islands at Portree.
Highland Region
Skye and Lochalsh District.

South Erradale, Gairloch, Ross-shire; Grampian, Highland and Islands at Dingwall.
Highland Region
Ross and Cromarty District.

South Galson, Isle of Lewis; Grampian, Highland and Islands at Stornoway.
Western Isles Islands Council.

South Glendale, Lochboisdale, Isle of South Uist; Grampian, Highland and Islands at Lochmaddy.
Western Isles Islands Council.

South Laggan, Spean Bridge, Inverness-shire; Grampian, Highland and Islands at Fort William.
Highland Region
Lochaber District.

South Queensferry, Edinburgh; Lothian and Borders at Edinburgh.
Lothian Region
City of Edinburgh District.

South Shawbost, Isle of Lewis; Grampian, Highland and Islands at Stornoway.
Western Isles Islands Council.

Southdean, Jedburgh, Roxburghshire; Lothian and Borders at Jedburgh.
Borders Region
Roxburgh District.

Southend, Campbeltown, Argyll; North Strathclyde at Campbeltown.
Strathclyde Region
Argyll and Bute District.

Southerness, Dumfries; South Strathclyde, Dumfries and Galloway at Dumfries.
Dumfries and Galloway Region
Nithsdale District.

Southmuir, Kirriemuir, Angus; Tayside, Central and Fife at Forfar.
Tayside Region
Angus District.

Southwick, Dumfries; South Strathclyde, Dumfries and Galloway at Dumfries.
Dumfries and Galloway Region
Nithsdale District.

Spean Bridge, Inverness-shire; Grampian, Highland and Islands at Fort William.
Highland Region
Lochaber District.

Speddoch, Dumfries; South
Strathclyde, Dumfries and
Galloway at Dumfries.
Dumfries and Galloway Region
Nithsdale District.

Spey Bay, Fochabers, Morayshire;
Grampian, Highland and Islands at
Elgin.
Grampian Region
Moray District.

Spinningdale, Bonar Bridge,
Sutherland; Grampian, Highland
and Islands at Dornoch.
Highland Region
Sutherland District.

Spittal of Glenshee, Perthshire;
Tayside, Central and Fife at Perth.
Tayside Region
Perth and Kinross District.

Spittal, Halkirk, Caithness;
Grampian, Highland and Islands at
Wick.
Highland Region
Caithness District.

Spittalfield, Perth; Tayside, Central
and Fife at Perth.
Tayside Region
Perth and Kinross District.

Sponish, Lochmaddy, Isle of North
Uist; Grampian, Highland and
Islands at Lochmaddy.
Western Isles Islands Council.

Spott, Dunbar, East Lothian;
Lothian and Borders at
Haddington.
Lothian Region
East Lothian District.

Springfield, Cupar, Fife; Tayside,
Central and Fife at Cupar.
Fife Region
North East Fife District.

Springholm, Castle Douglas,
Kirkcudbrightshire; South
Strathclyde, Dumfries and
Galloway at Kirkcudbright.
Dumfries and Galloway Region
Stewartry District.

Springside, Irvine, Ayrshire; North
Strathclyde at Kilmarnock.
Strathclyde Region
Cunninghame District.

Sprouston, Kelso, Roxburghshire;
Lothian and Borders at Jedburgh.
Borders Region
Roxburgh District.

St Abbs, Eyemouth, Berwickshire;
Lothian and Borders at Duns.
Borders Region
Berwickshire District.

St Andrews, Fife; Tayside, Central
and Fife at Cupar.
Fife Region
North East Fife District.

St Ann's, Lockerbie, Dumfriesshire;
South Strathclyde, Dumfries and
Galloway at Dumfries.
Dumfries and Galloway Region
Annandale and Eskdale District.

St Boswells, Melrose,
Roxburghshire; Lothian and
Borders at Selkirk.
Borders Region
Ettrick and Lauderdale District.

St Catherines, Cairndow, Argyll;
North Strathclyde at Dunoon.
Strathclyde Region
Argyll and Bute District.

St Combs, Fraserburgh,
Aberdeenshire; Grampian,
Highland and Islands at
Peterhead.
Grampian Region
Banff and Buchan District.

St Cyrus, Montrose, Angus;
Grampian, Highland and Islands at
Stonehaven.
Grampian Region
Kincardine and Deeside District.

St Fergus, Peterhead,
Aberdeenshire; Grampian,
Highland and Islands at
Peterhead.
Grampian Region
Banff and Buchan District.

St Fillans, Crieff, Perthshire;
Tayside, Central and Fife at Perth.
Tayside Region
Perth and Kinross District.

St Katherines, Inverurie,
Aberdeenshire; Grampian,
Highland and Islands at Aberdeen.
Grampian Region
Gordon District.

St Margaret's Hope, Orkney;
Grampian, Highland and Islands at
Kirkwall.
Orkney Islands Council.

St Martins, Perth; Tayside, Central
and Fife at Perth.
Tayside Region
Perth and Kinross District.

St Mary's, Orkney; Grampian,
Highland and Islands at Kirkwall.
Orkney Islands Council.

St Michael's, St Andrews, Fife;
Tayside, Central and Fife at
Cupar.
Fife Region
North East Fife District.

St Monance, Anstruther, Fife;
Tayside, Central and Fife at
Cupar.
Fife Region
North East Fife District.

St Mungo, Lockerbie,
Dumfriesshire; South Strath-
clyde, Dumfries and Galloway at
Dumfries.
Dumfries and Galloway Region
Annandale and Esdale District.

St Ninians, Stirling; Tayside,
Central and Fife at Stirling.
Central Region
Stirling District.

St Ola, Kirkwall, Orkney; Grampian,
Highland and Islands at Kirkwall.
Orkney Islands Council.

St Phillans, Skelmorlie, Ayrshire;
North Strathclyde at Kilmarnock.
Strathclyde Region
Cunninghame District.

St Quivox, Ayr; South Strathclyde,
Dumfries and Galloway at Ayr.
Strathclyde Region
Kyle and Carrick District.

St Vigeans, Arbroath, Angus;
Tayside, Central and Fife at
Arbroath.
Tayside Region
Angus District.

Staffin, Portree, Isle of Skye;
Grampian, Highland and Islands at
Portree.
Highland Region
Skye and Lochalsh District.

Stair, Mauchline, Ayrshire; South
Strathclyde, Dumfries and
Galloway at Ayr.
Strathclyde Region
Kyle and Carrick District.

Stand, Airdrie, Lanarkshire; South
Strathclyde, Dumfries and
Galloway at Airdrie.
Strathclyde Region
Monklands District.

Standburn, Falkirk, Stirlingshire;
Tayside, Central and Fife at
Falkirk.
Central Region
Falkirk District.

Stane, Shotts, Lanarkshire; South
Strathclyde, Dumfries and
Galloway at Hamilton.
Strathclyde Region
Motherwell District.

Stanley, Perth; Tayside, Central
and Fife at Perth.
Tayside Region
Perth and Kinross District.

Star, Glenrothes, Fife; Tayside,
Central and Fife at Kirkcaldy.
Fife Region
Kirkcaldy District.

Staxigoe, Wick, Caithness;
Grampian, Highland and Islands at
Wick.
Highland Region
Caithness District.

Steelend, Dunfermline, Fife;
Tayside, Central and Fife at
Dunfermline.
Fife Region
Dunfermline District.

Stein, Waternish, Dunvegan, Isle of
Skye; Grampian, Highland and
Islands at Portree.
Highland Region
Skye and Lochalsh District.

Steinish, Isle of Lewis; Grampian,
Highland and Islands at
Stornoway.
Western Isles Islands Council.

Stenhousemuir, Falkirk,
Stirlingshire; Tayside, Central and
Fife at Falkirk.
Central Region
Falkirk District.

Stenness, Stromness, Orkney;
Grampian, Highland and Islands at
Kirkwall.
Orkney Islands Council.

Stenscholl, Staffin, Portree, Isle of
Skye; Grampian, Highland and
Islands at Portree.
Highland Region
Skye and Lochalsh District.

Stenton, Dunbar, East Lothian;
Lothian and Borders at
Haddington.
Lothian Region
East Lothian District.

Stepps, Glasgow; Glasgow and Strathkelvin at Glasgow.
Strathclyde Region
City of Glasgow District.

Stevenston, Ayrshire; North Strathclyde at Kilmarnock.
Strathclyde Region
Cunninghame District.

Stewarton, Campbeltown, Argyll; North Strathclyde at Campbeltown.
Strathclyde Region
Argyll and Bute District.

Stewarton, Kilmarnock, Ayrshire; North Strathclyde at Kilmarnock.
Strathclyde Region
Kilmarnock and Loudoun District.

Stichill, Kelso, Roxburgh; Lothian and Borders at Jedburgh.
Borders Region
Roxburgh District.

Stilligarry, Isle of South Uist; Grampian, Highland and Islands at Lochmaddy.
Western Isles Islands Council.

Stirling; Tayside Central and Fife at Stirling.
Central Region
Stirling District.

Stirling, Peterhead, Aberdeenshire; Grampian, Highland and Islands at Peterhead.
Grampian Region
Banff and Buchan District.

Stobo, Peeblesshire; Lothian and Borders at Peebles.
Borders Region
Tweeddale District.

Stobs, Hawick, Roxburghshire; Lothian and Borders at Jedburgh.
Borders Region
Roxburgh District.

Stockinish, Isle of Harris; Grampian, Highland and Islands at Stornoway.
Western Isles Islands Council.

Stoer, Lochinver, Sutherland; Grampian, Highland and Islands at Dornoch.
Highland Region
Sutherland District.

Stonebyres, Lanark; South Strathclyde, Dumfries and Galloway at Lanark.
Strathclyde Region
Clydesdale District.

Stonefield, Blantyre, Glasgow; South Strathclyde, Dumfries and Galloway at Hamilton.
Strathclyde Region
Hamilton District.

Stonefield, Tarbert, Argyll; North Strathclyde at Campbeltown.
Strathclyde Region
Argyll and Bute District.

Stonehaven, Kincardineshire; Grampian, Highland and Islands at Stonehaven.
Grampian Region
Kincardine and Deeside District.

Stonehouse, Strathaven, Lanarkshire; South Strathclyde, Dumfries and Galloway at Hamilton.
Strathclyde Region
Hamilton District.

Stoneybridge, Isle of Uist;
Grampian, Highland and Islands at
Lochmaddy.
Western Isles Islands Council.

Stoneyburn, Bathgate, West
Lothian; Lothian and Borders at
Linlithgow.
Lothian Region
West Lothian District.

Stoneykirk, Stranraer,
Wigtownshire; South Strathclyde,
Dumfries and Galloway at
Stranraer.
Dumfries and Galloway Region
Wigtown District.

Stoneywood, Bucksburn,
Aberdeen; Grampian, Highland
and Islands at Aberdeen.
Grampian Region
City of Aberdeen District.

Stoneywood, Denny, Stirlingshire;
Tayside, Central and Fife at
Falkirk.
Central Region
Falkirk District.

Stormontfield, Perth; Tayside,
Central and Fife at Perth.
Tayside Region
Perth and Kinross District.

Stornoway, Isle of Lewis;
Grampian, Highland and Islands at
Stornoway.
Western Isles Islands Council.

Stow, Galashiels, Selkirkshire;
Lothian and Borders at Selkirk.
Borders Region
Ettrick and Lauderdale District.

Straad, Rothesay, Isle of Bute;
North Strathclyde at Rothesay.
Strathclyde Region
Argyll and Bute District.

Strachan, Banchory,
Kincardineshire; Grampian,
Highland and Islands at
Stonehaven.
Grampian Region
Kincardine and Deeside District.

Strachur, Cairndow, Argyll; North
Strathclyde at Dunoon.
Strathclyde Region
Argyll and Bute District.

Straiton, Loanhead, Midlothian;
Lothian and Borders at Edinburgh.
Lothian Region
Midlothian District.

Straiton, Maybole, Ayrshire; South
Strathclyde, Dumfries and
Galloway at Ayr.
Strathclyde Region
Kyle and Carrick District.

Stranraer, Wigtownshire; South
Strathclyde, Dumfries and
Galloway at Stranraer.
Dumfries and Galloway Region
Wigtown District.

Strath, Gairloch, Ross-shire;
Grampian, Highland and Islands at
Dingwall.
Highland Region
Ross and Cromarty District.

Strath Tummel, Pitlochry,
Perthshire; Tayside, Central and
Fife at Perth.
Tayside Region
Perth and Kinross District.

Strathaird, Broadford, Isle of Skye;
Grampian, Highland and Islands at
Portree.
Highland Region
Skye and Lochalsh District.

Strathaven, Lanarkshire; South
Strathclyde, Dumfries and
Galloway at Hamilton.
Strathclyde Region
Hamilton District.

Strathblane, Glasgow; Tayside,
Central and Fife at Stirling.
Central Region
Stirling District.

Strathcarron, Ross-shire;
Grampian, Highland and Islands at
Dingwall.
Highland Region
Ross and Cromarty District.

Strathconon, Muir of Ord, Ross-
shire; Grampian, Highland and
Islands at Dingwall.
Highland Region
Ross and Cromarty District.

Strathdon, Aberdeenshire;
Grampian, Highland and Islands at
Aberdeen.
Grampian Region
Gordon District.

Strathkanaird, Ullapool, Ross-
shire; Grampian, Highland and
Islands at Dingwall.
Highland Region
Ross and Cromarty District.

Strathkinnes, St Andrews, Fife;
Tayside, Central and Fife at
Cupar.
Fife Region
North East Fife District.

Strathlachan, Cairndow, Argyll;
North Strathclyde at Dunoon.
Strathclyde Region
Argyll and Bute District.

Strathmartine, Dundee; Tayside,
Central and Fife at Dundee.
Tayside Region
City of Dundee District.

Strathmiglo, Cupar, Fife; Tayside,
Central and Fife at Cupar.
Fife Region
North East Fife District.

Strathore, Kirkcaldy, Fife; Tayside,
Central and Fife at Kirkcaldy.
Fife Region
Kirkcaldy District.

Strathpeffer, Dingwall, Ross-shire;
Grampian, Highland and Islands at
Dingwall.
Highland Region
Ross and Cromarty District.

Strathrusdale, Alness, Ross-shire;
Grampian, Highland and Islands at
Tain.
Highland Region
Ross and Cromarty District.

Strathtay, Pitlochry, Perthshire;
Tayside, Central and Fife at Perth.
Tayside Region
Perth and Kinross District.

Strathy, Melvich, Thurso,
Caithness; Grampian, Highland
and Islands at Dornoch.
Highland Region
Sutherland District.

Strathyre, Callander, Stirlingshire;
Tayside, Central and Fife at
Stirling.
Central Region
Stirling District.

Strichen, Fraserburgh,
Aberdeenshire; Grampian,
Highland and Islands at
Peterhead.
Grampian Region
Banff and Buchan District.

Strollamus, Broadford, Isle of
Skye; Grampian, Highland and
Islands at Portree.
Highland Region
Skye and Lochalsh District.

Strombane, Isle of North Uist;
Grampian, Highland and Islands at
Lochmaddy.
Western Isles Islands Council.

Stromeferry, Strathcarron, Ross-
shire; Grampian, Highland and
Islands at Dingwall.
Highland Region
Ross and Cromarty District.

Stromness, Orkney; Grampian,
Highland and Islands at Kirkwall.
Orkney Islands Council.

Stronachlachar, Stirling; Tayside,
Central and Fife at Stirling.
Central Region
Stirling District.

Stronachullin, Ardrishaig, Argyll;
North Strathclyde at Dunoon.
Strathclyde Region
Argyll and Bute District.

Strond, Leverburgh, Isle of Harris;
Grampian, Highland and Islands at
Stornoway.
Western Isles Islands Council.

Strone, Dunoon, Argyll; North
Strathclyde at Dunoon.
Strathclyde Region
Argyll and Bute District.

Stronord, Newton Stewart,
Wigtownshire; South Strathclyde,
Dumfries and Galloway at
Stranraer.
Dumfries and Galloway Region
Wigtown District.

Stronsay, Orkney; Grampian,
Highland and Islands at Kirkwall.
Orkney Islands Council.

Strontian, Acharacle, Argyll;
Grampian, Highland and Islands at
Fort William.
Highland Region
Lochaber District.

Struan, Isle of Skye; Grampian,
Highland and Islands at Portree.
Highland Region
Skye and Lochalsh District.

Struan, Malaclate, Isle of North
Uist; Grampian, Highland and
Islands at Lochmaddy.
Western Isles Islands Council.

Strumore, Isle of North Uist;
Grampian, Highland and Islands at
Lochmaddy.
Western Isles Islands Council.

Struy, Beauly, Inverness;
Grampian, Highland and Islands at
Inverness.
Highland Region
Inverness District.

Stuartfield, Peterhead,
Aberdeenshire; Grampian,
Highland and Islands at
Peterhead.
Grampian Region
Banff and Buchan District.

Succoth, Arrochar, Dunbartonshire;
North Strathclyde at Dumbarton.
Strathclyde Region
Dumbarton District.

Sullom Voe, Shetland; Grampian,
Highland and Islands at Lerwick.
Shetland Islands Council.

Sumburgh, Shetland; Grampian,
Highland and Islands at Lerwick.
Shetland Islands Council.

Sunamul Island, Isle of Benbecula;
Grampian, Highland and Islands at
Lochmaddy.
Western Isles Islands Council.

Sunnyside, Coatbridge,
Lanarkshire; South Strathclyde,
Dumfries and Galloway at Airdrie.
Strathclyde Region
Monklands District.

Swainbost, Isle of Lewis;
Grampian, Highland and Islands at
Stornoway.
Western Isles Islands Council.

Swanston, Midlothian; Lothian and
Borders at Edinburgh.
Lothian Region
Midlothian District.

Swinton, Duns, Berwickshire;
Lothian and Borders at Duns.
Borders Region
Berwickshire District.

Swona, St Margaret's Hope,
Orkney; Grampian, Highland and
Islands at Kirkwall.
Orkney Islands Council.

Swordale, Evanton, Ross-shire;
Grampian, Highland and Islands at
Dingwall.
Highland Region
Ross and Cromarty District.

Swordale, Isle of Lewis; Grampian,
Highland and Islands at
Stornoway.
Western Isles Islands Council.

Symbister, Whalsay, Shetland;
Grampian, Highland and Islands at
Lerwick.
Shetland Islands Council.

Symington, Biggar, Lanarkshire;
South Strathclyde, Dumfries and
Galloway at Lanark.
Strathclyde Region
Clydesdale District.

Symington, Irvine, Ayrshire; North
Strathclyde at Kilmarnock.
Strathclyde Region
Cunninghame District.

Syre, Lairg, Sutherland; Grampian,
Highland and Islands at Dornoch.
Highland Region
Sutherland District.

Taeling, Dundee; Tayside, Central
and Fife at Dundee.
Tayside Region
City of Dundee District.

Tain, Ross-shire; Grampian,
Highland and Islands at Tain.
Highland Region
Ross and Cromarty District.

Talisker, Carbost, Isle of Skye;
Grampian, Highland and Islands at
Portree.
Highland Region
Skye and Lochalsh District.

Talmine, Tongue, Sutherland;
Grampian, Highland and Islands at
Dornoch.
Highland Region
Sutherland District.

Tangasdale, Castlebay, Isle of
Barra; Grampian, Highland and
Islands at Lochmaddy.
Western Isles Islands Council.

Tankerness, Orkney; Grampian,
Highland and Islands at Kirkwall.
Orkney Islands Council.

Tannadice, Forfar, Angus; Tayside,
Central and Fife at Forfar.
Tayside Region
Angus District.

Tantallon, East Lothian; Lothian
and Borders at Haddington.
Lothian Region
East Lothian District.

Taransay, Isle of Harris; Grampian,
Highland and Islands at
Stornoway.
Western Isles Islands Council.

Tarbert, Argyll; North Strathclyde at
Campbeltown.
Strathclyde Region
Argyll and Bute District.

Tarbert, Craighouse, Isle of Jura;
North Strathclyde at
Campbeltown.
Strathclyde Region
Argyll and Bute District.

Tarbert, Isle of Harris; Grampian,
Highland and Islands at
Stornoway.
Western Isles Islands Council.

Tarbet, Arrochar, Dunbartonshire;
North Strathclyde at Dumbarton.
Strathclyde Region
Dumbarton District.

Tarbolton, Mauchline, Ayrshire;
South Strathclyde, Dumfries and
Galloway at Ayr.
Strathclyde Region
Kyle and Carrick District.

Tarbrax, West Calder, West
Lothian; Lothian and Borders at
Linlithgow.
Lothian Region
West Lothian District.

Tarfside, Brechin, Angus; Tayside,
Central and Fife at Forfar.
Tayside Region
Angus District.

Tarland, Aboyne, Aberdeenshire;
Grampian, Highland and Islands at
Stonehaven.
Grampian Region
Kincardine and Deeside District.

Tarlogie, Tain, Ross-shire;
Grampian, Highland and Islands at
Tain.
Highland Region
Ross and Cromarty District.

Tarryblake, Huntly, Aberdeenshire;
Grampian, Highland and Islands at
Aberdeen.
Grampian Region
Gordon District.

Tarskavaig, Broadford, Isle of
Skye; Grampian, Highland and
Islands at Portree.
Highland Region
Skye and Lochalsh District.

Tarves, Ellon, Aberdeenshire;
Grampian, Highland and Islands at
Aberdeen.
Grampian Region
Gordon District.

Tarvie, Garve, Ross-shire;
Grampian, Highland and Islands at
Dingwall.
Highland Region
Ross and Cromarty District.

Taychreggan, Dalmally, Argyll;
North Strathclyde at Oban.
Strathclyde Region
Argyll and Bute District.

Tayinloan, Tarbert, Argyll; North
Strathclyde at Campbeltown.
Strathclyde Region
Argyll and Bute District.

Taynuilt, Argyll; North Strathclyde
at Oban.
Strathclyde Region
Argyll and Bute District.

Tayport, Fife; Tayside, Central and
Fife at Cupar.
Fife Region
North East Fife District.

Tayvallich, Lochgilphead, Argyll;
North Strathclyde at Dunoon.
Strathclyde Region
Argyll and Bute District.

Teangue, Armadale, Isle of Skye;
Grampian, Highland and Islands at
Portree.
Highland Region
Skye and Lochalsh District.

Teaninich, Alness, Ross-shire;
Grampian, Highland and Islands at
Tain.
Highland Region
Ross and Cromarty District.

Templand, Lockerbie,
Dumfriesshire; South Strath-
clyde, Dumfries and Galloway at
Dumfries.
Dumfries and Galloway Region
Annandale and Eskdale District.

Temple, Gorebridge, Midlothian;
Lothian and Borders at Edinburgh.
Lothian Region
Midlothian District.

Terregles, Dumfries; South
Strathclyde, Dumfries and
Galloway at Dumfries.
Dumfries and Galloway Region
Nithsdale District.

Teuchar, Turriff, Banffshire;
Grampian, Highland and Islands at
Banff.
Grampian Region
Banff and Buchan District.

Teviotdale, Hawick,
Roxburghshire; Lothian and
Borders at Jedburgh.
Borders Region
Roxburgh District.

Thankerton, Biggar, Lanarkshire;
South Strathclyde, Dumfries and
Galloway at Lanark.
Strathclyde Region
Clydesdale District.

The Oa, Port Ellen, Isle of Islay;
North Strathclyde at
Campbeltown.
Strathclyde Region
Argyll and Bute District.

Thornhill, Dumfriesshire; South
Strathclyde, Dumfries and
Galloway at Dumfries.
Dumfries and Galloway Region
Nithsdale District.

Thornhill, Stirling; Tayside, Central
and Fife at Stirling.
Central Region
Stirling District.

Thornley Park, Paisley; North
Strathclyde at Paisley.
Strathclyde Region
Renfrew District.

Thornliebank, Glasgow; North
Strathclyde at Paisley.
Strathclyde Region
Renfrew District.

Thornton, Kirkcaldy, Fife; Tayside,
Central and Fife at Kirkcaldy.
Fife Region
Kirkcaldy District.

Thorntonhall, Busby, Clarkston,
Glasgow; South Strathclyde,
Dumfries and Galloway at Paisley.
Strathclyde Region
Renfrew District.

Throsk, Stirling; Tayside, Central
and Fife at Stirling.
Central Region
Stirling District.

Thrumster, Wick, Caithness;
Grampian, Highland and Islands at
Wick.
Highland Region
Caithness District.

Thurso, Caithness; Grampian,
Highland and Islands at Wick.
Highland Region
Caithness District.

Tibbermore, Perth; Tayside,
Central and Fife at Perth.
Tayside Region
Perth and Kinross District.

Tigharry, Isle of North Uist;
Grampian Highland and Islands at
Lochmaddy.
Western Isles Islands Council.

Tighnabruaich, Argyll; North
Strathclyde at Dunoon.
Strathclyde Region
Argyll and Bute District.

Tighphuirst, Ballachulish,
Inverness-shire; Grampian,
Highland and Islands at Fort
William.
Highland Region
Lochaber District.

Tillicoultry, Clackmannanshire;
Tayside, Central and Fife at Alloa.
Central Region
Clackmannan District.

Tillietudlem, Kirkmuirhill,
Lanarkshire; South Strathclyde,
Dumfries and Galloway at Lanark.
Strathclyde Region
Clydesdale District.

Tillyfourie, Inverurie,
Aberdeenshire; Grampian,
Highland and Islands at Aberdeen.
Grampian Region
Gordon District.

Timsgarry, Isle of Lewis;
Grampian, Highland and Islands at
Stornoway.
Western Isles Islands Council.

Tinwald, Dumfries; South
Strathclyde, Dumfries and
Galloway at Dumfries.
Dumfries and Galloway Region
Nithsdale District.

Tipperty, Ellon, Aberdeenshire;
Grampian, Highland and Islands at
Aberdeen.
Grampian Region
Gordon District.

Tiroran, Isle of Mull; North
Strathclyde at Oban.
Strathclyde Region
Argyll and Bute District.

Toab, Deerness, Orkney;
Grampian, Highland and Islands at
Kirkwall.
Orkney Islands Council.

Tobermory, Isle of Mull; North
Strathclyde at Oban.
Strathclyde Region
Argyll and Bute District.

Toberonochy, Oban, Argyll; North
Strathclyde at Oban.
Strathclyde Region
Argyll and Bute District.

Tobson, Isle of Lewis; Grampian,
Highland and Islands at
Stornoway.
Western Isles Islands Council.

Todhills, Dundee; Tayside, Central
and Fife at Dundee.
Tayside Region
City of Dundee District.

Tolmachan, Isle of Harris;
Grampian, Highland and Islands at
Stornoway.
Western Isles Islands Council.

Tolob, Shetland; Grampian,
Highland and Islands at Lerwick.
Shetland Islands Council.

Tolstachaolais, Isle of Lewis;
Grampian, Highland and Islands at
Stornoway.
Western Isles Islands Council.

Tomatin, Inverness; Grampian,
Highland and Islands at Inverness.
Highland Region
Inverness District.

Tomdoun, Invergarry, Inverness-
shire; Grampian, Highland and
Islands at Fort William.
Highland Region
Lochaber District.

Tomich, Beauly, Inverness;
Grampian, Highland and Islands at
Inverness.
Highland Region
Inverness District.

Tomich, Cannich, Inverness;
Grampian, Highland and Islands at
Inverness.
Highland Region
Inverness District.

Tomintoul, Ballindalloch,
Morayshire; Grampian, Highland
and Islands at Elgin.
Grampian Region
Moray District.

Tong, Isle of Lewis; Grampian,
Highland and Islands at
Stornoway.
Western Isles Islands Council.

Tongland, Kirkcudbrightshire;
South Strathclyde, Dumfries and
Galloway at Kirkcudbright.
Dumfries and Galloway Region
Stewartry District.

Tongue, Lairg, Sutherland;
Grampian, Highland and Islands at
Dornoch.
Highland Region
Sutherland District.

Torastay, Cromore, Isle of Lewis;
Grampian, Highland and Islands at
Stornoway.
Western Isles Islands Council.

Tore, Muir of Ord, Ross-shire;
Grampian, Highland and Islands at
Dingwall.
Highland Region
Ross and Cromarty District.

Torgormack, Beauly, Inverness;
Grampian, Highland and Islands at
Inverness.
Highland Region
Inverness District.

Torloisk, Isle of Mull; North
Strathclyde at Oban.
Strathclyde Region
Argyll and Bute District.

Torlum, Isle of Benbecula;
Grampian, Highland and Islands at
Lochmaddy.
Western Isles Islands Council.

Torlundy, Fort William, Inverness-
shire; Grampian, Highland and
Islands at Fort William.
Highland Region
Lochaber District.

Tornaveen, Banchory,
Kincardineshire; Grampian,
Highland and Islands at
Stonehaven.
Grampian Region
Kincardine and Deeside District.

Tornegrain, Inverness; Grampian,
Highland and Islands at Inverness.
Highland Region
Inverness District.

Torphichen, Bathgate, West
Lothian; Lothian and Borders at
Linlithgow.
Lothian Region
West Lothian District.

Torphins, Banchory,
Kincardineshire; Grampian,
Highland and Islands at
Stonehaven.
Grampian Region
Kincardine and Deeside District.

Torrance, Glasgow; Glasgow and
Strathkelvin at Glasgow.
Strathclyde Region
City of Glasgow District.

Torranyard, Ayr; South
Strathclyde, Dumfries and
Galloway at Ayr.
Strathclyde Region
Kyle and Carrick District.

Torridon, Kinlochewe, Ross-shire;
Grampian, Highland and Islands at
Dingwall.
Highland Region
Ross and Cromarty District.

Torrin, Broadford, Isle of Skye;
Grampian, Highland and Islands at
Portree.
Highland Region
Skye and Lochalsh District.

Torrisdale, Campbeltown, Argyll;
North Strathclyde at
Campbeltown.
Strathclyde Region
Argyll and Bute District.

Torryburn, Dunfermline, Fife;
Tayside, Central and Fife at
Dunfermline.
Fife Region
Dunfermline District.

Tortarder, Portree, Isle of Skye;
Grampian, Highland and Islands at
Portree.
Highland Region
Skye and Lochalsh District.

Torthorwald, Dumfries; South
Strathclyde, Dumfries and
Galloway at Dumfries.
Dumfries and Galloway Region
Nithsdale District.

Torvaig, Portree, Isle of Skye;
Grampian, Highland and Islands at
Portree.
Highland Region
Skye and Lochalsh District.

Torwood, Larbert, Stirlingshire;
Tayside, Central and Fife at
Falkirk.
Central Region
Falkirk District.

Toscaig, Applecross, Achnasheen,
Ross-shire; Grampian, Highland
and Islands at Dingwall.
Highland Region
Ross and Cromarty District.

Tote, Portree, Isle of Skye;
Grampian, Highland and Islands at
Portree.
Highland Region
Skye and Lochalsh District.

Touch, Stirling; Tayside, Central
and Fife at Stirling.
Central Region
Stirling District.

Tough, Alford, Aberdeenshire;
Grampian, Highland and Islands at
Aberdeen.
Grampian Region
Gordon District.

Toward, Dunoon, Argyll; North
Strathclyde at Dunoon.
Strathclyde Region
Argyll and Bute District.

Townhead, Glasgow; Glasgow and
Strathkelvin at Glasgow.
Strathclyde Region
City of Glasgow District.

Townhead of Greenlaw,
Kirkcudbrightshire; South
Strathclyde, Dumfries and
Galloway at Kirkcudbright.
Dumfries and Galloway Region
Stewartry District.

Townhill, Dunfermline, Fife;
Tayside, Central and Fife at
Dunfermline.
Fife Region
Dunfermline District.

Trabboch, Mauchline, Ayrshire;
South Strathclyde, Dumfries and
Galloway at Ayr.
Strathclyde Region
Kyle and Carrick District.

Tranent, East Lothian; Lothian and
Borders at Haddington.
Lothian Region
East Lothian District.

Traquair, Innerleithen,
Peeblesshire; Lothian and Borders
at Peebles.
Borders Region
Tweeddale District.

Treslaig, Fort William, Inverness-
shire; Grampian, Highland and
Islands at Fort William.
Highland Region
Lochaber District.

Tresta, Shetland; Grampian,
Highland and Islands at Lerwick.
Shetland Islands Council.

Trinafour, Calvine, Perthshire;
Tayside, Central and Fife at Perth.
Tayside Region
Perth and Kinross District.

Trinity, Brechin, Angus; Tayside,
Central and Fife at Forfar.
Tayside Region
Angus District.

Trochry, Dunkeld, Perthshire;
Tayside, Central and Fife at Perth.
Tayside Region
Perth and Kinross District.

Troon, Ayrshire; South Strathclyde,
Dumfries and Galloway at Ayr.
Strathclyde Region
Kyle and Carrick District.

Troqueer, Dumfries; South
Strathclyde, Dumfries and
Galloway at Dumfries.
Dumfries and Galloway Region
Nithsdale District.

Trossary, Isle of South Uist;
Grampian, Highland and Islands at
Lochmaddy.
Western Isles Islands Council.

Tulliallan, Culross, Fife; Tayside,
Central and Fife at Dunfermline.
Fife Region
Dunfermline District.

Tullibardine, Auchterarder,
Perthshire; Tayside, Central and
Fife at Perth.
Tayside Region
Perth and Kinross District.

Tullibody, Alloa,
Clackmannanshire; Tayside,
Central and Fife at Alloa.
Central Region
Clackmannan District.

Tulliemet, Ballinluig, Perthshire;
Tayside, Central and Fife at Perth.
Tayside Region
Perth and Kinross District.

Tulloch, Roy Bridge, Inverness-
shire; Grampian, Highland and
Islands at Fort William.
Highland Region
Lochaber District.

Tullynessle, Alford, Aberdeenshire;
Grampian, Highland and Islands at
Aberdeen.
Grampian Region
Gordon District.

Tummel Bridge, Pitlochry,
Perthshire; Tayside, Central and
Fife at Perth.
Tayside Region
Perth and Kinross District.

Tundergarth, Lockerbie,
Dumfriesshire; South Strath-
clyde, Dumfries and Galloway at
Dumfries.
Dumfries and Galloway Region
Annandale and Eskdale District.

Turin, Forfar, Angus; Tayside,
Central and Fife at Forfar.
Tayside Region
Angus District.

Turnberry, Girvan, Ayrshire; South
Strathclyde, Dumfries and
Galloway at Ayr.
Strathclyde Region
Kyle and Carrick District.

Turriff, Banffshire; Grampian,
Highland and Islands at Banff.
Grampian Region
Banff and Buchan District.

Twatt, Orkney; Grampian, Highland
and Islands at Kirkwall.
Orkney Islands Council.

Twechar, Kilsyth, Glasgow; South
Strathclyde, Dumfries and
Galloway at Airdrie.
Strathclyde Region
Cumbernauld and Kilsyth District.

Tweedbank, Galashiels,
Selkirkshire; Lothian and Borders
at Selkirk.
Borders Region
Ettrick and Lauderdale District.

Tweedsmuir, Biggar, Lanarkshire;
Lothian and Borders at Peebles.
Borders Region
Tweeddale District.

Twynholm, Kirkcudbrightshire;
South Strathclyde, Dumfries and
Galloway at Kirkcudbright.
Dumfries and Galloway Region
Stewartry District.

Tyndrum, Crianlarich, Stirlingshire;
Tayside, Central and Fife at
Stirling.
Central Region
Stirling District.

Tynehead, Pathhead, Midlothian;
Lothian and Borders at Edinburgh.
Lothian Region
Midlothian District.

Tyningham, Dunbar, East Lothian;
Lothian and Borders at
Haddington.
Lothian Region
East Lothian District.

Tynron, Thornhill, Dumfriesshire; South Strathclyde, Dumfries and Galloway at Dumfries.
Dumfries and Galloway Region
Nithsdale District.

Tyrie, Fraserburgh, Aberdeenshire; Grampian, Highland and Islands at Banff.
Grampian Region
Banff and Buchan District.

Uachdar, Isle of Benbecula; Grampian, Highland and Islands at Lochmaddy.
Western Isles Islands Council.

Uddingston, Glasgow; South Strathclyde, Dumfries and Galloway at Hamilton.
Strathclyde Region
Hamilton District.

Uddstonehead, Strathaven, Lanarkshire; South Strathclyde, Dumfries and Galloway at Hamilton.
Strathclyde Region
Hamilton District.

Udny, Ellon, Aberdeenshire; Grampian, Highland and Islands at Aberdeen.
Grampian Region
Gordon District.

Udrigle, Laide, Gairloch, Ross-shire; Grampian, Highland and Islands at Dingwall.
Highland Region
Ross and Cromarty District.

Uidh, Vatersay, Isle of Barra; Grampian, Highland and Islands at Lochmaddy.
Western Isles Islands Council.

Uig, Isle of Lewis; Grampian, Highland and Islands at Stornoway.
Western Isles Islands Council.

Uig, Portree, Isle of Skye; Grampian, Highland and Islands at Portree.
Highland Region
Skye and Lochalsh District.

Uigen, Isle of Lewis; Grampian, Highland and Islands at Stornoway.
Western Isles Islands Council.

Ullapool, Ross-shire; Grampian, Highland and Islands at Dingwall.
Highland Region
Ross and Cromarty District.

Ullinish, Portree, Isle of Skye; Grampian, Highland and Islands at Portree.
Highland Region
Skye and Lochalsh District.

Ulva Ferry, Isle of Mull; North Strathclyde at Oban.
Strathclyde Region
Argyll and Bute District.

Unapool, Kylesku, Sutherland; Grampian, Highland and Islands at Dornoch.
Highland Region
Sutherland District.

Ungshader, Isle of Lewis; Grampian, Highland and Islands at Stornoway.
Western Isles Islands Council.

Uphall, Broxburn, West Lothian;
Lothian and Borders at Linlithgow.
Lothian Region
West Lothian District.

Uplawmoor, Glasgow; North
Strathclyde at Paisley.
Strathclyde Region
Renfrew District.

Upper Aird, Point, Isle of Lewis;
Grampian, Highland and Islands at
Stornoway.
Western Isles Islands Council.

Upper Barvas, Isle of Lewis;
Grampian, Highland and Islands at
Stornoway.
Western Isles Islands Council.

Upper Bayble, Isle of Lewis;
Grampian, Highland and Islands at
Stornoway.
Western Isles Islands Council.

Upper Carloway, Isle of Lewis;
Grampian, Highland and Islands at
Stornoway.
Western Isles Islands Council.

Upper Coll, Isle of Lewis;
Grampian, Highland and Islands at
Stornoway.
Western Isles Islands Council.

Upper Largo, Leven, Fife; Tayside,
Central and Fife at Cupar.
Fife Region
North East Fife District.

Upper Milavaig, Glendale, Isle of
Skye; Grampian, Highland and
Islands at Portree.
Highland Region
Skye and Lochalsh District.

Upper Shader, Isle of Lewis;
Grampian, Highland and Islands at
Stornoway.
Western Isles Islands Council.

Upper Sound, Shetland; Grampian,
Highland and Islands at Lerwick.
Shetland Islands Council.

Upper Yelts, Dollar,
Clackmannanshire; Tayside,
Central and Fife at Alloa.
Central Region
Clackmannan District.

Urgha, Isle of Harris; Grampian,
Highland and Islands at
Stornoway.
Western Isles Islands Council.

Urquhart, Elgin, Morayshire;
Grampian, Highland and Islands at
Elgin.
Grampian Region
Moray District.

Uskavagh, Isle of Benbecula;
Grampian, Highland and Islands at
Lochmaddy.
Western Isles Islands Council.

Uyeasound, Unst, Shetland;
Grampian, Highland and Islands at
Lerwick.
Shetland Islands Council.

Valasay, Isle of Lewis; Grampian,
Highland and Islands at
Stornoway.
Western Isles Islands Council.

Valtos, Culnacnock, Portree, Isle of
Skye; Grampian, Highland and
Islands at Portree.
Highland Region
Skye and Lochalsh District.

Valtos, Misvaig, Isle of Lewis;
Grampian, Highland and Islands at
Stornoway.
Western Isles Islands Council.

Vatersay, Castlebay, Isle of Barra;
Grampian, Highland and Islands at
Lochmaddy.
Western Isles Islands Council.

Vatisker, Isle of Lewis; Grampian,
Highland and Islands at
Stornoway.
Western Isles Islands Council.

Vatten, Dunvegan, Isle of Skye;
Grampian, Highland and Islands at
Portree.
Highland Region
Skye and Lochalsh District.

Vaul, Scarinish, Isle of Tiree; North
Strathclyde at Oban.
Strathclyde Region
Argyll and Bute District.

Vidlin, Shetland; Grampian,
Highland and Islands at Lerwick.
Shetland Islands Council.

Virkie, Shetland; Grampian,
Highland and Islands at Lerwick.
Shetland Islands Council.

Voe, Shetland; Grampian, Highland
and Islands at Lerwick.
Shetland Islands Council.

Walkerburn, Peeblesshire; Lothian
and Borders at Peebles.
Borders Region
Tweeddale District.

Wallacestone, Falkirk, Stirlingshire;
Tayside, Central and Fife at
Falkirk.
Central Region
Falkirk District.

Walls, Shetland; Grampian,
Highland and Islands at Lerwick.
Shetland Islands Council.

Wallyford, Musselburgh,
Midlothian; Lothian and Borders at
Edinburgh.
Lothian Region
Midlothian District.

Wamphray, Moffat, Dumfriesshire;
South Strathclyde, Dumfries and
Galloway at Dumfries.
Dumfries and Galloway Region
Annandale and Eskdale District.

Wanlockhead, Sanquhar,
Dumfriesshire; South Strath-
clyde, Dumfries and Galloway at
Dumfries.
Dumfries and Galloway Region
Nithsdale District.

Wardhouse, Insch, Aberdeenshire;
Grampian, Highland and Islands at
Aberdeen.
Grampian Region
Gordon District.

Warthill, Inverurie, Aberdeenshire;
Grampian, Highland and Islands at
Aberdeen.
Grampian Region
Gordon District.

Wartle, Inverurie, Aberdeenshire;
Grampian, Highland and Islands at
Aberdeen.
Grampian Region
Gordon District.

Wasbister, Rousay, Orkney;
Grampian, Highland and Islands at
Kirkwall.
Orkney Islands Council.

Waterbeck, Lockerbie,
Dumfriesshire; South Strath-
clyde, Dumfries and Galloway at
Dumfries.
Dumfries and Galloway Region
Annandale and Eskdale District.

Wateringhouse, Hoy, Orkney;
Grampian, Highland and Islands at
Kirkwall.
Orkney Islands Council.

Waterloo, Bankfoot, Perth;
Tayside, Central and Fife at Perth.
Tayside Region
Perth and Kinross District.

Waterloo, Breakish, Isle of Skye;
Grampian, Highland and Islands at
Portree.
Highland Region
Skye and Lochalsh District.

Waternish, Dunvegan, Isle of Skye;
Grampian, Highland and Islands at
Portree.
Highland Region
Skye and Lochalsh District.

Waterside, Kilmarnock, Ayrshire;
North Strathclyde at Kilmarnock.
Strathclyde Region
Kilmarnock and Loudoun District.

Watten, Wick, Caithness;
Grampian, Highland and Islands at
Wick.
Highland Region
Caithness District.

Weem, Aberfeldy, Perthshire;
Tayside, Central and Fife at Perth.
Tayside Region
Perth and Kinross District.

Weisdale, Shetland; Grampian,
Highland and Islands at Lerwick.
Shetland Islands Council.

Wellbank, Broughty Ferry, Dundee;
Tayside, Central and Fife at
Dundee.
Tayside Region
City of Dundee District.

Wellwood, Dunfermline, Fife;
Tayside, Central and Fife at
Dunfermline.
Fife Region
Dunfermline District.

Wemyss Bay, Renfrewshire; North
Strathclyde at Greenock.
Strathclyde Region
Inverclyde District.

West Barns, Dunbar, East Lothian;
Lothian and Borders at
Haddington.
Lothian Region
East Lothian District.

West Calder, West Lothian; Lothian
and Borders at Linlithgow.
Lothian Region
West Lothian District.

West End, Port Charlotte, Isle of
Islay; North Strathclyde at
Campbeltown.
Strathclyde Region
Argyll and Bute District.

West Gerinish, Isle of South Uist; Grampian, Highland and Islands at Lochmaddy.
Western Isles Islands Council.

West Helmsdale, Helmsdale, Sutherland; Grampian, Highland and Islands at Dornoch.
Highland Region
Sutherland District.

West Hynish, Scarinish, Isle of Tiree; North Strathclyde at Oban.
Strathclyde Region
Argyll and Bute District.

West Isle, Skerries, Shetland; Grampian, Highland and Islands at Lerwick.
Shetland Islands Council.

West Kilbride, Isle of South Uist; Grampian, Highland and Islands at Lochmaddy.
Western Isles Islands Council.

West Linton, Peeblesshire; Lothian and Borders at Peebles.
Borders Region
Tweeddale District.

West Saltoun, Pencaitland, East Lothian; Lothian and Borders at Haddington.
Lothian Region
East Lothian District.

West Sandwick, Yell, Shetland; Grampian, Highland and Islands at Lerwick.
Shetland Islands Council.

West Tarbert, Isle of Harris; Grampian, Highland and Islands at Stornoway.
Western Isles Islands Council.

West Wemyss, Kirkcaldy, Fife; Tayside, Central and Fife at Kirkcaldy.
Fife Region
Kirkcaldy District.

Wester Hailes, Edinburgh; Lothian and Borders at Edinburgh.
Lothian Region
City of Edinburgh District.

Westerdale, Halkirk, Caithness; Grampian, Highland and Islands at Wick.
Highland Region
Caithness District.

Westerkeld, Shetland; Grampian, Highland and Islands at Lerwick.
Shetland Islands Council.

Westerkirk, Langholm, Dumfriesshire; South Strathclyde, Dumfries and Galloway at Dumfries.
Dumfries and Galloway Region
Annandale and Eskdale District.

Westerton, Bearsden, Glasgow; North Strathclyde at Dumbarton.
Strathclyde Region
Dumbarton District.

Westfield, Bathgate, West Lothian; Lothian and Borders at Linlithgow.
Lothian Region
West Lothian District.

Westhaven, Carnoustie, Angus; Tayside, Central and Fife at Arbroath.
Tayside Region
Angus District.

Westhill, Inverness; Grampian,
Highland and Islands at Inverness.
Highland Region
Inverness District.

Westmuir, Kirriemuir, Angus;
Tayside, Central and Fife at
Forfar.
Tayside Region
Angus District.

Westquarter, Falkirk, Stirlingshire;
Tayside, Central and Fife at
Falkirk.
Central Region
Falkirk District.

Westray, Orkney; Grampian,
Highland and Islands at Kirkwall.
Orkney Islands Council.

Westruther, Gordon, Berwickshire;
Lothian and Borders at Duns.
Borders Region
Berwickshire District.

Weydale, Thurso, Caithness;
Grampian, Highland and Islands at
Wick.
Highland Region
Caithness District.

Whauphill, Newton Stewart,
Wigtownshire; South Strathclyde,
Dumfries and Galloway at
Stranraer.
Dumfries and Galloway Region
Wigtown District.

Whifflet, Coatbridge, Lanarkshire;
South Strathclyde, Dumfries and
Galloway at Airdrie.
Strathclyde Region
Monklands District.

Whins of Milton, Stirling; Tayside,
Central and Fife at Stirling.
Central Region
Stirling District.

Whistlefield, Garelochhead,
Dunbartonshire; North Strathclyde
at Dumbarton.
Strathclyde Region
Dumbarton District.

Whitburn, Bathgate, West Lothian;
Lothian and Borders at Linlithgow.
Lothian Region
West Lothian District.

Whitcastles, Lockerbie,
Dumfriesshire; South Strath-
clyde, Dumfries and Galloway at
Dumfries.
Dumfries and Galloway Region
Annandale and Eskdale District.

Whitchester, Duns, Berwickshire;
Lothian and Borders at Duns.
Borders Region
Berwickshire District.

Whitebridge, Foyers, Inverness;
Grampian, Highland and Islands at
Inverness.
Highland Region
Inverness District.

Whitecairns, Aberdeen; Grampian,
Highland and Islands at Aberdeen.
Grampian Region
City of Aberdeen District.

Whitecleuch, Crawfordjohn,
Lanarkshire; South Strathclyde,
Dumfries and Galloway at Lanark.
Strathclyde Region
Clydesdale District.

Whitecraig, Musselburgh, Midlothian; Lothian and Borders at Edinburgh.
Lothian Region
Midlothian District.

Whitecross, Linlithgow, West Lothian; Tayside, Central and Fife at Falkirk.
Central Region
Falkirk District.

Whiteface, Dornoch, Sutherland; Grampian, Highland and Islands at Dornoch.
Highland Region
Sutherland District.

Whitehall, Stronsay, Orkney; Grampian, Highland and Islands at Kirkwall.
Orkney Islands Council.

Whitehills, Banff; Grampian, Highland and Islands at Banff.
Grampian Region
Banff and Buchan District.

Whitehouse, Alford, Aberdeenshire; Grampian, Highland and Islands at Aberdeen.
Grampian Region
Gordon District.

Whitehouse, Tarbert, Argyll; North Strathclyde at Campbeltown.
Strathclyde Region
Argyll and Bute District.

Whitekirk, Dunbar, East Lothian; Lothian and Borders at Haddington.
Lothian Region
East Lothian District.

Whiteness, Shetland; Grampian, Highland and Islands at Lerwick.
Shetland Islands Council.

Whiterashes, Aberdeen; Grampian, Highland and Islands at Aberdeen.
Grampian Region
City of Aberdeen District.

Whithorn, Newton Stewart, Wigtownshire; South Strathclyde, Dumfries and Galloway at Stranraer.
Dumfries and Galloway Region
Wigtown District.

Whiting Bay, Brodick, Isle of Arran; North Strathclyde at Kilmarnock.
Strathclyde Region
Cunninghame District.

Whitletts, Ayr; South Strathclyde, Dumfries and Galloway at Ayr.
Strathclyde Region
Kyle and Carrick District.

Whitsome, Duns, Berwickshire; Lothian and Borders at Duns.
Borders Region
Berwickshire District.

Whittingehame, Haddington, East Lothian; Lothian and Borders at Haddington.
Lothian Region
East Lothian District.

Wick, Caithness; Grampian, Highland and Islands at Wick.
Highland Region
Caithness District.

Wigtown, Newton Stewart, Wigtownshire; South Strathclyde, Dumfries and Galloway at Stranraer.
Dumfries and Galloway Region
Wigtown District.

Wilkieston, Kirknewton, Midlothian; Lothian and Borders at Edinburgh.
Lothian Region
Midlothian District.

Wilsontown, Forth, Lanarkshire; South Strathclyde, Dumfries and Galloway at Lanark.
Strathclyde Region
Clydesdale District.

Winchburgh, Broxburn, West Lothian; Lothian and Borders at Linlithgow.
Lothian Region
West Lothian District.

Windy Yet, Stewarton, Ayrshire; North Strathclyde at Kilmarnock.
Strathclyde Region
Kilmarnock and Louden District.

Windygates, Leven, Fife; Tayside, Central and Fife at Kirkcaldy.
Fife Region
Kirkcaldy District.

Wishaw, Lanarkshire; South Strathclyde, Dumfries and Galloway at Hamilton.
Strathclyde Region
Hamilton District.

Wiston, Biggar, Lanarkshire; South Strathclyde, Dumfries and Galloway at Lanark.
Strathclyde Region
Clydesdale District.

Wolfhill, Perthshire; Tayside, Central and Fife at Perth.
Tayside Region
Perth and Kinross District.

Woodend, West Lothian; Lothian and Borders at Linlithgow.
Lothian Region
West Lothian District.

Woodhead, Turriff, Banffshire; Grampian, Highland and Islands at Banff.
Grampian Region
Banff and Buchan District.

Woodside, Aberdeen; Grampian, Highland and Islands at Aberdeen.
Grampian Region
City of Aberdeen District.

Woodside, Coupar Angus, Perthshire; Tayside, Central and Fife at Perth.
Tayside Region
Perth and Kinross District.

Woodville, Arbroath, Angus; Tayside, Central and Fife at Arbroath.
Tayside Region
Angus District.

Woolfords, West Calder, West Lothian; Lothian and Borders at Linlithgow.
Lothian Region
West Lothian District.

Woolmet, Dalkeith, Midlothian; Lothian and Borders at Edinburgh.
Lothian Region
Midlothian District.

Wormit, Newport-on-Tay, Fife;
Tayside, Central and Fife at
Cupar.
Fife Region
North East Fife District.

Wyre, Orkney; Grampian, Highland
and Islands at Kirkwall.
Orkney Islands Council.

Yarrow, Selkirk; Lothian and
Borders at Selkirk.
Borders Region
Ettrick and Lauderdale District.

Yetholm, Kelso, Roxburghshire;
Lothian and Borders at Jedburgh.
Borders Region
Roxburgh District.

Yetts of Muckart, Dollar,
Clackmannanshire; Tayside,
Central and Fife at Alloa.
Central Region
Clackmannan District.

Ythanbank, Ellon, Aberdeenshire;
Grampian, Highland and Islands at
Aberdeen.
Grampian Region
Gordon District.

Ythanwells, Huntly, Aberdeenshire;
Grampian, Highland and Islands at
Aberdeen.
Grampian Region
Gordon District.